The Roots of *Walden* and the Tree of Life

Gordon V. Boudreau

Vanderbilt University Press
Nashville / 1990

Published in 1990 by Vanderbilt University Press
Printed in the United States of America

Library of Congress Cataloging-in-Publication Data

Boudreau, Gordon V., 1929–
The roots of Walden and the tree of life / Gordon V. Boudreau.
p. cm.
ISBN 0–8265–1235–6 (alk. paper)
Includes bibliographical references.
1. Thoreau, Henry David, 1817–1862. Walden. 2. Thoreau, Henry David, 1817–1862—Symbolism. 3. Emerson, Ralph Waldo, 1803–1882—Influence—Thoreau. 4. Tree of life in literature. 5. Nature in literature. I. Title.
PS3048. B6 1990
818′.303—dc20 90–12297
CIP

For Grace . . .
. . . and the Holy Spirit

Now the parable is this:
the seed is the word of God.
Luke 8:11

Contents

Writings of Thoreau Cited Parenthetically in the Text, by Abbreviation

C *The Correspondence of Henry David Thoreau.* Edited by Walter Harding and Carl Bode. New York: New York Univ. Press, 1958.

CC *Cape Cod.* Edited by Joseph J. Moldenhauer. Princeton: Princeton Univ. Press, 1988.

CP *Collected Poems of Henry Thoreau.* Enlarged ed. Edited by Carl Bode. Baltimore: Johns Hopkins Press, 1964.

EEM *Early Essays and Miscellanies.* Edited by Joseph J. Moldenhauer and Edwin Moser, with Alexander C. Kern. Princeton: Princeton Univ. Press, 1975.

Huck "Huckleberries." Edited by Leo Stoller. 1970. Reprinted in *The Natural History Essays.* Edited by Robert Sattelmeyer. Salt Lake City: Peregrine Smith, 1980.

J *The Journal.* Vols. 7–20 of The Writings of Henry David Thoreau. 20 vols. Walden Edition. Boston: Houghton Mifflin, 1906; herein cited by the alternate numbering, I-XIV.*

LJ *Consciousness in Concord: The Text of Thoreau's Hitherto "Lost Journal" (1840–1841) Together with Notes and a Commentary.* Edited by Perry Miller. Boston: Houghton Mifflin, 1959.

MW *The Maine Woods.* Edited by Joseph J. Moldenhauer. Princeton: Princeton Univ. Press, 1972.

PJ, I *Journal, Volume 1: 1837–1844.* Edited by Elizabeth Hall Witherell, William L. Howarth, Robert Sattelmeyer, and Thomas Blanding. Princeton: Princeton Univ. Press, 1981.*

PJ, II *Journal, Volume 2: 1842–1848.* Edited by Robert Sattelmeyer. Princeton: Princeton Univ. Press, 1984.*

RP *Reform Papers.* Edited by Wendell Glick. Princeton: Princeton Univ. Press, 1973.

W, V *Excursions and Poems.* Vol. 5 of *The Writings of Henry David Thoreau.* Boston: Houghton Mifflin, 1906.

Wa *Walden.* Edited by J. Lyndon Shanley. Princeton: Princeton Univ. Press, 1971.

Wk *A Week on the Concord and Merrimack Rivers.* Edited by Carl Hovde. Princeton: Princeton Univ. Press, 1980.

*When quoted matter is followed by both J and PJ, the first citation indicates the quoted source.

Writings of Emerson Cited Parenthetically in the Text, by Abbreviation

CW *The Collected Works of Ralph Waldo Emerson.* Edited by Alfred R. Ferguson et al. 4 vols. Cambridge: Harvard Univ. Press, 1971–87.

EL *The Early Lectures of Ralph Waldo Emerson.* Edited by Stephen E. Whicher, Robert E. Spiller, and Wallace E. Williams. 3 vols. Cambridge: Harvard Univ. Press, 1959-72.

EW *The Complete Works of Ralph Waldo Emerson.* 12 vols. Centenary Ed. Boston: Houghton Mifflin, 1903.

JMN *The Journals and Miscellaneous Notebooks of Ralph Waldo Emerson.* Edited by William H. Gilman et al. 16 vols. Cambridge: Harvard Univ. Press, 1960-82.

L *The Letters of Ralph Waldo Emerson.* Edited by Ralph L. Rusk. 6 vols. New York: Columbia Univ. Press, 1939.

Preface

IN THE MID 1960's, several years after beginning my full-time teaching career at Le Moyne College, nearly every freshman in the required composition course was reading either R. W. Chambers' *Thomas More* or Henry David Thoreau's *Walden,* the latter in the attractive and durable Riverside Edition with Sherman Paul's fine introduction. Having finished my dissertation on Herman Melville in the late 1960's, I was invited by Father John Lahey, S. J., to "get up" a lecture on Thoreau's *Walden* on the strength of my being the resident scholar of the period. As I began to ponder the possibilities, I recalled a little essay written by a freshman at Marquette University, Rita Prudlow, titled "Going to the Roots—Radical," which appeared in the 1959 issue of Marquette's *Fresh Ink: A Magazine of Freshman Writing,* and was used as a supplemental text in teaching the course for the 1959-60 academic year. Though having served at Marquette on the Freshman Magazine Committee that made the selection, I never met Rita Prudlow, but she symbolizes those countless students, some of them now nameless or faceless, who, over the years, have been a continual stimulation in the growth of this study, two chapters of which (6 and 8) have been repeated in slide-lecture format in the classroom for the past eighteen years. Classroom experience, the invitation of a congenial colleague, and a recollection of a 500-word freshman essay—an extended definition of "radical"—all these produced a roughed-out lecture titled "Going to the Roots: The Radicalism of *Walden,*" first given to Le Moyne students, then revised and given as a public lecture, "*Walden*–A Radical Myth," as a Greyfriar lecture at Sienna College in 1971.

To be sure there are other debts, one to a now retired colleague, Ed Mullen, who introduced me to Walter Harding, founder of the Thoreau Society, who in turn asked me if I had read Thoreau's journals when I didn't know of their existence. So I began to read them. Later Professor Harding would enable me to work at Concord, first on an exploratory trip in the summer of 1970, then as a participant in his NEH seminar on biography and the transcendentalists in the summer of 1977. I am also most grateful to Anne McGrath, curator of the Thoreau Lyceum, whose enthusiasm for Thoreau was so infectious, and whose invitation to lecture at the Lyceum then, and several times thereafter, gave me a sense of audience and excitement, never more so than when I shared the program with my son, Vincent, whose talk on the animals of *Walden* had an affectionate wisdom far beyond the years of one who had just graduated from college. Anne in turn in those first days introduced me to Tom Blanding, now the president of the Thoreau Society, who had just graduated from Marlboro College with an honors thesis on Thoreau, and seemed to have a sixth sense in perceiving and comprehending my reading of a crucial passage in Thoreau's "Spring." As with a legion of Thoreauvians, I, too, am grateful to Marcia Moss of the Concord Free Library for her generosity in sharing the wealth of her extensive knowledge about the works of Concord authors. Likewise I am indebted to the Starr Library of Middlebury College, and especially to Robert Buckeye, Curator, for permission to examine their special collection and quote from a manuscript.

I am grateful as well to the Le Moyne community, to the Research and Development Committee, and to a succession of academic deans who have supported my attempts to publish a study so repeatedly and extensively revised, deepened, but also delayed over a period of twenty years. To them I am grateful for their unfaltering support—in sabbatical semesters, a one-time reduction of course load, and the expense of numerous manuscript preparations and mailings. I also want to thank various directors of university presses for having rejected this study at earlier stages, though to say so might sound sardonic, which at the time of rejection might well have described my prevailing mood. I realize that such early versions, had any been published, might now seem an embarrassment. I also am grateful to my numerous readers, mostly anonymous, whose reports—some of them wise and penetrating, some of them narrow and without imagination—have encouraged or provoked me to persist.

Here at Le Moyne, a succession of colleagues has urged me on in this work, perhaps no one more so than Barbara Clarkson, whose perdurable judgment of the worth of my study has kept me at it. Others have encouraged me over the years—Professors Bill Cunningham, Neil Novelli, the late Bill Forrest, Pat Segedy, Randy Fertel, Roger Lund, and Michael Suarez, S.J., my most recent "in house" reader. My thanks as well go to the library staff at Le Moyne for their help, especially for their efficiency in obtaining inter-library loans. I have been blessed by a succession of conscientious typists and personal computer assistants of uncommon affability and competence—Maryann DeMichelle, Joan Mattes, Barbara Poole, and most recently and especially, Sharyn Knight. They affirm that the spirit of collegiality, where it exists, is often most pervasive in the humbler, and often least appreciated positions, without which a college could not function.

Finally, I owe my deepest gratitude to my wife Grace, who, having so much to do with the growth of this book through her discerning and demanding intelligence as a reader, also gave me the will to persist through so many rejections. She will not, when it is finally published, be able to understand a word of it. Her reading must come hereafter, in a revised edition. And to our sons and daughters—Joe, Vin, Maura, Kris, Sue, Gordy, and Lou—each of whom, having been herded around Walden Pond en masse, is marching to the sound of a different drummer. I trust they heard it first in the magic circle of the family "dinner," if they could there hear anything at all, and that if they now put an ear to the table, they might hear the faint rappings of a bug whose metamorphosis is proceeding apace. I trust all will sit again at that festive board, perhaps with clean fingernails all around.

GORDON V. BOUDREAU
Le Moyne College
Syracuse, N. Y.

I

Prologue

Photograph of "Sand Foliage from Deep Cut on Railroad, Concord, Massachusetts," taken March 17, 1900, by Herbert W. Gleason

1

Of Passages and Determination

There are, I take it, in each man's history insignificant
passages which he feels to be to him not insignificant;
little coincidences in little things,
which touch all the springs of wonder. . . .

Ralph Waldo Emerson, ltr. to Mary Moody
August l, 1826, L, I, 170

I was determined to know beans.

Wa, 161

IN 1843, the line of the railroad that was to run from Boston to Fitchburg was constructed alongside the western edge of Walden Pond, a mile south of the village of Concord, Massachusetts. A few rods toward the village from where the tracks skirted the pond, a low wooded hill necessitated a cut in the earth to permit the laying of the railbed. Achieved by cheap labor of Irish immigrants, this cut, about a quarter of a mile long and thirty to forty feet deep (PJ, II, 384), came to be known as the "Deep Cut." Not only did it create a passage for the iron horse whose sides would pare the edge of the clear, spring-fed waters of Walden, it also permitted commerce in an ice harvest gleaned from the pond's surface. Less than two years after the track was laid, on a piece of property called "The Briars" that Ralph Waldo Emerson had recently bought, Henry David Thoreau, America's most notorious squatter, began a sojourn of "twos"—two years, two months, and two days—an experiment in living that, seven years after leaving the pond, he would convert to *Walden,* a literary expression of oneness.[1]

In the process of achieving such an integration, Thoreau made use of the railroad, sometimes for matters mundane and practical, as when taking its right-of-way for the most convenient passage to his home in the village, sometimes for purposes transcendent and literary, as when making its locomotive serve symbolically in *Walden* both as a disrupter of an ideal pastoral life and as an exemplar of the heroic that fronts not only the essentials of life, but the assaults and discontents of winter as well.[2] Even the railroad's exuviae—especially its exuviae—served Thoreau: the shack of an Irishman who had worked on the railroad supplying him with some boards for his cabin, the smoke rising from the locomotive directing his gaze skyward to an azure-tinted heaven. But the exuviae that served him best ran underground—not that "underground railroad" for which he was a sometimes conductor helping to transport men of quiet desperation on a passage from enforced servitude toward the North Star and prospects of freedom, but that ground under and adjacent to the iron tracks and "sleepers," ground of clay and sand in the Deep Cut. There the thaw first effected an eruption, seemingly of Nature's bowels, then, as though touched by "all the springs of wonder"—to borrow Emerson's phrase in the epigraph to this chapter—was converted into an expression of exuberance and joy.

The Deep Cut "passages" upon which the study that follows ultimately concentrates are multiple—passages through which the train moved in its journeying, and through which Thoreau moved almost daily on his treks to and from the village; passages in the "Spring" chapter of *Walden* that describe the thawing bankside of the Deep Cut as "sand foliage" and bring *Walden* to "its climax in a slime of sand" (LJ, 126), as Perry Miller has astutely observed; and passages of a psychological nature that express the characterology of Thoreau. For in the latter half of the twentieth century the sand foliage passages have become a critical proving ground for Freudian and Eriksonian critics, the Freudians especially regarding them as evidence of an obsessive and rejective personality determined by infantile experience. A less procrustean reading—expressed by the title of Gail Sheehy's popular *Passages: Predictable Crises of Adult Life* (1976)—points toward a more recent and holistic manner of interpreting the sand foliage passages as stages in the development of a personality. In 1977 Richard Lebeaux, in *Young Man Thoreau,* offered an Eriksonian study that concluded with Thoreau's move to Walden Pond in 1845. A former student of Erik Erikson, Lebeaux acknowledged his debt to the author of *Young Man Luther,* in his title as well as in his terminology and procedure in studying a "great man." But when Lebeaux completed his psychobiographical examination of Thoreau's life with *Thoreau's Seasons* (1984), his indebtedness had shifted to Daniel J. Levinson's *The Seasons of a Man's Life* (1978), from which he derived his title, the theme of generativity, and the cycle of the seasons. Interestingly, Sheehy's *Passages,* which appeared two years earlier than Levinson's *Seasons,* had drawn from Levinson's preliminary pioneering studies in the Adult Life Cycle, an indebtedness readily acknowledged. In *Thoreau's Seasons,* Lebeaux probes the passages on the Deep Cut as evidence of Thoreau's generativity, projections of Thoreau's psyche at a stage through which he is attempting to forge a passage.[3] In chapter 9, I survey the extensive critical and psychobiographical treatment of the passages on the sand foliage in the Deep Cut that appear in the "Spring" chapter of *Walden.*

But these sand foliage passages also provide a means of drawing aside the curtain from the mystery of artistic creation to reveal something of the passage from the unconscious to the conscious in the creative process. In "The Poet" Emerson states, "Art is the path of the creator to his work" (JMN, IX, 71; CW, III, 22); and he goes on to remark, "By God it is in me and must go forth of me." No mere expletive, his "By God" expresses a sense of being used as an instrument of divine revelation. Similarly in Thoreau's case, the mystery of the genesis of *Walden* is profoundly religious. The impression made by the Deep Cut, turned to expression, validates the ambiguity of "the creator" in Emerson's statement: *Walden* is an expression of an enthusiast in the radical sense of that word (*en-theos*), and Thoreau saw himself as an agent ("By God") to express creation's meaning or as a procreator in an act that has to do chiefly with seeing with new vision. Especially in the chapter "Spring," *Walden* lays claim to being considered not only a book of Revelation—as Emerson intended in his own book *Nature*—but a book of Genesis as well.

In his earliest extant journal entry describing the sand foliage in the Deep Cut, written in the first spring after he left Walden Pond, Thoreau wonderingly pondered that curious expression in the thawing bankside—roots, as he saw them—and queried: "Whither may the sun of new spring lead them on—These roots of ours[?]" (PJ, II, 383). Some two decades of intermittent pondering have persuaded me that at and in the Deep Cut passages Thoreau, by linguistic mimicry of nature's expression, impels his readers to examine what was there emergent in "these roots of ours" by the use of depth agronomy and etymology rather than depth psychology. In the chapters that follow, I trace the emergence of the vegetal and linguistic roots of *Walden* as they burgeon toward expression in Thoreau's life and in his art. Continuing to follow these roots would lead him to respond to two principles or laws of Nature operative in his life and in his art, the law of currents and the law of vegetation.

Thoreau was drawn to emulate both laws by his determination to live a "*purely* sensuous life" (Wk, 382). In two of the three great adventures of his life, viewed from a literary perspective, he devoted himself to a deep experience of these laws: he committed himself first to the current of a sluggish river that meandered through his native town before it joined a more boisterous stream tumbling from White Mountain sources, and next, to the vegetation in a field beside his Walden Pond cabin where he cultivated beans so assiduously as to suspect, in moments of rapture, that "it was no longer beans that I hoed, nor I that hoed beans" (Wa, 159).[4] He wanted the earth to say "beans" instead of "grass." And so, in a narrowly economic sense, and in a mother tongue, it did. But when at the end of his first growing season he harvested his annual crop, he had intimations that a perennial crop—a father tongue of "tropes and expression, to serve a parable-maker one day" (Wa, 162)—remained to be harvested. In his second season he would cultivate fewer beans; but in the interval between leaving the pond and publishing *Walden* seven years later, he would cultivate his tropes and expression in imagination, in "some upland pasture— where the John's / wort grew" (PJ, I, 352; J, I, 304). During that interval, his imagination was rooted and attenuated along a fine network that ran from his beanfield to the eruption of earth in the bankside where the roots of plants configured into the roots of words so that the flowing mixture of sand and clay became a place of response to the presumably rhetorical question Emerson had raised, "What was it that nature would say?" (CW, I, 14).

If Thoreau was obsessed with the thawing bankside, as few critics would now deny, it was not so much because he projected into it his private, subconscious torments; rather, it was because the bankside provoked him to study, read, and articulate that peculiar natural expression of those same laws of currents and vegetation to which he had already responded in life. To his peeled eye and pointed ear, the earth, which in a mother tongue had said "beans," in a "father tongue" (Wa, 101) now uttered the word "lobe" (Wa, 306), itself a product of the law of currents and the law of vegetation. In that single word the laws he had seen, heard, and followed in a kind of generating and organic ecstasy coalesced to find expression, not simply in a personality, but in a poem called *Walden* that gave the lie to a couplet wrung out of earlier dejection: "My life has been the poem I would have writ, / But I could not both live and utter it" (Wk, 343). He would. He did. For in the Deep Cut he had discovered "not the workman whom we have hired, with whom we love so well to talk, but the workman whose work we are" (Wa, 134).

In the several "passages" here under scrutiny, Thoreau articulated these two laws in a linguistic mimicry of nature and its concealed Creator, thereby gaining the right to be regarded as America's most thoroughly radical (and radicle) author. As projected in the persona of *Walden,* Thoreau's artistic Self, his identity, his being, is fairly "grounded" in this railroad "interval." Through the interval of space from where he had cultivated beans as well as thoughts and expression, to where the railroad made the Deep Cut, he seemed to extend his roots beneath the soil of his consciousness. Similarly, his organic radicalism was spanning the interval of time between *A Week on the Concord and Merrimack Rivers* (1849) and *Walden* (1854), the two books he published in his lifetime.

In the study of the genesis of *Walden* that follows, I consider *A Week on the Concord and Merrimack Rivers* an early version of *Walden,* one whose underlying roots generate as its informing central archetype the tree of the Fall, the discovery of whose meaning is the climactic event in Thoreau's first book. Through two centuries of American experience in New England, the tree of the Fall had indicated a guiding principle of Puritan theology and culture. Early in his journal Thoreau quoted the first verse of the *New England Primer,* which was meant to be not so much written upon but scored into the tabula rasa of tender New England minds as they came upon the first letter of the alphabet with its rhymed rubric: "In Adam's fall / We sinned all." But upon that text, which the *Primer* illustrated with a rough sketch of Adam and Eve in postlapsarian shade at the tree of the Fall, he at once imposed a seemingly playful reversion: "In the new Adam's rise / We shall all reach the skies" (J, II, 153). Then, with scarcely a hitch in his walked style, he added, "The Arbor-Vitae, or tree of life,—is what we want," and by so doing projected the archetypal symbol of *Walden,* the antithesis of the tree of the Fall. Thus *Walden* may be construed as a radical revision of *A Week,* a positive print from the negative of Thoreau's first book, the emanations of an instrument, finely tuned, that set to music the untold silence with which *A Week* concludes.

In what lies ahead, I examine the roots of Thoreau's radical genius, tracing them to where they surface in the sand foliage passages first pioneered by Perry Miller, who there found Thoreau's genius obsessive, self-deceptive—in short, lying.[5] Still, it is ground Thoreau found "dear to lie in" in a fabulous and truthful way, ground he pioneered in a determined, deliberate, and radical way, rather than obsessively and mendaciously. Or if "obsessive" is the operative word to describe his directive impulse, it is so paradoxically and in its roots: "Latin *obsidere* . . . to sit down before, besiege, beset: *ob,* on + *sedere* to sit" (American Heritage Dictionary, hereafter cited as AHD). These Latin roots of "obsess" emphasize what is rudimentary and paradoxical in *Walden*: in "Where I Lived and What I Lived For," Thoreau reports his determination to take up a "residence" [*re* + *sedere,* "to sit back," "remain sitting" (AHD), same root as "obsess"] or "*sedes*" (Wa, 81) in order to seek, track down, corner, delve for, discover, and eventually proclaim the meaning of life, if such he could find. Had he not hinted such speculative obsessiveness in remarking, "I long ago lost a hound, a bay horse, and a turtle-dove, and am *still* on their trail" (Wa, 17; emphasis added)? And isn't "still" particularly paradoxical in this context? Suggesting that while he is ever moving on their trail, he is profoundly arrested in speculation over their trailings? For Thoreau was not hounded out to Walden Pond. Rather, he was the hound who, sensing that every aspect of nature had concealed meanings, called attention to them by going "on point" with every fibre of his being—"*still* on their trail"—in a manner to demonstrate that "Sympathy with Intelligence" (W, V, 239) he prized more than knowledge itself. Or, to shift metaphorical ground again, Thoreau went to Walden Pond in order to go "on the mount," as he once punned in coming upon such words as "transport" and "ecstasy" (J, IV, 466-67) in the book of Richard C. Trench, an English philologist who would muse at length over the notion "that we like what is like."[6] And are not Thoreau's writings aspiring sermons "on the mount," though uttered from where the valleys smile, rather than depressing odes to dejection, even if uttered from the mountaintops? And doesn't he offer his contemporaries, of every age, a timeless Pisgah view of a promised land, a temple of Concord, a brave new world—within? And of a dawn we might never have glimpsed except for his words?[7]

For surely *Walden* is not the record of a fugitive life—obsessed and desperate—from one man's contemporaries, from society, from woman, perhaps from one's own self, but a purposeful, emphatic, determined journey into the deeps of self. And having returned from travels deep in Concord, Thoreau offers *Walden* as a spiritual alarm clock, a pulse-stirring drum, a brazen bugle that calls us to awaken, wash the film from our eyes, and see—speculate—on the very ground upon which we stand—or sit. From his own "*sedes*" by Walden Pond—his "sit," as Whitman would have called it—Thoreau took up a speculative life most deliberate—in economics, agriculture, politics, botany, zoology, anthropology, philology, and theology. He speculated in opposition to "the most sacred laws of society" (Wa, 323) it might seem, but not in the merely negative and skulking way of the judgment Emerson once impatiently rendered when learning that Thoreau would not pay his taxes.[8] Rather, he did so "through obedience to yet more sacred laws" (Wa, 323), as he writes in the conclusion of *Walden.* If he first sensed them as "faint intimations" only, "fallings from us, vanishings," as Wordsworth put it in a poem that came so readily to the lips of a Transcendentalist, it may be they were intimations of those "grandest laws" that were "continually being executed" next to us: "We seek to perceive them, and we do not see them; we seek to hear them, and we do not hear them; identified with the substance of things, they cannot be separated from them" (Wa, 134). In a voice emphatically not passive, but reflexive and deliberate, Thoreau declared he "was determined to know beans" (Wa, 161).

*

In the midst of his Walden experience, Thoreau had gone "on the mount" quite literally, setting out from his Walden Pond retreat on the last day of August 1846, for his first trek into the Maine woods, and then, on the slope of Mt. Katahdin, leaving his party of fellow excursionists for a solitary ascent of Maine's highest peak. In traversing that "drear and grim" (PJ, II, 336) slope, he climbed across rocks strewn about so thickly that it seemed to have "rained rocks" (PJ, II, 339). So shattering was his sense of "Vast, Titanic, inhuman Nature" (MW, 64) while on the mount that the ground of his being seemed to fall away to "Chaos and Old Night" (MW, 70). On the starkly barren elevation above the tree line, some vital part of his nature seems to have abandoned him "through the loose grating of his ribs," and he was stung by Nature's witheringly personal blast, which is in no way deflected by a generic "him" and "you":

> She [Nature] does not smile on him as in the plains. She seems to say sternly, why came ye here before your time? This ground is not prepared for you. Is it not enough that I smile in the valleys? I have never made this soil for thy feet, this air for thy breathing, these rocks for thy neighbors. I cannot pity nor fondle thee here, but forever relentlessly drive thee hence to where I *am* kind. (MW, 64)

And kin. And like. For unlike the valley of the Deep Cut, it was alien ground for Thoreau to lie in, not receptive or productive of the *mythus,* a place, far from his magic circle, where "the principle of vegetation was hard put to it" (MW, 61). Having earlier translated *Prometheus Bound* for *The Dial,* he could find no ground for his own translation on that mountaintop, for "it was a place . . . to be inhabited by men nearer of kin to the rocks and to wild animals than we" (MW, 70-71). Nor did he feel kin to a Titan or Christ, benefactors of mankind pinioned in suffering on mountain tops, for his was a celebrative "identity," made to "smile in the valleys," or in Nature's intervals, rather than on her pinnacles. In 1851 he would write, "Mythology is the crop which the Old World bore before its soil was exhausted. The West is preparing to add its fables to those of the East. . . . The soil in which those fables grew is deep and inexhaustible" (J, II, 145-46). But at the top of Katahdin, the "unhandselled globe" (MW, 70) had not yet generated any soil to lie in, or from which to grow New World fables; and there Thoreau "felt the presence of a force not bound to be kind to man" (MW, 70).

In "Greek Myth: Prometheus on Ktaadn," Robert D. Richardson, Jr., considers Thoreau's description of the boulder-strewn landscape on Katahdin similar to "the descriptions of the thawing clay bank in *Walden,* when [Thoreau] felt himself in the laboratory of the world." But in Thoreau's description of his confrontation with wild nature at the summit of the mountain, Richardson sees an attempt "to puzzle out his own condition with the help of Aeschylus' great figure of Prometheus." He argues that though Prometheus is "crucial to 'Ktaadn,' . . . it is very little in evidence in the finished work." Richardson finds "all allusion to Prometheus' cry from the rock or Christ's from the cross" to be withheld, in order to convey the actuality of Thoreau's "experience on the mountain."[9]

But while Richardson sees Thoreau as sublimating the mythic and religious in his experience on the mount, a subterranean counter-current just as surely indicates mythic and religious forces at work and emergent in his journal during the period of composition of "Ktaadn." Just a few days after returning to Walden Pond, Thoreau was pondering "the naked the embalmed unburied death of Jerusalem—! In Tasso's poem [*Jerusalem Delivered*] I trust some things are sweetly buried" (PJ, II, 353). But were they? For after an excision from his journal—nine-tenths of a page—he resumed with a recollection of his experience on Katahdin and a complete reversal of moods about the "death of Jerusalem": "—Some unaffected tears shed by a pilgrim on Mt. Calvary within the week.—" (PJ, II, 353). Something having happened on that forbidding rocky summit in Maine ran so disturbingly beneath the level of his consciousness that it required a reassessment of the "death of Jerusalem"? In his journal he then writes, but now as a deeply affected spectator, of a pattern of human suffering and atonement in the "mythus," more particularly Christian than Greek, which culminated on a barren summit and upon a paradoxical tree of life:

> To the old mythology one memorable addition is due to this era—the Christian fable—With what pains and tears and blood these centuries have woven the christian fable—and added that to the mythology of mankind! The New Prometheus.
>
> With what miraculous consent and patience is this mythus stamped on the memory of the race?
>
> Nations and centuries combine to dress old truth in a new garb—to adorn it and set it forth. (PJ, II, 353)

While "unhandselled" (MW, 70) Nature might chastise him on the mount, it would woo him in valleys dear to lie in. And in the soil of his own deep Concord, the rudiments of a tree of life for a New Adam were already beginning to stir, perhaps dressing part of an "old truth in a new garb." As he would put it in "Huckleberries":

> When the husk gets separated from the kernel, almost all men run after the husk and pay their respects to that. It is only the husk of Christianity that is so bruited and wide spread in this world, the kernel is still the very least and rarest of all things. There is not a single church founded on it. To obey the higher law is generally considered the last manifestation of littleness. (Huck, 212)

Tracing the characterology of Thoreau's expression has made me ever more aware of the shaping influence of his Concord neighbor and mentor, Ralph Waldo Emerson, whose role as surrogate father—intellectual, spiritual, and artistic as well as familial—may well be the basis of their alienation in the early 1850s. While Emerson was absent lecturing, Thoreau had been a live-in handyman with the Emerson family, so much so that in the affections of young Waldo Emerson he seems to have supplanted the natural father. Earlier still, when Thoreau had become homesick in Staten Island while tutoring the children of Emerson's brother William, he had written to Lidian Emerson what could only be called "a love letter" (C, 121), which Lidian "was almost ashamed to show" to Henry's family (JMN, XV, 490).[10] Though one senses strong tracings of an Oedipal complex in this affair, at a deep level they suggest not so much a sexual but an intellectual and artistic rivalry with and displacement of the father figure.

But Thoreau's rivalry with Emerson was not so much over the hand of Lidian as over that of Nature, for which Emerson had professed the prior claim, though from the elevation of his lecture platform. Thoreau, however, was the more persistent, attentive, and intimate wooer. Having been nudged by Emerson's *Nature* to attend to what Nature would say, then journalizing the veracity of Emerson's claim in "The American Scholar" that "Know thyself" and "Study nature" are ultimately the same (CW, I, 55), Thoreau listened to the whispered sweet nothings of Nature with an ear so rapt as to contradict Emerson's appraisal that he had chosen to be "the bachelor of thought & nature," and was "near to the old monks in their ascetic religion!" (JMN, XV, 261). In 1851 Thoreau, perhaps with a sidelong glance at Emerson, confided in his journal that he was more the husbandman than the bachelor of Nature:

> The intellect of most men is barren. They neither fertilize nor are fertilized. It is the marriage of the soul with Nature that makes the intellect fruitful, that gives birth to imagination. . . . The man of intellect only, the prosaic man, is a barren, staminiferous flower; the poet is a fertile and perfect flower. (J, II, 413-14)

By February 1, 1852, Thoreau was complaining of the "cold words" of a friend on whom he had relied—plainly Emerson—and went on to write:

> While we preach obedience to human laws and to that portion of the divine laws set forth in the New Testament, the natural laws of genius, of love and friendship, we do not preach nor insist upon. . . . How much of seeming recklessness, even selfishness, is to be explained by obedience to this code of the divine laws! (J, III, 262)

Did not such obedience entail the leaving of father and mother even, including intellectual and artistic parents? And was this not especially the case for one who had apprenticed himself to the advocate of Self-

Reliance? Emerson once asserted that he did not wish to "bring men to me, but to themselves. I delight in driving them from me" (JMN, XIV, 258). But inevitably there were pain, anger, and confusion in their estrangement. Instructed by Emerson, Thoreau must follow the lead of his own unconscious genius, one that would lead him beyond the mosaic patterning of his expression—as in *A Week*—to the organic one that would shape *Walden.* Perhaps Emerson lacked the ability to see such value in the mature work of his onetime disciple. Shortly after the publication of *Walden,* he wrote that "a man can only write one book. That is the reason why everybody begs readings & extracts of the young poet until 35" (JMN, XIII, 348). This seems to accord with Emerson's treatment of Thoreau as writer, first clamoring for extracts for the pages of *The Dial,* then nearly oblivious to the genius of *Walden,* published when Thoreau had just turned thirty-seven.

The peculiar genius of Emerson had led him to the lecture platform: in speaking, not in writing, the aura of inspiration radiated about the ex-minister. Once he tried to convince Thoreau of his sense of ecstasy in public speaking: "I went to the public assembly, put myself in the conditions, & instantly feel this new craving,—I hear the voice, I see the beckoning of this Ghost." But, as he also commented, "H. D. T., with whom I talked of this last night, does not or will not perceive how natural is this, and only hears the word Art in a sinister sense" (JMN, IX, 71). After following the lead of Emerson by lecturing in Providence on December 6, 1854, Thoreau vented his irritation privately the next day: "I would rather write books than lectures. That is fine, this coarse" (J, VII, 79). Whatever posthumous amendments Emerson made about the genius of Thoreau relate mainly to his life and journal expressions, not to his artistic masterpiece—*Walden.*

Still, with Thoreau safely in his grave, Emerson seemed to sense what he had first failed to notice in the "literary task" Thoreau had set himself to—that his journals were a cache of love letters of unsuspected intimacy. In reading them, Emerson acknowledged that Thoreau shows

> muscle, & ventures on & performs feats which I am forced to decline. In reading him, I find the same thought, the same spirit that is in me, but he takes a step beyond, & illustrates by excellent images that which I should have conveyed in a sleepy generality. (JMN, XV, 353)

In 1857 Emerson recorded a brief thaw in their relationship following a walk with Thoreau on the first of May, during which Thoreau had deftly fashioned a naturalist's specimen box from a strip of white birch bark. Attempting to stir up a resurgence of camaraderie, Emerson wrote in his journal: "We will make a book on walking, 'tis certain, & have easy lessons for beginners. 'Walking in ten Lessons' " (JMN, XIV, 137). Emerson would never make such a book, but Thoreau, who regularly walked three or four hours a day, did so with essays, including "Walking," collected for a posthumous volume aptly titled *Excursions.* Emerson went on to remark, in absolute innocence of whatever artistic or Oedipal innuendos a Freudian might there discern, that "H. [Henry] had found, he said, lately a fungus which was a perfect Phallus; & in the books one is noted *Obscoenum.*" Thoreau was so reserved in overreaching Emerson for the hand of Nature that his gesture of dismissal, an equivalent fig, was almost certainly unconscious.

*

In an illuminating study of Emerson, Joel Porte judged "Emerson's bond with Thoreau . . . far more personal" than that with Carlyle, for "their friendship touched his thought and feelings in more vital ways."[11] It was a friendship, coming at the right time, that touched Thoreau's emerging genius in ways so directive as to risk being taken for granted. Having lately discovered this to be the case, I have paired these Concord neighbors from time to time, with an admitted bias for Thoreau. For those of a contrary bias, I plead as indulgence Emerson's nearly matchless generosity of spirit.

Finally, though I may seem to have come full circle in my estimation of Thoreau and the psychologists, particularly the determinists, in finding an Oedipal relationship between these two major figures in our heritage, there is an important difference at the crossroads. Oedipus came to his fated encounter at a place where three roads met because he was in flight from an evil announced by the oracle at Delphi. Thoreau's encounter with his surrogate father came about because he was in pursuit of his own genius, which he was determined to grasp. Oedipus was determined in spite of the fact—perhaps because of the fact—that he was looking over his shoulder, and ran headlong into what he wished to avoid at all costs. Thoreau was determined because of the fact that he was looking ahead to discover at all costs what was there. Emerson may have discovered that all nature was a revelation, a sphinx to unriddle; it remained for Thoreau to see, almost clean through, to a side of Nature's sentence that the sand foliage in the Deep Cut riddled, and that he there divined by seemly deliberation.[12] *Walden* is the expression of what he divined, the fulfillment of a journal observation that "it is vastly easier to discover than to see when the cover is off" (PJ, I, 183; LJ, 166). This study traces the process of that discovery and the myth it generated in our nation's most thoroughly religious radical.

II

Half Way the Law of Currents

2

Emerson: With Frost in the Current

Whilst the abstract question occupies your intellect, nature brings it in the concrete to be solved by your hands.

Emerson, *Nature* (CW, I, 44)

IN *Studies in Classic American Literature,* D. H. Lawrence tellingly observed that the rhythm of American art activity is dual, "a disintegrating and sloughing of the old consciousness" and "the forming of a new consciousness underneath."[1] Though Poe, as he remarked, had only the "disintegrative vibration," Emerson and Thoreau surely had both. Moreover, Emerson, who stands as representative man in the period of America's intellectual coming of age he is credited for inaugurating, once defined the age of puberty as "the passage from the Unconscious to the Conscious" (JMN, IV, 348). One expression of this dual process Emerson exemplified is travel taken in obedience to "some deep, inward voice of religious belief"—again the words are Lawrence's: "Obeying from within."[2] As Joel Porte has convincingly demonstrated, Emerson's "orientation" in traveling seems to have been eastward, though there were obviously some retrograde movements.[3] Thoreau's was persistently westward, with the sun, though inclined somewhat to the Southwest, from where the Native American's thawing spirit (Manitou) emanated. In "Walking," Thoreau generalized that "we go eastward to realize history and study the works of art and literature, retracing the steps of the race; we go westward as into the future, with a spirit of enterprise and adventure," one with the sun, the "Great Pioneer," which sets in "the garden of the Hesperides . . . foundation of all those fables" (W, V, 215).

These personal inclinations are perhaps best exemplified by the deviation each put upon a proposal to travel to the West Indies for reasons of health. On the brink of such a journey, Emerson in 1832 wrote to his brother of an abrupt change of plans, for "in a few hours the dream changed into a purpureal vision of Naples & Italy" (L, I, 359). But Thoreau, advised to journey to the West Indies in search of health in 1861, perversely headed west, as if reading "West Indies" with a deadpanned literalness to justify a trip to the frontier in western Minnesota where he caught a glimpse of the Sioux in their native place (C, 615). In his "Eastering," Emerson would follow the lengthened shadows of historical Christianity to their projecting sources; in his Westering, Thoreau would discern in "our shadows . . . an insensible perspiration toward the sun," which he emulated in a writing style whose "volatile truth" (Wa, 325) rose above the inadequacy of words in their residual statement. Emerson felt his religion, historically, as the tie that binds, though its sacrament no longer proved nourishing to him; Thoreau, who had early and quietly signed off from his church, felt no ties to a formal creed, though he was nourished by an umbilical cord to an extravagant and unbounded West, "white on the chart" (Wa, 321), and found communion in daily nibbling the crust of the earth. But at a stage of passage when they began to discern and follow the deep currents of their independent lives, both, too, had encounters with an early frost.

*

By late spring, 1832, the temperature of Emerson's spirit had descended to the bulb after the death of his first wife, Ellen. No longer able to administer the Lord's Supper in good faith, in a "week of moral excitement" when the "Thermometer Says Temperate"—it was June 2—Emerson nonetheless found it "Cold, cold" (JMN, IV, 27). He had found those "Reasoning Machines" (JMN, II, 238)—of Locke, Clarke, and Hume—"bare reason, cold as cucumber" (L, I, 174). Before year's end, having resigned his pastorate, he was radically disoriented from what he would come to confess was the "corpse-cold Unitarianism . . . of Brattle Street & Boston" (JMN, IX, 381), and departed from that "icehouse of Unitarianiam" (JMN, VIII, 182) on Christmas Day. By timing as well as compass heading, he had embarked on an "Eastering" journey that would put him in Rome during Holy Week.

But once in Europe, Emerson was affected by both vibrations, the historical tradition of Christianity and the unfolding God within. When his foot first touched Old World soil at Malta, he pointedly wrote of entering Europe "at the little end so we shall admire by just degree from the Maltese architecture up to St. Peter's" (JMN, IV, 116). Arriving in Rome, Emerson attended Palm Sunday services at the Sistine Chapel in the morning, visited St. Peter's that afternoon, and still later at the Chiesa Nuova listened to music sung so beautifully by a choir of "mutilated [castrated] wretches" that it was "painful to hear them" (JMN, IV, 153). In the Sistine Chapel three days later, he heard the *Miserere* sung, as if drawn from an instrument "more like the Eolian harp than any thing else" (JMN,

IV, 154). On Holy Thursday the "forms" of the liturgy he witnessed struck him more powerfully than he expected; and he longed, in vain as it turned out, to hear from Pope Gregory but "a single sentence or a single word" (JMN, IV, 155) that might bear the traces of his own life's experience. On Easter morning at St. Peter's, he was again moved, first by the unveiling (apocalypse) of the statuary at the celebration of Christianity's greatest triumph, and then by the Pope's benediction to all points of the compass, which he found a "sublime spectacle" (JMN, IV, 157). In Florence several weeks later, he felt a painful longing to revisit St. Peter's, "which I can never more behold" (JMN, IV, 169).

Leaving Italy he entered Switzerland, pausing at Lausanne on the shores of Lake Leman where he visited the summerhouse of Edward Gibbon—one of those sceptics who had turned "the sweetwaters to bitter" (JMN, II, 108)—had written *Decline and Fall* (JMN, IV, 194). He went on to the birthplace of Calvinism—Geneva, a city that straddled not only the currents of the Rhone River at its source, but also those countercurrents of Western man's self-demeaning and self-glorifying instincts set to a flow from Geneva by John Calvin and Jean-Jacques Rousseau. Emerson found little to gratify his religious imagination there, however, and cryptically noted that "the Established Church of Geneva is now Unitarian & the three Calvinistic clergymen of the city are ejected" (JMN, IV, 195). The aggregation of evidence to show a propensity in historical Christianity to decline and fall so distressed Emerson that he nearly canceled a most reluctant visit to Ferney and the chateau of Voltaire, "king of the scorners" (JMN, IV, 194). But in Paris, a gradual resuscitation of spirits occurred, and when Emerson crossed the channel, he would turn to the English Romantic poets for spiritual nourishment.

Notwithstanding his apparent failure to discover an affecting spiritual thaw at the historical sources of his religious heritage, Emerson was nonetheless able to strike the optative note a year after his return to New England: "What a benefit if a rule could be given whereby the mind could at any moment *east* itself, & find the sun" (JMN, V, 38). He had done so—was in the process of doing so—in writing *Nature,* the "book of Revelation of our St. Radulphus," as Oliver Wendell Holmes called it, which proposes a radical orientation of man with nature.[4] What enabled him to do so had come about in part through his visit to the Jardin des Plantes in Paris, and in part by his responses—delayed in both cases—to Goethe and Coleridge. In journeying through Sicily and Italy, Emerson had been guided by the *Italienische Reise* of the Weimar sage, recently deceased, who had advised Waldo's older brother in a private interview to stick to his ministerial calling.[5] Twice in his Italian journeys Emerson had passed through Padua, where he took the time to attend a lecture on anatomy at the University, but made no mention of the famous Botanical Gardens where Goethe, in beholding a fan palm, had had his ineradicable epiphany of the metamorphosis. Goethe had not himself understood the import of his visionary gleam until he recalled, forty-five years later, that till then his studies of the variation of plant types had only suggested a grouping

under one concept, [so that] it gradually became clear to me that the concept could also be valid in a higher sense; a challenge which hovered in my mind at that time in the sensuous form of a supersensuous archetype. . . . Only a person who has himself experienced the impact of a fertile idea, be it original, or communicated to him or engrafted by others, will understand what passionate activity is stirred in our minds, what enthusiasm we feel, when we glimpse in advance and its totality something which is later to emerge in greater and greater detail in the manner suggested by its early development. . . . I was bound to be occupied with it, if not exclusively, nevertheless during the rest of my life.[6]

Not till Emerson stood in the Jardin des Plantes did he sense something of the compelling ocular evidence of the metamorphosis that had moved Goethe so powerfully; and then he hungered to be convinced that his destiny, like Goethe's, was to be a naturalist. The next year he strained for "the glimmering of the pure plastic Idea . . . what Goethe sought in his Metamorphosis of Plants" (JMN, IV, 288).[7] It was a debt Emerson acknowledged to Goethe for the rest of his life: in 1850 "Goethe" was the final chapter in the architecture of *Representative Man,* in the preface of which Emerson invoked Goethe's peculiar archetype by calling man "that noble endogenous plant which grows, like the palm, from within outward" (CW, IV, 4); in 1853, as Moncure Conway reported, Emerson had in his study two statuettes and a portrait of Goethe, and even a cat by that name.[8] Looking back upon his career in 1876, Emerson in "Poetry and Imagination" repeatedly and prominently mentions the metamorphosis to suggest an identity of thought and nature:

Nature is itself a vast trope, and all particular natures are tropes. . . . All thinking is analogizing, and it is the use of life to learn metonomy. The endless passing of one element into new forms, the incessant metamorphosis, explains the rank which the imagination holds in our catalogue of mental powers. The imagination is the reader of these forms. (EW, VIII, 15)

In the same essay, Emerson singles out Goethe as having preeminently realized this analogy: "Science does not know its debt to imagination. Goethe did not believe that a great naturalist could exist without this faculty" (EW, VIII, 10).

By writing that "in poetry we say we require the miracle" (EW, VIII, 16), Emerson suggests that for him nature's "everflowing metamorphosis" expressed tropically (by a turn) the miracle of the translation of spirit into form, of breath into word. To the high priest of American Transcendentalism, here was the "transubstantiation, the conversion of daily bread into the holiest symbols" (EW, VIII, 35), for in his mind the metamorphosis supplanted the Unitarian symbol of transubstantiation that he could not embrace within the received forms of worship in the months leading to his first journey to Europe. In the winter of 1866-67, Emerson reflected in his journal:

> The word *miracle,* as it is used, only indicates the savage ignorance of the devotee, staring with wonder to see water turned into wine, & heedless of the stupendous fact of himself being there present. If the water became wine, became fire, became a chorus of angels, it would not compare with the familiar fact of his own perception. Here he stands, a lonely thought, harmoniously organized into correspondence with the Universe of mind & matter.[9] (JMN, XVI, 54)

Emerson's response to Coleridge, similarly delayed, seems to have deepened and expanded in his lifetime.[10] Taking leave of Europe on September 1, 1833, Emerson at Liverpool summed up his satisfaction in having traveled through Malta, Sicily, Italy, Switzerland, France, England, and Scotland, and in seeing "the men I wished to see,—Landor, Coleridge, Carlyle, Wordsworth," even though they all seemed deficient "in insight into religious truth," without an "idea of that species of moral truth which I call the first philosophy" (JMN, IV, 78-79). But once at sea and homeward bound, he was at work to remedy that deficiency, for in the little "book about nature" (JMN, IV, 237) growing under his hand, he was to start a new faith and a new career for the edification of his country no less than himself. Twenty-one months later, still at work on his collection of essays "chiefly upon Natural Ethics," he wrote to Frederic Henry Hedge of his attempt to bring "a pebble or two to the edification of the new temple whilst so many wise hands are demolishing the old" (L, I, 447). His "new temple" may well derive from one of his favorite authors, Francis Bacon, who two centuries earlier had proposed building a new and profane "temple of Salamon" for a community of scientists who were to use inductive reasoning (the "new philosophy") to establish a relationship between man and nature that would redound to man's utility.[11]

In the sensational and empirical philosophy of John Locke, the Baconian aspiration seemed to have found its spokesman. But Locke, who in New England had been made to sustain a sense of order in the temples of worship guarded by such stalwarts as the elder Channing, proved a stultification to the high hopes of young Unitarian idealists flushed with a Kantian enthusiasm. In his investigation, Emerson, like Bacon, proposed to interrogate creation in order to develop "an original relation to the universe" (CW, I, 7), organized the first half of his seminal study on the uses of the world, quoted Bacon's "good thoughts are no better than good dreams, unless they be executed," and mentioned the herald of inductive thought by name in "Language" (CW, I, 22). But unlike Bacon, Emerson required a supersensual utility of nature; and for this a "clearer reason" (CW, I, 33) than Locke's opened his eye to the "great apparition, that shines so peacefully around us" (CW, I, 7). That Reason, that wise eye, came through, or was certainly reinforced by, Coleridge.

Soon after returning from England, Emerson had come upon an article by Frederic H. Hedge, "Coleridge's Literary Character," in the *Christian Examiner* for March 1833. There Hedge cogently rehearsed the distinction between reason (the intuitive faculty) and understanding (the logical or discursive faculty) in his discussion of the two characteristics of genius—originality and form. In an access of enthusiasm, Emerson wrote to his brother Edward of the article as "a living leaping Logos," and of Hedge as an "unfolding man" (L, I, 401-2), the former phrase suggesting a "present expositor of the divine mind" (CW, I, 39), as he would write in *Nature,* the latter the unfolding organic metaphor that has come to be nearly synonymous with Transcendental art activity. In a second letter to Edward, six months later, Emerson wrote of the understanding and the "eternal Reason," mentioning Milton, Coleridge, and the Germans who, he said, had first drawn the distinction "between Reason & Understanding" (L, I, 412) that had come to the Transcendentalists via James Marsh's edition of Coleridge's *Aids to Reflection.*

In *Nature,* Emerson uses Coleridge's terminology in defining the understanding as the faculty that "adds, divides, combines, measures," and Reason as the faculty that "transfers all these lessons into its own world of thought, by perceiving the analogy that marries Matter and Mind" (CW, I, 23). While in "Beauty," the third chapter of *Nature,* Emerson renders the insight of Reason with an abstract "perception" (CW, I, 13), in chapter 6, "Idealism," he invokes ocular imagery to discriminate between the "unrenewed understanding" and Reason: "Until this higher agency intervened, the animal eye sees, with wonderful accuracy, sharp outlines and colored surfaces. When the eye of Reason opens, to outline and surface are at once added, grace and expression" (CW, I, 30). Ocular imagery dominates the concluding chapter as well: not only in title ("Prospects," from *speculo,* I see), but in subject matter the chapter is visionary, its final paragraph beginning, "So shall we come to look at the world with new eyes," and concluding that man shall enter his kingdom over nature "without more wonder than the blind man feels who is gradually restored to perfect sight" (CW, I, 44-45). Thus when Christopher Cranch "unerringly picked" Emerson's "transparent eyeball" for caricature, he discerned an "eye of Reason" (CW, I, 30) essentially Coleridgean.[12]

Although the ocular image aptly suggests the dominant mode of perception, of insight, of Reason, it inadequately conveys the dynamic relationship between subject and object that Emerson characteristically renders in terms of flowing. In all but one of the chapters of *Nature*—"Spirit" is the exception—fluxional metaphors appear, many of them prominently. In the opening paragraph of "Introduction," for example, Emerson writes of the "floods of life [which] stream around and through us, and invite us by the powers they supply," and wonders, this being so, why we should "grope among the dry bones of the past" (CW, I, 7); in "Prospects" he writes of instances of Reason's authority as occasions of "an instantaneous in-streaming causing power" (CW, I, 43), and in "Commodity" of "this ocean of air above, this ocean of water beneath . . . the endless circulations of the divine charity [which] nourish man" (CW, I, 11). Even in the "transparent eyeball" passage, ocular imagery is immediately succeeded by fluxional: "The currents of the Universal Being circulate through me; I am part or particle of God" (CW, I, 10).

Given Emerson's predilection for images of flowing, critics have aptly named "Idealism" the "bridge chapter" over which he labored to "pontificate" between nature as an object of sense and as a manifestation of spirit.[13] In its first five paragraphs Emerson disposes of the question "whether nature outwardly exists" by an act of faith: "God never jests with us, and will not compromise the end of nature, by permitting any inconsequence in its procession" (CW, I, 29). Then distinguishing among the senses, the "unrenewed understanding," and Reason, Emerson asserts that a simple "mechanical" shift in point of view can give man a "low degree of the sublime" (CW, I, 31). But only "Reason," he insists, enables an experience of the true sublime, "unfixes the land and the sea, makes them revolve around the axis of his primary thought."

Mention of "mechanical" and "primary thought" brings to mind the central paired terms in Coleridge's literary criticism—the "mechanic" and "organic," and the "primary imagination" and the "secondary imagination."[14] In the chapter Emerson finds it relevant to quote from Shakespeare's *The Tempest* in an attempt to illustrate a "transfiguration which all material objects undergo through the passion of the poet" (CW, I, 32). Embedded in the passage he quotes are the terms of Coleridge's hierarchy of senses, understanding, and reason, and the central image of the passage is that of flowing:

The charm dissolves apace,
And, as the morning steals upon the night,
Melting the darkness, so their rising *senses*
Begin to chase the ignorant fumes that mantle
Their clearer *reason.*

Their *understanding*
Begins to swell: and the approaching tide
Will shortly fill the *reason*able shores
That now lie foul and muddy.
(CW, I, 33; emphasis added)[15]

What lends credence to such an interpretation is that little more than a year after the publication of *Nature,* Emerson confided in his journal that "the most random word can be set in a place by a philosopher. Why then should we think it strange that critics of today should find wonderful ideal truth in Shakespeare's Tempest . . . [?]" (JMN, V, 382). In citing *The Tempest,* Emerson is suggesting that a means of bridging the flood between phenomenal and noumenal nature is insight, and that the circulation of the tide is Reason's flow through creation, which our understanding should imbibe so that it might "swell" in a manner to suggest imagination's organic, rather than fancy's merely mechanic, metaphor of the growth of the mind.

In "Prospects," ocular motif conjoins with flowing to form a parable of Emerson's own construction:

Once he [man] was permeated and dissolved by spirit. He filled nature with his overflowing currents. Out from him sprang the sun and moon; from man, the sun; from woman, the moon. The laws of his mind, the periods of his actions externized themselves into day and night, into the year and the seasons. But, having made for himself this huge shell, his waters retired; he no longer fills the veins and veinlets; he is shrunk to a drop. He sees, that the structure still fits him, but fits him colossally. Say, rather, once it fitted him, now it corresponds to him from far and on high. (CW, I, 42)

In Emerson's seminal book of a movement Joel Porte called "simply organicism in an American setting," one might expect to come frequently upon the metaphor of vegetation to suggest the growth of the mind.[16] Sampson Reed's "Oration on Genius," delivered in 1821 but not published until 1849, contended that "the mind of the infant contains within itself the first rudiments of all that will be hereafter, and needs nothing but expansion, as the leaves and branches and fruit of a tree are said to exist in the seed from which it springs."[17] Emerson heard that address, given at his Harvard Commencement on August 21, 1821, and he "secured a copy, which he considered a treasure, and praised the work throughout his life as the creation of an original mind."[18] In *Growth of the Mind* (1829), Reed had challenged directly the Lockean metaphor of the mind as a tabula rasa by supposing it seminal and organic:

There prevails a most erroneous sentiment that the mind is originally vacant, and requires only to be filled up; and there is reason to believe that this is most intimately connected with false conceptions of time. The mind is originally a most delicate germ whose husk is the body, planted in this world that the light of heaven may fall upon it with a gentle radiance and call forth its energies.[19]

Though the matter of Emerson's *Nature* offered bountiful opportunity for elaborating vegetal metaphors, the few that do occur seem merely to assert a relationship between mind and nature, in a manner generally abstract and tendentious only. Following the "transparent eyeball" paragraph, Emerson writes that "the greatest delight which the fields and woods minister, is the suggestion of an occult relation between man and the vegetable. I am not alone and unacknowledged. They nod to me and I to them" (CW, I, 10). He goes on to assert in "Language" that this relationship is "not fancied by some poet, but stands in the will of God" (CW, I, 22). In this provocative chapter, he suggests that such a "radical correspondence" may be found in language, for "every word which is used to express a moral or intellectual fact, if traced to its root, is found to be borrowed from some material appearance" (CW, I, 18). In such operative words as "relation," "radical," and "root," one senses a drift from abstraction to image; and when in "Discipline" Emerson declares that "all organizations are radically alike" (CW, I, 26), the vegetal image is near to hand since he has just described the moral law at the center of nature as it "radiates to the circumference. It is the pith and marrow of every substance." Even here "marrow" confounds the evolving vegetal metaphor hinted by "pith"; and one can find a developed similitude of growing only in "Spirit," where it suggests an image of flowing as well:

The Supreme Being, does not build up nature around us, but puts it forth through us, as the life of the tree puts forth new branches and leaves through the pores of the old. As a plant upon the earth, so a man rests upon the bosom of God; he is nourished by unfailing fountains, and draws, at his need, inexhaustible power. (CW, I, 38)

What dictates the skeletal form of *Nature,* bones protruding, is the faculty of understanding with a tradition of sermonizing by firstlies and secondlies. But burgeoning images of flowing and growing signal the imagination's anticipation of a metamorphosis occurring neither in word nor in trope in the whole of *Nature.*[20]

Within a year after his little book appeared, however, Emerson, in "The American Scholar," would use the metamorphosis, both in word and in trope. To be sure, the one occurrence of the word conveys a sense of what Daniel Shea calls a "regressive metamorphosis," which in turn suggests a lapse—"Man is thus metamorphosed into a thing, into many things" (CW, I, 53).[21] Nonetheless, the address offers a richly elaborated figure of progressive or generative metamorphoses:

> The new deed is yet a part of life,—remains for a time immersed in our unconscious life. In some contemplative hour, it detaches itself from the life like a ripe fruit, to become a thought of the mind. Instantly, it is raised, transfigured; the corruptible has put on incorruption. . . . In its grub state, it cannot fly, it cannot shine,—it is a dull grub. But suddenly, without observation, the selfsame thing unfurls beautiful wings, and is an angel of wisdom. (CW, I, 60)

Emerson was here beginning to demonstrate what he had written in "Prospects": "Whilst the abstract question occupies your intellect, nature brings it in the concrete to be solved by your hands" (CW, I, 44).

One feature of the "old consciousness" Emerson was sloughing off concerned dead or moribund language. Perry Miller once observed that a notable difference between the romantic revolutionary in England and in America was that, while the former's thrust was against the poetic diction of the Neoclassical age, nobody in America had so tyrannized over native taste as had Alexander Pope.[22] But in a nation whose early literature, especially in New England, derived from a rigorous cultivation of the divine word, a strong case could be made for the tyranny of the Bible. Its translators and through them its preachers raised pulpit oratory to a fine, if prolonged, art. And that most popular of allegorical "novels," *Pilgrim's Progress,* affected a biblical dialogue that proved irresistible even to the utilitarian sensibilities of Benjamin Franklin. Certainly it helped put the conversational stamp on the works of such as Cooper, Melville and, especially, Hawthorne (see JMN, VII, 244-45).

Like Wordsworth and Coleridge in the "Preface" to the *Lyrical Ballads,* Emerson in the first chapter of *Nature* had proposed to recover a "poetical sense" of nature, an "integrity of impressions made by manifold natural objects" that "few adult persons" (CW, I, 9) have maintained. Subsequently in "Language," he wrote of how the "corruption of man is followed by the corruption of language" until "new imagery ceases to be created, and old words are perverted to stand for things which are not." But it is for wise men to "pierce this rotten diction and fasten words again to visible things; so that picturesque language is at once a commanding certificate that he who employs it, is a man in alliance with truth and God" (CW, I, 20). In supplying instances of such language use, Emerson suggests himself as that wise man, and *Nature* as his attempted Apocalypse.

In another sense, however, *Nature* was the first shovel in Emerson's efforts to unearth a book of Genesis. From the "Language" chapter of *Nature* through "The American Scholar," "The Divinity School Address," and "Self-Reliance" to "The Poet," Emerson would attempt not only to perceive as luminous the passageway of spirit into nature, but also to trace the process whereby the intimations of the miraculous fade away, those "voices which we hear in solitude . . . but [which] grow faint and inaudible as we enter into the world" (CW, II, 29). In these essays and addresses, Emerson is at work defining, in order to slough off, those stultifying outside influences—a foreign culture, an historical Christianity, conformity, consistency—to attend to the voice of "God . . . here within" (CW, II, 41), so that he might rely on the deep radical "Self" as the "word made flesh" (CW, II, 43). In "The Divinity School Address," Emerson attacked the tyranny of the Bible, though obliquely, by taking issue with the "Hebrew and Greek Scriptures" for their lack of "epical integrity" (CW, I, 92), and excoriated those spiritless ministers who preached "as if God were dead" (CW, I, 84). He described at length one such "formalist"—almost certainly the Reverend Barzillai Frost of Concord—who had not learned the secret of his profession, "namely, to convert life into truth" (CW, I, 85-86). It was the very complaint he had made about Pope Gregory at the Easter services in Rome.

Ordained on February 1, 1837, at the Unitarian church in Concord where he had been called to serve as colleague to Dr. Ezra Ripley, Emerson's stepgrandfather, the Reverend Barzillai Frost (1804-58) then served from 1837 to 1857. They were years of special significance for Emerson and Thoreau, both in their evolving careers as Transcendentalists and artists, and in their relationship. At the time of Frost's arrival in Concord, Thoreau was about to finish his formal education at Harvard, and stimulated by keeping a journal, he began to draw knowledge from nature at first hand. At the same time, as Conrad Wright has convincingly demonstrated, Emerson was entering a final stage in his crisis of vocation. Having resigned from the Second Church in Boston in 1832, he had nonetheless supplied the pulpit at East Lexington on a regular basis, and exchanged with other ministers as well. Emerson was present at the ordination of Frost, who within a few months had settled into such unrelieved sterility and monotony in his preachments that he symbolized for Emerson a lack of the true religious sentiment and a dependence on dogma, especially concerning miracles.

The "final climax of Emerson's crisis of vocation" came on Sunday, March 18, 1838, when Emerson complained in his journal of the "formalist" preacher.[23] To Emerson it seemed that the minister could speak only about miracles, while in the snowstorm outside the miracle of nature was plain to see. Thus, while "the snowstorm was real, the preacher [was] merely spectral" (JMN, V, 463). There is fine irony here, as Joel Porte points out, in that "the preacher should seem *spectral* compared even to the frigid and ghostly reality of snow," and that Emerson's description of the "Reverend Barzillai *Frost* should increase our sense of how intricate is his play of imagination here."[24] But a few days later, when Emerson received his invitation from the senior class of the Divinity School of Harvard to give the "customary discourse," he had in his journal a draft of the pivotal experience that he would generalize in calling each future minister to become "a newborn bard of the Holy Ghost" (CW, I, 90) by preaching to the people of "his life,—life passed through the fire of thought" (CW, I, 86).[25] Although Emerson was too full of the milk of human kindness to mention Frost by name—even in his journal—the implied contrast with the snowstorm outside suggests that the latest representative of a religious heritage, who stood in the pulpit Emerson himself might well have filled, symbolized institutionalized religion's assumption that the revelation was over. The contrast between this killing Frost and "the fire of thought" could hardly be greater.

Neither Wright nor Porte seems cognizant of a further intricacy in a play of imagination about Frost's baptismal name—Barzillai. But it seems to have been common, encyclopedic knowledge that the biblical name (a friend of David, in II Samuel 19) had some connection with "*barzel*," "iron, strong," or "son of iron."[26] It is unlikely that such a witty fellow as James Russell Lowell, who in the early summer of 1838 was rusticated from Harvard and placed in the care of the Frost family, would miss the meaning. In fact, Lowell referred to his host as "Bar" in his correspondence, and once quizzed him about the probable reason for a parishioner's standing up during the good reverend's sermon. "Bar" responded that the man was probably unaccustomed to "intellectual exertion," and was therefore "unable to follow a train of ideas." Lowell's amused reaction was: "What a capital expression that is for such a railroadlike mind as Bar's! which has the same train travelling over & over it again [&] again." Lowell's rustication at Concord had enabled him to walk with Emerson, and it may be that they joked together over "Bar" Frost as the very antithesis of flowing, especially since the maiden name of Bar's young wife, Stone, reinforced the pun. Moreover, such high jinks seem to have been elaborated by a visit from Nathan Hale, Jr., Lowell's classmate. When Hale wrote Lowell of the Frosts' generous hospitality, he could not resist a punning inversion of the meaning of the reverend's name, complaining that the bed of "Bar" Frost was "*too soft* for this *hot weather*," and facetiously proposing to arrange for him to preach at Andover in order to get "a taste of the delights of feathers, and ther. 90° in the shade—."[27]

However "Bar" Frost reacted to Emerson's address—and Emerson did send him a copy (JMN, XII, 180)—many of the other Unitarian ministers sat bolt upright. Andrews Norton was so provoked that he called it "the Latest Form of Infidelity," for in his estimation it struck "directly at the root of faith in Christianity, and indirectly of all religion, by denying the miracles attesting the divine mission of Christ."[28] In his address Emerson had dealt with miracles in an exasperatingly elusive way—especially given their importance to the older generation of Unitarians—suggesting that miracles seemed "ridiculous" (CW, I, 80) because they addressed the senses, not "the aspiration of society." Moreover, Emerson said that Christ "*spoke* of miracles; for he felt that man's life was a miracle, and all that man doth, and he knew that this daily miracle shines, as the man is diviner" (CW, I, 81; emphasis added), which seems a considerable distortion of how miracles are "reported" in the New Testament. "But the very word Miracle, as pronounced by Christian churches," continued Emerson, "gives a false impression; it is Monster. It is not one with the blowing clover and the falling rain."

Randall Stewart has pointed out that in the address Emerson does not deny the divinity of Christ; rather, he denies the exclusiveness of that divinity, attributing the divine not to Christ alone among men, but to every man who, like Christ, would be "true to what is in you and me" (CW, I, 81).[29] Similarly, Emerson seems not to deny the miraculous but to assert that everything is miraculous. Later in the address he says that "to aim to convert a man by miracles, is a profanation of the soul. A true conversion, a true Christ, is now, as always, to be made by the reception of beautiful sentiments" (CW, I, 83). His recovery from this somewhat cloying turn of phrase is clarifying: "It is true that a great and rich soul, like his, falling among the simple, does so preponderate, that, as his did, it names the world." Such statements, elaborated more fully in "The Poet," suggest that in Emerson's view the New Testament miracles should give way to the miracle of language, and the true "conversion" is the naming of the world, a task for the poet-priest.

In "The Poet," Emerson would deal with man not partial but whole, capable of perceiving—undistracted by restrictive influences—and also of articulating the word, for a man "is only half himself, the other half is his expression" (CW, III, 4). Midway through "The Poet," Emerson avails himself of etymological resources as a means of drawing nigh the point of naming, writing that

> language is made up of images, or tropes, which now, in their secondary use, have long ceased to remind us of their poetic origin. But the poet names the thing because he sees it, or comes one step nearer to it than any other. This expression, or naming, is not art, but a second nature, grown out of the first, as a leaf out of a tree. (CW, III, 13)

In his figure of a leaf, one notes an organic rendering of Coleridge's distinction between primary and secondary imagination:

> The primary IMAGINATION I hold to be the living Power and prime Agent of all human Perception, and as a repetition in the finite mind of the eternal act of creation in the infinite I AM. The secondary Imagination I consider as an echo of the former. . . .[30]

If the Word was in the beginning, it was there that the miracle of language occurred, or had already occurred, and *illo tempore* signified a passage of spirit into form, breath into word, "as a leaf out of a tree." Emerson's leaf is but one of a veritable forest of organic tropes in this deeply textured essay.

But Emerson goes on to invoke the metamorphosis—the word occurs seven times—often with an accompanying and "tropical" flow. In one paragraph he suggests Reason's eye effects a supersensual conversion:

As the eyes of Lyncaeus were said to see through the earth, so the poet turns the world to glass, and shows us all things in their right series and procession. For, through that better perception, he stands one step nearer to things, and sees the flowing or metamorphosis; perceives that thought is multiform; that within the form of every creature is a force impelling it to ascend into a higher form; and, following with his eyes the life, uses the forms which express that life, and so his speech flows with the flowing of nature. (CW, III, 12)

In the next paragraph he draws an analogy between the accompanying flow and baptism to suggest a decidedly religious character in the metamorphosis:

What we call nature, is a certain self-regulated motion, or change; and nature does all things by her own hands, and does not leave another to baptize her, but baptizes herself; and this through the metamorphosis again. (CW, III, 13)

Daniel Shea has remarked that "The Poet" is Emerson's "richest development of the theme of metamorphosis," and as a corollary, it seems to me, is his most radical religious expression.[31] With rapturous intensity Emerson there fixes upon that "holy place . . . where Being passes into Appearance, and Unity into Variety" (CW, III, 9), and describes the miracle of transubstantiation in terms of the metamorphosis. The religious intent of the Poet was to translate the "throbs and heart-beatings" of impression so that "thought may be ejaculated as Logos, or Word" (CW, III, 23). As "Sayers," poets had, as their holy end, to become "liberating gods. Men have really got a new sense, and found within their world, another world, or nest of worlds; for, the metamorphosis once seen, we divine that it does not stop" (CW, III, 17).

As an expression of Reason rather than understanding, "The Poet" is Emerson's closest approximation to the miracle of language, and this through a richly textured metaphor, metonomy, and metamorphosis meant to span the space between language and nature. Still, the essay concludes with the vapid pronouncement that "forms with transparent boundaries" are "outlets into celestial space" (CW, III, 24). In the summer of 1841, the period of "The Poet," Emerson had delivered "one of his most intense and orphic orations, 'The Method of Nature,' proclaiming ecstasy and metamorphosis as the ruling principles of the universe."[32] During the same period he had propounded in his "Oversoul" an aerial metaphor indicating that while he had indeed followed a metaphorical flowing and growing to their coalescence in a metamorphosis, he had, in the meantime, lost his grip on the suggestive radical and root metaphors that seemed emergent in his earlier essays and addresses. Perhaps Emerson was himself, with Bronson Alcott, something of an "airplant" afflicted with a family proclivity to etherealize, and a need therefore to hold on hard to the huckleberry bushes.[33] In "The Transcendentalist," Emerson acknowledged as much in confessing that his life was "superficial, takes no root in the deep world" (CW, I, 213), and in "The Poet" seemed to side with Timaeus in affirming that a man is "a heavenly tree, growing with his root, which is his head, upward . . . " (CW, III, 18). Except for his persistent and ineradicable influence, Emerson might seem to exemplify the seed sown on rocky ground that grows for a time, then shrivels up and dies. More fairly, he exemplifies the sower of the seed that flowered in New England.

If this appraisal seems somewhat unfair to Emerson personally, perhaps it is so because of an anticipated contrast with his "disciple" Thoreau, whose hold on the huckleberry bushes as well as his rootedness in Concord was absolutely tenacious. In fact, on precisely those two issues they differed, Emerson complaining of Thoreau's choice for captaining a huckleberry party instead of engineering for all America, and tolerant—but barely, and that chaffingly—of Thoreau's penchant for "referring everything to the meridian of Concord . . ." (EW, X, 480, 468). At a time when Emerson was propounding his Oversoul, Thoreau was drawn to the Undersoul, punningly, and perhaps contentiously, writing in "My Boots" of an "inward lustre that bespeaks / An open sole," a lustre with

> a worthier glory far
> Than that which gilds the outmost rind with darkness
> visible—
> Virtues that fast abide through lapse of years,
> Rather rubbed in than off. (PJ, I, 88; J, I, 60)

In negotiating the distance from priest to poet, in part by a significant trip to Europe, Emerson had not only broken free from the preachments of Frost in the currents of his individual and collective religious experience; he had found in those currents the substance of a metamorphosis into a religion that, as his Oversoul suggests, was tied to a lofty ideal. That burgeoning ideal no doubt worked its influence on Thoreau, who in the fall of 1837, under the aegis of Emerson, launched his literary career by beginning his own journal. Within five weeks, however, Thoreau was turning his attention from what was aloft to what was underfoot. And there he found a variety of frosts in nature whose preachments might somehow indicate the current of his own life, if he could somehow serve as their translator, thaw them, make them flow. Perhaps nature's frost, in its varied forms, held the key to his identity.

3

Thoreau: With Frost at the Source

And the Spirit of God moved upon the face of the waters.
Genesis 1:2

As A STUDENT at Harvard College in the mid-1830s, Thoreau seems already to have waved aside the "cold tea of Unitarianism" (JMN, IX, 339) that he would formally decline in 1841; thus his religious metabolism was relatively unaffected by such frost as influenced Emerson's religious experience. Nor did he, like Emerson's generation, "have to break the way from Locke to Coleridge," for he inherited the terminology and the ideas of Transcendentalism that derived from the English Romantic movement.[1] Moreover, he sensed his good luck in being born in the nick of time, and in the very place where Transcendental Reason and the organic metaphor would earn a local habitation and a name. When and where Emerson and Thoreau first met are uncertain; but by early 1837, Emerson had advanced Thoreau's cause for financial assistance at Harvard in a letter to President Josiah Quincy. On his part, Thoreau seems already to have caught the visionary gleam from Emerson's *Nature*, as had so many of his classmates. And though he may not have been present at Emerson's Phi Beta Kappa Address "The American Scholar," given to his graduating class (of 1837) on August 31, he must have been pleased and flattered by the generous friendship extended by his neighbor in Concord.[2]

Back home in Concord that fall, Thoreau began what was to become a two-million-word journal spanning twenty-four years of his life by cryptically recording its origin: " 'What are you doing now?' he asked. 'Do you keep a journal?' So I make my first entry today" (J, I, 3). Almost certainly the "he" was Emerson, who would doubtless have made Goethe and Coleridge fit subject matter of their first lengthy conversations. Soon, in fact, they were studying German together, and Thoreau's first journal entry, for October 22, concludes with a sentence probably fed to him directly by Emerson, who three months earlier had recorded in his own journal the same *"Es ist alles wahr wodurch du besser wirst"* (JMN, V, 346-47; PJ, I, 5; J, I, 3) that concluded Thoreau's first titled entry, "On Solitude."[3] On October 16 Emerson had gone to Walden Pond where he read Goethe at its shore. Almost at once he drew his willing disciple to the obligatory encounter with "the cow from which all [the Transcendentalists'] milk was drawn" (JMN, XI, 382), as Emerson would later remark of Goethe. The first thirty pages of Thoreau's published *Journal* are awash in Goethean draughts. But after four months, that source suddenly goes dry, and Thoreau is off, as he later wrote, "to extract from Nature whatever nutriment she can furnish. . . . I milk the sky and the earth" (J, V, 478).[4] He would consider Goethe at length again in *A Week on the Concord and Merrimack Rivers* (1849), raiding these journal entries and a lecture on poetry he read before the Concord Lyceum in 1843 (EEM, 172) to do so, but with his tutored enthusiasm strictly reined in. Margaret Fuller, who had inveigled Emerson into studying German, was an early Goethean enthusiast; but her reluctance to publish Thoreau in the pages of *The Dial* may have contributed to Thoreau's judgment, in *A Week,* that Goethe lacked genius and dwelt "in the regions of the understanding" (Wk, 143) rather than the imagination. There Thoreau went on to complain that while Goethe always looks at nature with a reference to art, the man of genius, the true Artist, "detects and applies the law from observation of the works of Genius, whether of man or nature" (Wk, 328). And then Thoreau—almost alone among the Transcendentalists—put Goethe behind him once and for all by charging that he left "a thin varnish or glaze" (Wk, 376) over his work and by preferring Chaucer to Goethe as the boatman who would convey him from a stream of thought back to a stream of life.[5]

And what of the influence of Samuel Taylor Coleridge, that other channel to American Transcendentalism set to a surge by James Marsh's American edition of *Aids to Reflection* (1829)? Already familiar with the Coleridgean "fancy," "imagination," and "reason," Thoreau had borrowed Coleridge's *Letters, Conversations, and Recollections* from the Harvard library in the summer of 1837.[6] In 1839 he was intrigued by Coleridge's experiment of strewing sand on a metallic plate, then sounding a harmonic chord over it, which made the grains assume the patterns of "circles, and other geometrical figures" that a discord would at once destroy. Characteristically, Thoreau derived a moral meaning from that natural fact: "The brave man is such a point of relative rest, over which the soul sounds ever a harmonic chord" (PJ, I, 97; J, I, 104-5). On January 19, 1841, he notes that "Coleridge, speaking of the love of God, says—'He that loves, may be sure he was loved first' " (PJ, I, 222; LJ, 214), and builds a miniature essay on that theme. Later that month he quotes Coleridge briefly (PJ, I, 230; J, I, 175), and the next month somewhat petulantly matches strides by remarking, "Coleridge observed the 'landscapes made by damp on a white-washed wall' and so have I" (PJ, I, 268; J, I, 217).

Although the journals of Thoreau in the 1840s are fragmentary, they contain quotations from Coleridge's *Table Talk, Aids to Reflection,* and *The Statesman's Manual;* and notebooks and reading lists he kept also refer to *Confessions of an Inquiring Spirit* and *Letters, Conversations, and Recollections.* Recently, Robert Sattelmeyer and Richard A. Hocks have argued that Thoreau's reading of Coleridge's *Theory of Life* in late 1848, shortly after its publication, had a "catalytic effect" (p. 281) on him comparable to that of the Jardin des Plantes on Emerson, for it provided Thoreau with "a philosophical underpinning" for "adopting the study of natural history, along with writing, as the principle occupation of his life."[7] While I dispute their contention that Coleridge is *the* catalyst for Thoreau at this crucial time of redirection and integration—unlike Emerson, he was in the process of becoming a naturalist—I agree that for Thoreau, "as for Coleridge, the law would always precede the phenomena that demonstrated it" (p. 282); but Thoreau had already glimpsed the demonstration of such law in the frost vegetation, almost a dozen years before reading Coleridge's *Theory.* Indeed, as if in recognition of extravagance in their claim, Sattelmeyer and Hocks also call for an assessment of "the books and the thinkers that actually furnished Thoreau with the points d'appui of his natural history studies" (p. 270). The answer was forthcoming almost at once with an excellent intellectual biography by Robert D. Richardson, Jr., *Henry Thoreau: A Life of the Mind.*[8] There Richardson persuasively demonstrates both the breadth and the depth of Thoreau's readings—like Coleridge, he was "a chain reader" (p. 245)—at this time of integration in which Coleridge was one of a number of important influences that included Alexander von Humboldt. But in the winter of 1851-52 during the pivotal period when the shape of *Walden* was being converted from the mechanic to the organic, Thoreau surely had the English poet-critic in mind when, observing in great detail the flight of a hawk, he concluded, "Flights of imagination, Coleridgean thoughts" (J, III, 144).

But New Year's Day found Thoreau contesting the opinion, reported by Chalmers, that Coleridge "wanted ideas which he could see all round and not such as he must look at away up in heavens." Having taken regular moonlight walks the previous summer, Thoreau was out of patience with Coleridge's view that "ideas that soar above the earth cannot be seen all around," to which he responds:

> They are moonshine, are they? Very well, then, do your night travelling when there is no moon to light you; but I will be thankful for the light that reaches me

from the star of least magnitude. I will be thankful that I see so much as one side of a celestial idea, one side of the rainbow and the sunset sky, the *face* of God alone. (J, III, 173-74)[9]

Nearly four months later, in citing the story of how a friend of Titian defended painting against the sculptor's charge of its being an incomplete art, he found a response to Coleridge. The painter in the story had produced the figure of

a warrior, who, having his back turned towards the spectator, stood looking at himself in a fountain, in whose limpid waters his full front figure was reflected. At the left of the warrior was suspended his suit of polished steel armor, in which was mirrored, with exact fidelity, the whole of his left side. At the right was painted a looking-glass, which reflected that side,

and by this means, the artist "won the wager." Thoreau retorts triumphantly, "So I would fain represent some truths as roundly and solidly as a statue, or as completely and in all their relations as Barbarelli his warrior,—so that you may see round them" (J, III, 464-65).

Only once more in the Journal is Coleridge mentioned by name (J, III, 328). There is an obligatory passing tribute in his essay on Carlyle (EEM, 223, 248, 258), but even that small praise was later undermined by his statement in *Walden* that he did not "propose to write an ode to dejection, but to brag as lustily as chanticleer in the morning" (Wa, 84). Still, the bravado of dismissal is mollified by an 1857 letter in which Thoreau encourages B. B. Wiley to "read Coleridge again & further—skipping all his theology," and also "DeQuincey's reminiscences of Coleridge & Wordsworth" (C, 478). And as with so many of the Transcendentalists, Thoreau from time to time alludes to Coleridge's Dejection Ode, and may at other times be thinking of the central images suggested by "The Aeolian Harp"—both Emerson and Thoreau owned such harps—and perhaps also by "Frost at Midnight."[10]

And where did such signings off and crowings leave a budding Transcendentalist in those times when, as Perry Miller put it, "Coleridge . . . and [the] shining blades of German steel" went "flashing through the brains of the young men" (LJ, 49)? Closer, it would seem, to his native town and the river that influenced it. Even as he pored over Goethe under Emerson's tutelage, rendering chunks of *Torquato Tasso* and *Italienische Reise* into what threatened to become a commonplace book, he was broadening the range of his expression on grounds more immediate to nature. A few pages into his journal, in an entry sandwiched between quotations from *Italienische Reise,* Thoreau fingered the pulse, "the jugular vein of Musketaquid. Who knows how much of the proverbial moderation of the inhabitants was caught from its dull circulation" (PJ, I, 12; J, I, 10).

In other passages near the source of his journal, his expression appropriates the metaphor and mood of running water. On November 3, for instance, he dreamily muses of launching himself on the stream of thought: "If one would reflect let him embark on some placid stream, and float with the current. He cannot resist the Muse" (PJ, I, 10; J, I, 8). Before his first November of journalizing runs out, he writes of looking "around for thoughts when I am overflowing myself" (PJ, I, 15; J, I, 13). Had he simply, however unconsciously, appropriated Emerson's sense of life as "primarily a flux and a becoming," a sense that so carried over into Emerson's expression that, according to F. O. Matthiessen, his essays "tended to deliquesce, like that on the Over-Soul, which is compared to water no less than a dozen times"? Matthiessen's appraisal that Emerson "saw himself, in a recurrent image, *standing* on the bank of a river *watching* the endless current upon which floated past him objects of all shapes and colors" is instructive in underscoring the different responses of Emerson and Thoreau to the flowing.[11] If Emerson was content to look on from the bankside and throw transcendental bridges from shore to shore, Thoreau so thirsted for flowing waters that he would be content with nothing short of immersion. To fulfill that thirst he would soon commit himself to the waters of the Concord and Merrimack rivers with his brother John, first to float upon that stream of time, and then, by a process of reflective artistry, to become one with the law of currents, with the "liquid lapse of thought."

*

First, however, he would have to get beyond the frost at his journal sources. In his entry for November 9, 1837, under a trite heading "Still streams run deepest," Thoreau at first seems to choose floating with the current by quoting from *England's Helicon,* but then ponders an actual frozen rill that had somehow caught his fancy in the magic circle of his wanderings. At one level, the suppressed rill mirrors his own barely murmuring expression: "The early frosts bridge its narrow channel, and its querrulous [sic] note is hushed. . . . But there are souls whose depths are never fathomed." And he continues in a way to suggest Emerson's characteristic bankside view:

> We get a distant view from the precipitous banks, but never a draught from their mid-channels. Only a sunken rock or fallen oak, can provoke a murmur—And their surface is a stranger to the icy fetters which bind fast a thousand contributory rills. (PJ, I, 10; J, I, 8-9)

A succession of entries then constitute Thoreau's first journal "affair" with some aspect of nature, his attention being riveted by various configurations of "icy fetters." Between November 28 and December 23, 1837, in five separate entries comprising nearly 40 percent of the content of his journal for the period, Thoreau writes on "Hoar Frost & Green River" (Nov. 28; PJ, I, 15-16; J, I, 13-14), "Jack-Frost" (Dec. 15; PJ, I, 18; J, I, 16-17), "Frozen Mist" (Dec. 16; PJ, I, 18-19; J, I, 17-18), and "Crystals" (on both Dec. 19 and 23; PJ, I, 21-22; J, I, 20-22). By way of analogy with "frost vegetation," he describes rhubarb crystallizing in a bowl (Dec. 22; PJ, I, 22; J, I, 21). In late January, in what will become characteristic of these accounts of extended and heightened relationships, Thoreau concludes with a coda on "Hoar Frost" (PJ, I, 26; J, I, 26). It seemed to him that such crystallizations were evidence of a single law organizing the "ghost leaves" and the "green ones whose forms they assume," and further, that "vegetation is a kind of crystallization" (PJ, I, 18; J, I, 16), the "ice at swampbridge," like the frost, being "checquered with a kind of mosaic work" (PJ, I, 21; J, I, 20).

Nor was this a merely transient affair, for in his *Dial* essay "Natural History of Massachusetts" five years later, Thoreau would draw on his journal for the winter of 1837, and especially December, as a time in which "the Genius of vegetation seemed to hover by night over its summer haunts with unusual persistency," making the circumstances "unusually favorable" for the study of "a new department of vegetable physiology, what may be called crystalline botany" (W, V, 126-28). Such remarks indicate that Thoreau's reflections were more nearly fanciful and mechanic than imaginative and organic (in the Coleridgean sense), even though "Frost at Midnight" may have worked some of its magic over his first journal flirtation. In the same *Dial* essay, he contends that the crystalline structure in nature inclines to the foliate, and can be found in animate as well as inanimate nature. In recalling the frost and the vegetation whose pattern it imitated, he perceived the expression of a law "one and invariable, and every plant in the spring pushed up into and filled a permanent and external mould, which, summer and winter forever, is waiting to be filled." He further extended the notion by pondering whether it would be "as philosophical . . . to consider all growth, all filling up within the limits of nature, but a crystallization more or less rapid?" (W, V, 126-28).

The very next year, in a lecture on poetry ("Homer. Ossian. Chaucer") read at Concord Lyceum, Thoreau alluded to the phenomenon again. But by then the operative law of nature he detected seemed to have shifted from the crystalline and mechanic to the organic, as is suggested by his ruminations over the character of nature's "genius." In discriminating between two classes of poet, one of genius and the other of "intellect and taste," Thoreau finds the former is one with "the stream of inspiration, which bubbles out, now here, now there, now in this man, now in that. It matters not through what ice-crystals it is seen, now a fountain, now the ocean stream running under ground" (EEM, 171-72). And in the same paragraph he mentions the "measured step" of the poet of "intellect and taste," which is not "instinct with life," one such instance being Goethe. Thus, six years after being drawn to the phenomenon of crystalline frost, his imaginative eye had penetrated beneath its frozen surface to where a "stream of inspiration" flowed. Such penetration is the very hallmark of Thoreau's peculiar genius.

The topic of genius stands near the top of any list of the preoccupations of the American Transcendentalists, and it gives rise to amusing moments, as when Margaret Fuller in discussing the women's issue queried in what was, for her at least, a question totally rhetorical: "Who would be a goody that could be a genius?" (JMN, V, 407). For instance, Emerson possessed a copy of Sampson Reed's oration "On Genius" years before its publication. He also held a high opinion of Hedge's essay "Coleridge's Literary Character" (1833)—which spelled out the two characteristics of genius as originality and form. In addition, in a journal Encyclopedia for 1824-35 (JMN, VI, 195-97) under the heading of "Genius," Emerson gathered excerpts from various sources, including four from Coleridge and two from Goethe. Finally, he gave a lecture titled "Genius," first delivered in early 1839 (JMN, VII, 165). All these testify to the persistent appeal of genius as a topic of compelling interest to Emerson. But we are wrong to suppose that a genius was, for the Transcendentalist, one who expressed a personality that broke all conventions, all laws, as is sometimes thought to be the case. For Emerson, and even more particularly for Thoreau, genius might be either one who discerned certain laws of nature and faithfully gave expression to them or the power within a person that was an expression of such laws. Thus genius was either the medium or the message, perhaps both. When Emerson quotes from Hazlitt's *Table-Talk* that "Genius or originality is for the most part some strong quality in the mind answering to & bringing out some new & striking quality in Nature," he touches on a characteristic of genius that Hedge called originality; and in quoting Goethe's "Genius is that power of man which by acting & doing gives laws & rules" (JMN, VI, 196), he underscores the principle of form, not freely given by the artist, but transmuted from laws detected in nature to inform his own statement—in art as in life. For Thoreau, too, especially as exemplified in his prolonged reflections upon the frost vegetation, genius was both a manifestation of a "new & striking quality in Nature" and an answering "strong quality in the mind": in "Natural History" he wrote of the "Genius of vegetation" (W, V, 126) that hovered over December; in his lecture on poetry he spoke of the poet "of genius" who is one with "the stream of inspiration" (EEM, 171, 172), though at first, to Thoreau's eye, hidden beneath the frost.

*

As a very young man who sensed that his thoughts had "an ebb & flow," Emerson had wondered "whether any laws fix them & what the laws are" (JMN, II, 153). Thirty-four years later, conscious of the course his own expression had taken, he had developed an angle of vision, a perspective, a "Philosophy" of two laws, that of "*Identity*," from the "fact that *metaphysical faculties & facts are the transcendency of physical*," and that of "Flowing" (JMN, XIV, 191). In the metamorphosis and the flowing, we see the persistency with which such laws governed and directed his expression, no less than his perception. But given the fact that he demurred in actually becoming a naturalist in order to take up a place of vantage *from* the bankside (I write metaphorically here of an artistic viewpoint Emerson assumed in lecturing on nature), the "sources" of these two laws in his works derive from "influences" more literary than natural. Even at the Jardin des Plantes, his eye was drawn to perceive the metamorphosis by a pattern of arrangement of the plants, a suggestively imposed organization, not nature unmediated.

And what of the flowing? Almost a year to the day before Thoreau embarked with his brother on what would be the first leg of a journey on the Concord and Merrimack rivers, Emerson, at sundown, had a kind of epiphany at the top of Dr. Ripley's hill, which overlooked not only the Old Manse where he had written a good deal of *Nature,* but also the battlefield at North Bridge and the sweep of the Concord River through the Great Meadow toward Ball's Hill. At that height of vantage he "renewed [his] vows to the Genius of that place." Looking toward the west, he saw

> a deposite [sic] of *still light,* not radiant. Then I beheld the river like God's love journeying out of the grey past on into the green future. Yet sweet & native as all those fair impressions on that summit fall on the eye & ear, they are not yet mine. I cannot tell why I should feel myself such a stranger in nature. (JMN, VII, 74)

Perhaps he had already foreclosed on the possibility of a literal voyaging on the Concord River because of his age—he was thirty-five—and his state both as a married man and as one still dignified at times by the title "Reverend." His lecture career having been launched in 1833 with a series on natural history, at age thirty-five he now wrote that "after thirty a man is too sensible of the strait limitations which his physical constitution sets to his activity. The stream feels its banks, which it had forgotten in the run & overflow of the first meadows" (JMN, VII, 71). Already Emerson seems to have resigned himself to the bankside, and two years later remarked that "infancy, youth, receptive, aspiring, with religious eye looking upward, counts itself nothing & abandons itself to the flowing instruction, flowing from all sides. But the man & woman of seventy assume to know all . . ." (JMN, VII, 380).

Fourteen years younger than Emerson, Thoreau, on the near side of thirty-five on the very day of Emerson's vision of the "*still light*" above the beckoning river, disclosed his readiness to abandon himself to the "flowing instruction" in writing: "How unaccountable the flow of spirits in youth. . . . Dam it up you may, but dry it up you may not, for you cannot reach its source" (PJ, I, 56; J, I, 59). In the first February of his journalizing, Thoreau had written of the difficulty of subjecting oneself "to an influence. It must steal upon us when we expect it not—and its work be all done ere we are aware of it" (PJ, I, 28; J, I, 28). The advantage Thoreau had over Emerson was not just his youth and his "physical constitution"—he, too, had a "mouse in the chest"—but his readiness. The stretch of the river beheld by Emerson would, for Thoreau, be the first leg of a journey, a "flowing instruction" expressive of nature's genius through the law of currents.

When Hawthorne, living at the Old Manse, was a boating companion of Thoreau, he was uncertain in which direction the languid Concord actually flowed. But Thoreau, who had observed the sluggish river closely, could remark on its evidence that "life is current and not stagnant" (PJ, I, 170; LJ, 152). In a Thalesian mood in April, 1838, Thoreau wrote that the beginnings of philosophy are "marvelous . . . —We can imagine a period when 'Water runs down hill' may have been taught in the schools" (PJ, I, 187; LJ, 172). But when he later drew an analogy between love and water, the relationship suggested was in terms of fluid essentially static, expressive of a "law of mechanics." Love "never fails," he wrote, for

> just as high as the waters rise in one vessel just so high they will rise in every other with which there is communication—either direct or under ground or from above the stars. Love is beside in some such independent fluid element in respect to our vessels, which still obeyes [sic] only its own and not our lawes [sic] by any means, without regard to the narrow limits to which we would confine it. (PJ, I, 493)

That Thoreau uses "vessel" here to signify a container of fluids indicates the static qualities in his notion, and hints at what he might mean, elsewhere, by characterizing man as a "hydrostatic paradox" (PJ, I, 267; J, I, 216). Moreover, Thoreau's conjoining of love and fluid might express a lofty sentiment, but it was bad physics, at least to the Aristotelian school, which held that the love or affection of water was for the lowest place.

But when Thoreau devoted himself to the "flowing instruction," he apprehended that what governed the law of currents was the law of gravity. In a journal entry of the period 1842-44, he wrote in a way to reveal his comprehension of the four elements that constituted the Elizabethan world picture, with clear awareness of the moral significance in that picture: it was "wholesome" to contemplate the natural laws, "as gravity heat—light—moisture—dryness" (PJ, II, 85; J, I, 467). His inclusion of the law of gravity, which Newton had discovered after the age of Shakespeare, shows a discernment of the principle by which Nature endlessly converts water in stasis into the dynamic condition of flowing, and thereby permits the man who would be a "vessel" to float on its currents as well as contain it. Since Thoreau believed "there is no exclusively moral law—there is no exclusively physical law" (PJ, II, 241), might he not find moral significance in discerning that the law of gravity caused the current? He suggests as much in remarking that near the headwaters of the Merrimack, the waters had poured down the hillside into the stream, "falling all the way, not discouraged by the lowest fall—for it intends to rise again. There are earth air fire & water—very well, this is water. down it comes that is the way with it" (PJ, II, 267). If this was an "enlightened moment" in which the scientific laws of nature were converted to "morality and modes of divine life" (PJ, I, 468), did it not suggest that "gravity," not "love," is what the stream stands for, or according to which it runs?

In the course of his own life from the completion of his fluvial voyage to the death of his brother John, Thoreau's means of coping with "gravity" were the timeless ones of youth and high spirits. In the spring of 1841, he wrote that "Virtue is boyant and elastic," spelling *buoyant* in a way to invoke a pun at the expense of "gravity," and went on to write, "Virtue . . . stands without effort and does not feel gravity—but sin plods and shuffles— Newton needed not to wait for an apple to fall to discover the attraction of gravitation—it was implied in the fall of man" (PJ, I, 305).[12] Still, "boyancy" enabled one both to float upon the stream of life, even though its currents were expressive of the genius of gravity, and to ride clear of the rapid whirlpools expressive of that genius. Thus "boyancy," like the rivulet source of the Merrimack, was "not discouraged by the lowest fall—for it intends to rise again" (PJ, II, 267).

But what was the basis for such an "intended" rise? Was it self-determined? Or responsive to other laws of nature, so far unexpressed if in fact discovered? Were there countercurrents in the stream of time to the general fall? Refreshing returns to the sources, each return a timeless overturning of the law of gravity and succeeding fall—the lapse—of the streams of life? What of the law of evaporation, which might give the promise of unremitting springs to the lapsing current? Perhaps without fully understanding the relationship implied between natural and spiritual law, Thoreau had described in his journal one such moment during his voyage, when his attention was riveted to the bankside:

> The banks of the Merrimack are steep and clayey for the most part and trickling with water—and where a spring oozes out a few feet above the level of the river, the boatmen cut a trough out of a slab with their axes and place it so as to receive the water, and fill their jugs conveniently. Bursting out from under the root of a pine or a rock, sometimes this purer and cooler water is collected into a little basin close to the edge of and level with the river—a fountain head of the Merrimack.—
>
> so near along lifes [sic] stream lie the fountains of innocence and youth—making fertile the margin of its turbid stream. Let the voyageur replenish his vessel at these uncontaminated sources.—Some youthful spring perchance still empties with tinkling music into the oldest river, even when it is falling into the sea. I imagine that its music is distinguished by the river gods from the general lapse of the stream and falls sweeter upon their ears in proportion as it is nearer the sea.
>
> As thus the evaporations of the river feed these unsuspected springs which filter through its banks so our aspirations fall back again in springs upon the margin of our life's stream to refresh and purify it. (PJ, II, 27-28)

From the bankside Emerson had gazed upon the flowing river, but "with religious eye looking upward" (JMN, VII, 380), perhaps too ready to soar. "Blessed is the day when the youth discovers that Within and Above are synonyms" (JMN, IV, 365), he had written after the crest of his thirtieth year in a way to anticipate his "Oversoul." Thoreau himself seems to have given in to the same inclination by offering as the climax of *A Week* an interpolated account of his ascent of Mt. Saddleback, where the voyager's aspirations run counter to the genius of gravity to find expression in cloudy vapors, evaporations. But from within the stream he had gazed *at* the bankside as well, and there he discerned the "uncontaminated sources" of a spring to which his "vessel" had sailed and with which his "vessel" might be filled. Here was a bankside expression of nature that anticipated the thawing bank in the "Spring" chapter of *Walden,* where the law of currents converts to formulate a paradox—a reversal—not only hydrostatic, but hydrodynamic as well. In a word, nature, not Coleridge, was the radical "influence" in Thoreau's education.

In tracing the course of Thoreau's "flowing instruction," I have suggested that he characteristically put behind him such literary influences as Goethe and Coleridge. The influence of Emerson, however, cannot so readily be dismissed, and Thoreau's efforts to do so are as little convincing as is his claim that he enjoyed the spectacle of the fire he had accidentally set while boiling fish at the shore of Fairhaven Pond.[13] Early in his relationship with Emerson, when the wax was most susceptible to the impression of flowing—it was but a few days before Emerson's vision from the bankside—Thoreau himself had had an arresting revelation of the meaning of a river:

> For the first time it occurred to me this afternoon what a piece of wonder a river is.—A huge volume of matter ceaselessly rolling through the fields and meadows

of this substantial earth— . . . One would think that, by a very natural impulse, the dwellers upon the headwaters . . . would follow in the trail of their waters to see the end of the matter. (PJ, I, 55; J, I, 58-59)

Within a year, Thoreau had so far freed himself from the "icy fetters" at the source of his journal that he had traced the "trail of . . . waters to see the end of the matter." But he would not actually see the sources of his stream of inspiration until he gazed more deeply and conjecturally at the bankside.

Meanwhile Emerson, having traced one revelation to its source in historical Christianity, came to an "end of the matter" in his "Divinity School Address." There the attenuating stream of the revelation of a divine word seemed to give way to a swelling current of Self-Reliance. But from his bankside perspective as aspiring poet-priest whose disassociation from the current of religious tradition was painful, he raised an issue that distressed his deep self: "Am I a hypocrite, who am disgusted by vanity everywhere, & Preach self trust every day?" It was an unsettling issue of the time, and Melville would treat it with bottomless irony at the expense of Emerson in a fluvial adventure titled *The Confidence-Man.* Even in the 1950s the issue remained so completely unsettling to Randall Stewart that he found in Emerson's espousal of Self-Reliance an antithesis both of Christian humility and of the democratic principle, and Emerson therefore the arch-heretic of our nation's religious and political heritage.[14] Pondered at depth, in the light of liberation theology and of Christ's statement that "the kingdom of God is within" (Luke 17:21), Emerson's bankside appraisal now seems genuinely paradoxical, rather than contradictory and subversive—a hydrostatic paradox, though uttered from the side of the stream.

In the process of rejecting one revelation of the Word of God, Emerson had first broken from the tradition by acting upon his inability, as a minister of the Word, to accept the Lord's Supper as a commemoration of the miracle of transubstantiation, and then by his radical impatience with the "pronounced" miracles of historical Christianity, as he conceived them. His growing sense of mission as poet-priest attending and articulating the miracle of language, or prophesying the arrival of such a poet-priest, had its own countercurrent, however. At times it seemed to Emerson that having assumed the role of American Scholar in declaring that "Life is our dictionary," he felt that the dictionary had instead become his life. The day after John and Henry Thoreau completed their voyage, Emerson, with a sting of envy and remorse, complained of living under the tyranny of "an Age of Words."

We are shut up in schools & college recitation rooms for ten or fifteen years & come out at last with a bellyfull of words & do not know a thing. We cannot use our hands or our legs or our eyes or our arms. We do not know an edible root in the woods. We cannot tell our course by the stars nor the hour of the day by the sun. It is well if we can swim & skate. We are afraid of a horse, of a cow, of a dog, of a cat, of a spider. Far better was the Roman rule to teach a boy nothing that he could not learn standing. Now here are my wise young neighbors [John and Henry] who instead of getting like the wordmen into a railroad-car where they have not even the activity of holding the reins, have got into a boat which they have built with their own hands, with sails which they have contrived to serve as a tent by night, & gone up the river Merrimack to live by their wits on the fish of the stream & the berries of the woods. (JMN, VII, 238)[15]

Nor did his mood soon vanish, for in an entry spanning September 14-17, he wrote of his hatred for "editors, preachers, & all manner of scholars," and his preference for such tradesmen as "a blacksmith, a truckman, a farmer"; and of his sense that "we die of words. We are hanged, drawn, & quartered by dictionaries" (JMN, VII, 240). A few days later, still under the spell, he stated that "all conversation among literary men is muddy" (JMN, VII, 242), and the waters did not seem to clarify until he walked "toward Fairhaven with H. T." (JMN, VII, 249), as he reported near the end of that entry, and asserted, a day or two later, that "a walk in the woods is only an exalted dream" (JMN, VII, 252).

It was but a year after his rivial voyage that Thoreau wrote, "Truth is always paradoxical" (PJ, I, 143; J, I, 153), and some months later defined man as "the hydrostatic paradox—the counter-poise of the system" (PJ, I, 267; J, I, 216). What he meant by this not altogether transparent remark included being open to the influence of water, just as his calling *A Week* "hypaethral" meant open to the influence of the ether, of the heavens, and only in part because it was written out of doors. In calling man "hydrostatic," he may also be suggesting his attempt to arrest, codify, capture, in a safe abstraction, the response of man to the "influence" of water, even as in the opening months of his journalizing he tried to define nature's operations as so many crystallizations, though he likewise "tried to fancy that there was a disposition in these crystallizations to take the form of the contiguous foliage" (PJ, I, 22; J, I, 22). The "crystalline particles" were there duplicated in the currents frozen into "ice at swamp-bridge" (PJ, I, 21; J, I, 20), and in a hoar frost that covered every "leaf and twig . . . with a sparking ice armor" (PJ, I, 26; J, I, 26), almost as if the frost vegetation was nature's imagistic rendering of the minister of Concord who, for Emerson, exemplified the petrifaction of the spirit in the word—Rev. Barzillai ("son of iron") Frost.

For Thoreau, however, the frost near the source of his youthful expression was susceptible to genial influences that silently murmured below. By 1842 he had found that "though nature's laws are more immutable than any despot's yet to our daily life they rarely seem rigid, but we relax with license in summer weather—" (PJ, I, 396; J, I, 354). Ten years later, on January 1, 1852, Thoreau fairly bristled because "Mr. [Rev. Barzillai] Frost did not like Mrs. S—'s lecture last night; did not like what she said about the clergy. Said it was too *transcendental* for him. This is the profane swearing of such men" (J, III, 171). Before the end of the month he would snipe at the Reverend Mr. Frost twice more in suggesting that he is a type of those who deal with the letter of the word, and not the spirit, and that "Frost and Anger [?] might preach forever" to honest men, without effect. In the same entry he goes on to write that "in this movement of the waters, the sectarians and formalists are left floating on chips and slivers of doctrine. In preaching . . . they make the mistake of preaching or writing on the letter and not the meaning of the letter, the creed and not the life" (J, III, 230), and thus preach a denial of "the Spirit of God [that] moved upon the face of the waters" (Genesis 1:2).

When the frost of Thoreau's youth so soon gave way to melting influences, it converted the vessel of man from a hydrostatic to a hydrodynamic paradox, provided he embarked on the stream of life. This notion had provoked a journal verse in 1844:

> I fain would stretch me by the highway side,
>   To thaw and trickle with the melting snow,
> That mingled soul & body with the tide
>   I too might through the pores of Nature flow.
>
> (PJ, II, 116; J, I, 477)

In articulating the process by which ice and frost would "thaw and trickle" into running streams, within and without, Thoreau, even in name, invites a contrast with the Reverend Mr. Frost. For if "Frost" hinted a spiritless attenuation, a freezing of the influence of Christianity when severed from nature, "Thoreau" suggests the influence of natural springs undefiled and freely running. In articulating his name, Thoreau would express the process by which Thor—Norse god associated with frost—gave way to Thaw—expressive of the natural influences in running waters, the sense of which was contained in the second syllable (-eau, F. water) of Thoreau's name. Thus in the articulating streams flowing through the traveler deep in Concord, there was, even nominally, an influence to make of man a hydrostatic paradox, and thereby "help to forward the new spring along" (PJ, II, 116; J, I, 477).

4

A Week: Lapse of the Current, Tree of the Fall

It is a beautiful illustration of the law of obedience, the flow of a river, the path for a sick man. . . .

"A Winter Walk" (W, V, 66)

IN A JOURNAL entry of 1841 that he would use in *A Week on the Concord and Merrimack Rivers,* Thoreau wrote of "motions everywhere in nature," which must surely be "the circulations of God. The flowing sail, the running stream, the waving tree . . ." (J, I, 302). In the voyage with his brother John in the late summer of 1839, he had consigned himself to those circulations—current motions expressive halfway in "the running stream," halfway in "the flowing sail"—and in "boyant" spirits had passed beneath a "waving tree" that seemed the very type of an Edenic tree of life.[1] But though this high-spirited voyage was the basis for Thoreau's first book, what called it into being was the death of his brother John on January 11, 1842. This came about when, on New Year's Day, John slightly nicked the tip of the ring finger of his left hand while stropping his razor, nicked it "just deep enough to draw blood," as Thoreau's biographer relates.[2] Ten days later, the effects of this nick having stilled his mortal circulations, John Thoreau lay dead of lockjaw, and the "boyancy" of Thoreau's remembered voyage turned to gravity, the tree of life to the tree of knowledge and death, tree of the Fall. The shock to Henry, who suffered psychosomatic symptoms of the disease, was further intensified by the death of six-year-old Waldo Emerson from scarlet fever on January 24, and he continued "silent and depressed . . . for a long, long while."[3] Even years later, Thoreau could not hear his brother's name without choking back the tears.

As for Emerson, the death of Waldo "seems to have been the end of something essential," according to Jonathan Bishop, and terminated his first creative period.[4] Bewildered by his loss, Emerson tried to articulate his isolation in "Experience":

> What opium is instilled into all disaster! It shows formidable as we approach it, but there is at last no rough rasping friction, but the most slippery sliding surfaces. . . . There are moods in which we court suffering, in the hope that here, at least, we shall find reality, sharp peaks and edges of truth. But it turns out to be scene-painting and counterfeit. The only thing grief has taught me, is to know how shallow it is. That, like all the rest, plays about the surface, and never introduces me into the reality, for contact with which, we would even pay the costly price of sons and lovers. Was it Boscovich who found out that bodies never come in contact? Well, souls never touch their objects. An innavigable sea washes with silent waves between us and the things we aim at and converse with. Grief too will make us idealists. In the death of my son, now more than two years ago, I seem to have lost a beautiful estate,—no more. I cannot get it nearer to me. . . . Nothing is left us now but death. We look to that with a grim satisfaction, saying, there at least is reality that will not dodge us. (CW, III, 28-29)

Joel Porte has ably demonstrated how, from its opening paragraphs, "Experience" expresses in "a series of metaphoric correlatives for a version of the Fall" a sense of lapsing that Emerson cannot contain, a mood of the "forsaken," the "*emptied*," and of being "*out of touch*" that replicates the "numbed sense" in the opening of John Keats's "Ode to a Nightingale."[5] Late in the essay Emerson seems to recover by contending that "the life of truth is cold . . . but it is not the slave of tears, contritions, and perturbations" (CW, III, 46); but that claim seems undercut by his propounding that "the Fall of Man"—a religious doctrine with which he never had patience—was the fall into self-consciousness, "the discovery we have made, that we exist" (CW, III, 43), which may be a way of stating his discovery, in the death of his son, that we will not always exist, that indeed we are mortal. No longer, at any rate, is Emerson concerned with pontificating the unbridged distance that yawns between subject and object as he had been in *Nature,* but now presents the cup of Lethe in proposing that since "we live amid surfaces, . . . the true art of life is to skate well on them" (CW, III, 35).[6]

If "Experience" is Emerson's attempt to skate on the frozen surface of life, it is a kittlybending effort above the fact of death so thinly filmed over. Thoreau's *A Week,* his belated memorial to his brother, is, on the other hand, a grudging yet unblinking admission of the consequences of the Fall, and in one of his verse epigraphs, Thoreau invoked his unnamed brother as muse and guiding spirit in the journey ahead:

> Where'er thou sail'st who sailed with me,
> Though now thou climbest loftier mounts,
> And fairer rivers dost ascend,
> Be thou my Muse, my Brother—.
>
> (Wk, 3)

So committed, Thoreau in *A Week* makes a mighty effort to convert the consequences of a razor's nick from "Here lies" to "There rises" (Wk, 170), and to climb loftier mounts, to ascend fairer rivers than those on the literal journey; but he never quite succeeds, and no one was more aware of the short fall than himself. His celebration of a transcendental friendship subsides into a discussion of "Silence . . . , a balm to our every chagrin" (Wk, 392), though no restorative, following which is the paean to silence in the book's closure. The publication of *A Week* seemed almost to intensify that silence: of the 1000 copies printed, 706 came back to Thoreau from his publisher four years later to swell to more than 900 the number of books in his personal library (J, V, 459). But he had made his first volume "a mole whereon the waves of Silence may break" (Wk, 393), and he would bend his ear to hear what resounding waves might next come to it.

By June 1, 1853, well into the stream of inspiration in writing *Walden*, Thoreau seems to have distanced his personal losses sufficiently to see in the beautiful pincushion galls on white oaks a symbol of his first book:

> Through our temptations,—aye, and our falls,—our virtues appear. As in many a character,—many a poet,—we see that beauty exhibited in a gall, which was meant to have bloomed in a flower, unchecked. . . . The poet cherishes his chagrins and sets his sighs to music. This gall is the tree's "Ode to Dejection." (J, V, 210)

And extending the figure by an allusion to a dejected Hamlet (1. 4. 23-38), Thoreau writes:

> How oft it chances that the apparent fruit of a shrub, its apple, is merely a gall or blight! How many men meet with some blast in the moist growing days of their youth, and what should have been a sweet and palatable fruit in them becomes a mere puff and excrescence. . . .

The death of John in the "moist growing days" of his youth was cause enough for Thoreau's dejection (from L. *dejectus* . . . to cast down). And though *dejecta* refers to "excremental matter; feces" (AHD), Thoreau particularizes the apple in suggesting that what should have been a sweet and palatable fruit might become a mere puff and excrescence, a "Dead Sea apple," thus an apple of Dejection and Discord rather than of Concord.

And yet . . . the fluvial travel that is the basis of *A Week* was intended to be from Concord, Massachusetts, to Concord, New Hampshire, and return. On the opening page Thoreau focuses on "Concord" in a way to establish a mythic dimension to their journey from a home port settlement that was "commenced in a spirit of peace and harmony" (Wk, 5), to an intended port of call that they "persisted" in referring to as "*New* Concord" (Wk, 303). Near book's end, reinforcing the musical undertones of his mythic journey, Thoreau follows his discussion of silence by suggesting that though *A Week* had not set "his sighs to music" (J, V, 210), it may have been instrumental in preparing him for the deeper harmonies of *Walden*, for "a good book is the plectrum with which our else silent lyres are struck" (Wk, 392). Thus while the trip was to have run from Concord to Concord on a horizontal plane, vertically it ran beyond the range of Thoreau's powers to articulate deeper harmonies, unheard melodies—or discords.

Discord—Concord; dissonance—harmony; soundness—and silence. One of the nagging problems in dealing with *A Week* is Thoreau's confounding of purposes: it is, as Lawrence Buell so rightly puts it, "a very hard book to hold in one's mind."[7] And in reading it we would be well advised to heed D. H. Lawrence's admonition to pay less attention to the avowed purpose of an author than to the "running undercurrent" of his book.[8] That Thoreau's first book is expressive of the law of currents is both natural and clear: Stephen L. Tanner finds its recurring pattern of imagery runs to "current motions."[9] One of these is the current of the times, which comprises the adventures of the two voyagers and their historical predecessors on or adjacent to the river—and Thoreau puns frequently on "current events" in this connection. Another is the current of the eternities—the voyager's thoughts, speculations, dreams, and the mythic and timeless condition toward which they aspire.

Content to quote as "current" an historian's opinion that the "springs" of the "dead" Concord River (Wk, 61) are near Hopkinton, Maine (Wk, 5), Thoreau then sets his own course to the springs of the "living" Merrimack (Wk, 88) above New Concord, to which he will journey in a way, as Kevin P. Van Anglen remarks, "to reverse the decay inherent in civilized life and letters by moving to the sources of words as well as the things, and breathing life into them once more."[10] But the fluvial journey terminated at Hookset (what fine ironies in a name!), the journey to New Concord being completed by land. And the goal of exploring the Mt. Agiocochook source of the Merrimack is, in the book, displaced by a lengthy interpolated account of an ascent of Mt. Saddleback in "Tuesday," rather early to be effective as a climax.[11] In the idealized, dreamlike ascent, Thoreau suggests a transition from mountain top to cloud, source of all rivers:

> Low-anchored cloud,
> Newfoundland air,
> Fountain-head and source of rivers,
> Dew cloth, dream drapery. . . .
> (Wk, 191)

As projected in the book's epigraph, this destination is of "loftier mounts" and "fairer rivers" (Wk, 3) than on the stream of time. But at Mt.

Agiocochook (Washington), literally loftier than Saddleback, Thoreau stops short of the source of "fairer rivers," myth, dreams, burgeoning language, the first leaf of the book of Genesis, comes abruptly upon a version of the Fall, and flees in precipitous haste back to Concord.

*

Like Emerson in *Nature,* Thoreau in *A Week* faced the problem of bridging the gap between the real and the ideal, the fact and the truth. How was he to negotiate the interval between the stream of life, current events, and the stream of thought? Between time, with its discords, and eternity, with its lofty or deep concords? While Emerson did so by focusing on a mode of perception, speculating on a transparent eyeball as his means of transport, Thoreau and his brother fashioned their means of transportation with their own hands, calling the results of their craft *Musketaquid,* Indian for *Concord,* and forming it in obedience to the two currents within which their pilgrimage took its course—water and air. "If rightly made," Thoreau noted, the ideal boat "would be a sort of amphibious animal, a creature of two elements, related by one half its structure to some swift and shapely fish, and by the other to some strong-winged and graceful bird" (Wk, 16). At one level, he was dealing with such practical means of propulsion as oars and sails, the fins and wings of his amphibian craft. But figuratively he was dealing with the hypaethral characters of air (spirit) and water (time, current events) in which his craft sailed, and by which, in the composition of *A Week,* he plied his writer's craft. Thus while Emerson, the bankside pontificator, had struggled with one recalcitrant span, Thoreau, the navigator, coursed upon the stream he would later go a-fishing in, the sails of his "craft" in the meantime filling—perhaps puffing out from time to time—with soaring inspirations. But Thoreau judged their vessel insufficiently inspired, a "dull waterfowl" that "availed itself of the old law that the heavier shall float the lighter," and therefore obedient more to the law of fish than of birds, though proving "a sufficient buoy for our purpose" (Wk, 16).

At moments *A Week* expresses a masterful confluence of the two streams, as when in the last paragraphs of "Thursday" the two voyagers awake in the night "still eking out [their] dreams with half-awakened thoughts," and then remember that they "lay on the bank of the Merrimack, and not in [their] chamber at home." Thoreau revives the moment with a delicious intermingling of sibilants and liquids:

> With our heads so low in the grass, we heard the river whirling and sucking, and lapsing downward, kissing the shore as it went, sometimes rippling louder than usual, and again its mighty current making only a slight limpid trickling sound, as if our water-pail had sprung a leak, and the water were flowing into the grass by our side. (Wk, 332)

Oftener, however, Thoreau's streams seem to flow on parallel planes, connected chiefly by the desire that they be connected. Flowing with the river, Thoreau at one point looks aloft speculatively—at "rivers of stars," Milky Ways—and senses that below, too, flow "rivers of rock," "rivers of ore" (Wk, 331), yet we do not see them. Such speculative passages in *A Week* seemed digressive to James Russell Lowell, who found them like "snags jolting us headforemost out of our places as we are rowing placidly up stream or drifting down";[12] and Walter Harding's classroom edition fosters this view in separating narrative from speculative "streams" by different typeface.[13]

Notwithstanding their hypaethral aspirations for "Newfoundland air, / Fountain-head and source of rivers," the current motions of Thoreau's book arrive not at the springs of life, but at their fall. In tone, structure, and major symbol, this book expresses a lapsarian journey, a fall. At the launching out described in the last paragraph of the introductory chapter, Thoreau suggests his readiness to commit himself to the lapse of time:

> I had often stood on the banks of the Concord, watching the lapse of the current, an emblem of all progress, following the same law with the system, with time, and all that is made; the weeds at the bottom gently bending down the stream, shaken by the watery wind, still planted where their seeds had sunk, but ere long to die and go down likewise; the shining pebbles, not yet anxious to better their condition, the chips and weeds, and occasional logs and stems of trees, that floated past, fulfilling their fate, were objects of singular interest to me, and at last I resolved to launch myself on its bosom, and float whither it would bear me. (Wk, 12-13)

And having begun *A Week* by emphasizing the lapse of the current, Thoreau concludes by emphasizing the lapse of the season in a way to complement and intensify the elegiac note of the launching out, making a transcendental pun in remarking that "the Fall had commenced."[14] The last day of the return voyage is attended by signs of a "change in the weather" (Wk, 334), and even the faces of men lining the banks make it clear that "the Fall had commenced" (Wk, 335). In Thoreau's Thanatopsis, not only were the leaves "fast ripening for their fall," but the very thoughts of the voyagers "began to rustle" (Wk, 336).

To be sure the season of spring need not figure in a book about a journey that took place in late summer—but the anticipated voyage to the "springs" of the Merrimack having failed to materialize, the change accompanying the arrival of fall is not simply a change in mood, it is a replication of the biblical myth of the Fall of man. Early in *A Week* Thoreau had challenged "the word . . . to fall back on innocence" with the recommendation to "fall forward rather on to whatever there is there" (Wk, 77). At the point in the journey where he should realize his goal of arriving at a prelapsarian state where springs not fail, he is brought up against the slope of a forbidding mountain, its name in upper case type—"AGIOCOCHOOK" (Wk, 314)—staring him down as if a chastening New World version of the Roman god Terminus—"Thus far and no further." For at the genesis of the Merrimack, and by extension of the stream of time and of man's imagination, he falls forward upon the consequences of the great Fall, quoting from George Herbert's "Virtue" in a way to emphasize the lapsed condition of man:

> Sweet days, so cool, so calm, so bright,
> The bridal of the earth and sky,
> Sweet dews shall weep thy fall to-night,
> For thou must die.
> (Wk, 314)[15]

He might momentarily film a thin ice over this mortal fact by punning that sparrows are always "*chipper,* never infirm," but only until truth breaks in:

> We do not see their bodies lie about; yet there is a tragedy at the end of each one of their lives. They must perish miserably; not one of them is translated. True, "not a sparrow falleth to the ground without our Heavenly Father's knowledge," but they do fall, nevertheless. (Wk, 224)

Elsewhere he would pun incessantly and paradoxically over the fate of "Rear Admiral Van" (Wk, 170), a fate most grave.[16] His aspirations forestalled through such discoveries, and dejected by the warning that all must fall, Thoreau sums up his overland return to riverside in a single clause—"When we returned to Hooksett, a week afterward" (Wk, 314)—and from there the voyage home is a precipitous, hasty descent to Concord, "the discovery of fall [being] the single most important event in *A Week*. . . ."[17]

An analogous discovery in the recounted journey was the tree of the Fall. After setting sail in hopes of reaching a prelapsarian state of content along a pastoral valley running from Concord to Concord, they had passed beneath an enormous basswood tree, the "*tilia Americana,* also called the lime or linden . . . a new tree to us" (Wk, 158), which seemed to promise entry to a Garden of Eden. Thoreau details the riches of this New World autotype of the Edenic tree of life, not only in recent times, but in history and myth as well—its uses for fisherman's matting, ropes, peasant's shoes, nets, coarse cloth, roofs of cottages, baskets, paper, bucklers, sounding-boards, panels for carriages, cradles, sugar, honey, a kind of chocolate, medicine, and charcoal. As they sail under its canopy seeing the "sky through its chinks," the "meaning and idea of the tree stamped in a thousand hieroglyphics on the heavens" (Wk, 159) had come home to them.

But what Thoreau finds in the course of the journey, or perhaps in the lapse of time between its completion and the publication of *A Week,* is a tree of knowledge, tree of the Fall. In "Sunday" he might find affirmation of a beneficent tree of life in such "still lines" as Virgil's " '*Strata jacent passim sua quaeque sub arbore poma.*' / The apples lie scattered everywhere, each under its tree" (Wk, 90). But in "Monday" he finds "wrecks of ancient apple trees" (Wk, 160) near the dents in the earth where stood the houses of the first white settlers of Nashua; at Tyngsboro an apple tree with a nail marking the disastrous height of the flood waters of 1785; and nearby, "Elisha's apple-tree" (Wk, 356), which marked the grave of a friendly Indian killed by his own race, his lost grave revealed when a flood, archetypal sign of mankind's continual lapsing, settled the earth to reveal the place of burial. Moreover, after noting that the tree against which the brains of Hannah Dustan's infant had been dashed out was an apple tree (Wk, 321), Thoreau generalizes that "there have been many who in later times have lived to say that they had eaten of the fruit of that apple-tree" (Wk, 324). Thus the journey of *A Week,* which can be charted on a horizontal plane that runs from Concord to Concord, can in imagination be projected on a vertical plane that overlays the tree of knowledge. For having ascended in the "rivers of sap" (Wk, 331) to the highest "branches" of the Merrimack, Thoreau there came upon the apples of Discord, Sodom's apples, the bitter taste of which is the knowledge of death at first, the fact of death at last. And from the highest "branches" of this riparian tree from which he had plucked and tasted a forbidden fruit, Thoreau descends along its trunk in rivers of sap to old Concord, dutifully fastening his boat at the base of the same wild apple tree to complete a ritual of "current motions" in a way to symbolize that "the Tree of Knowledge is a Tree of Knowledge of good and evil" (Wk, 362), a tree of the Fall.[18]

But though the silence with which *A Week* concludes finds its interpretation in part through the fastening of the boat to the trunk of the tree of the Fall, a tantalizing hope endures that the Fall might perhaps be fortunate, might lead to *Walden's* "Spring." Paul David Johnson has pointed out that

> the final lines . . . [which] suggest the brothers' return as a departure . . . fall upon a note of spring: "We leaped gladly on the shore, drawing [the boat] up and fastening it to the wild apple tree, whose stem still bore the mark which its chain had worn in the spring freshets." (Wk, 393)[19]

This hope seems not only to grow out of Thoreau's discovery of the lapse of man and the fruit of its arboreal symbol; it seems to germinate from the very word "lapse," within which Thoreau finds the rudiments of a redemptive hope to spring and fructify in *Walden.*[20]

I have earlier mentioned Thoreau's commitment to the "lapse of the current" at the moment of embarking, when the weeds at the bottom, reflecting Thoreau's doleful state, are bending with the stream and "Shaken by the watery wind." Though still planted, they are "erelong to die and go down likewise" (Wk, 12-13). Other occasions in which Thoreau makes use of "lapse" to suggest temporality and death likewise convey a redemptive hope. Consider, for example, the implicit redemptive potential in time suggested by "in the lapse of ages, Nature will recover and indemnify herself" (Wk, 62), in "Sunday"; and "There is something even in the lapse of time by which time recovers itself" (Wk, 351), in "Friday." In "Monday" the "materials and hints" furnished by a colony of ants permit Thoreau to elaborate his thoughts about an "equally progressive splendor . . . in the lapse of the divine periods" (Wk, 158). Here Thoreau puns on "periods" to suggest divine "sentences" (meanings) as well as durations of time in sacred history (where history by definition is of divine meaning). Elsewhere he suggests that only by the patient work of the imagination can a divine "sentence" be redeemed from time. In the final chapter, Thoreau discusses the "stream of inspiration" and its product, maintaining that the "true finish" of old books (cf. the Goethean varnish) is partly the "work of time. . . . A work of genius is rough-hewn from the first, because it anticipates the lapse of time, and has an ingrained polish, which still appears when fragments are broken off, an essential quality of its substance" (Wk, 376-77). Just so with *A Week.* At the moment, however, such speculations are but the waking dream of one voyager who falls back into silence, as does the book at its conclusion.[20]

But in the dawning hours Thoreau's ear did catch a redemptive note in the falling stream of time that intimated the note of eternal spring, though with an impression insufficient for the budding poet to turn to expression. Thoreau puzzled over his dawning awareness to write:

> So near along life's stream are the fountains of innocence and youth making fertile its sandy margin; and the voyageur will do well to replenish his vessels often at these uncontaminated sources. Some youthful *spring,* perchance, still empties with tinkling music into the oldest river, even when it is *falling* into the sea, and we imagine that its music is distinguished by the river gods from the general *lapse* of the stream, and *falls* sweeter on their ears in proportion as it is nearer to the ocean. As the evaporations of the river feed thus these unsuspected *springs* which filter through its banks, so, perchance, our aspirations *fall back again in springs* on the margin of life's stream to refresh and purify it. (Wk, 193; emphasis added. See also PJ, II, 27-28 cited earlier.)

At this moment of awakening on the sandy margin of life's stream, Thoreau's aspiration is to "fall back again in springs" even before he falls forward onto the fact of death. Thus the mythic poem that Thoreau composes in *A Week* is "A Fall" (Lapse), even while "Nature, who is superior to all styles and ages, is now, with pensive face, composing her poem . . . with which no work of man will bear to be compared" (Wk, 377). In *Walden* Thoreau would attend to the sounds of the rills from such "unsuspected springs" as filtered through another bankside "on the margin of life's stream" (Wk, 193), and learn to "read" them as a resounding antithesis of the Fall he fronted so unblinkingly in *A Week.*

*

In minor as well as major patterns, Thoreau organizes *A Week* to suggest such polarities as innocence and guilt, the ideal and the fallen, the aspiration and the lapse. One such polarity is that of fish and fowl. The "fish principle in Nature" was first expressed by the vessel he and his brother had built: by the color of its bottom half, green, and by its oars and rudder—the boat's fins and tail. In the book itself, two fish, the shad and the pickerel, illustrate this principle. In what Lawrence Buell describes as a "mock-tragic lament" for the shad, Thoreau implies a personal relationship with this fish, "full of instinct, which is thy faith . . . armed with a just cause," but "in this backwards spring" literally "dammed" from rising to its source of life.[21] By cutting a swath, a *transjectus,* across the river's current, commerce had sealed the fate of the shad from its true home, and likewise the fisherman from plying his proper trade, turning him into a fieldworker who, because he has imbibed too deeply from spirits hidden in a bottle, undulates "like a serpent" as he mows the field, and expects only to be cut down himself by the Great Mower (Wk, 35). The pickerel, on the other hand, strike the note of expectation. In describing them, Thoreau anticipates the fabulous Walden pickerel about whom he would sing a panegyric as the "animalized nuclei" of Walden Pond, dwelling so deeply in an elemental spring, God's drop, as to be translated from profane to sacred meanings—transcendentalized. Looking deep into the river, in "Tuesday" Thoreau discerns the form of a pickerel amidst the rocks, "lying low in the transparent water,—eager to double some distant cape, to make some great bend as in the life of man, and see what new perspectives would open" (Wk, 232).

Thoreau here suggests that these are fish who have not yet taken the turn, are not "tropical" (trope: "Latin *tropus,* from Greek *tropos,* a turn, way, manner" [AHD]) though they have not been dammed (or damned) like the shad, and are thus still hopeful of rounding the cape, taking a turn. In the third epigraph of *A Week* Thoreau evokes this image in referring to his brother as "the only permanent shore, / The cape never rounded, nor wandered o'er" (Wk, 3), perhaps to hint that what is rounded is not only the cape of death, but of good hope as well. As he worked over the "Spring" chapter of *Walden,* Thoreau, in describing the thawing bankside, would try to force a rounding of the cape through a personification; his attempt, which survives in the Bibliophile Edition, reads, "The whole face is a continuous broad shore, and narrow below, to which the chin is a Cape of Good Hope."[22] In *Walden* he will eventually favor an organic means of translation in a multiple expression of leaves, though in its "Conclusion" he will retain a symbolic antithesis of Good Hope at Cape Horn in Tierra del Fuego, a land of infernal fire, and by implication hopelessness, more than a mere ocean away. In any case in *A Week,* neither Thoreau's boat, nor the shad, nor even the pickerel round the cape, make the "tropical" turn to reach the shores of spring, so that like Thoreau, the fish principle founders, at least temporarily, on the fall.

But the rightly made vessel of the Thoreau brothers expressed principles of the fowl no less than of the fish. The blue upper half of its hull and its expansion of sail expressed its relationship to the ethereal currents, as if it were "some strong-winged and graceful bird" (Wk, 16). Thus the craft of Thoreau launched for a journey expressed halfway this principle as well. And though no single bird long holds sway over Thoreau's rivers in *A Week,* perhaps the most extensive description, and one in which the relationship with the persona is most temptingly suggested, is that of the smaller bittern at the beginning of "Wednesday," which prepares the way for an extended essay on friendship, the thematic center of the book. A bird of the "oldest Thalesian school . . . [who] believes in the priority of water to the other elements" (Wk, 235), the bittern is characterized by Thoreau as "the genius of the shore . . . moping along its edge . . . with ever an eye on us." The coalescence of bird and persona is strengthened by Thoreau's accompanying poem "My life is like a stroll upon the beach" (Wk, 241). Both are literal and "littoral" ("Of or existing on a shore. . . . [Latin *Littoralis* . . . from *litus* . . . shore]" [AHD]) strollers who have aspirations for a far (tropical) shore, as suggested in the second epigraph of *A Week:* "I am bound, I am bound, for a distant shore, / By a lonely isle, by a far Azore" (Wk, 3).[23] The bittern is no "strong-winged and graceful bird" like the soaring hawk in "Spring" (Wa, 316-17), but a lugubrious bird "moping" along the shore, or maintaining its low flight over the river, risking neither climb toward the sun, with the hawk, nor dive into the deep, like the risible loon of *Walden:* clearly, the bittern is a bird of the horizontal, rather than the vertical, plane.

Still, the bittern's lowly aspirations seem reinforced symbolically by the "lofty and silent flight" of *two* herons silhouetted against the sky, "a symbol for the ages to study" (Wk, 390). In a sense, the bittern is to the youthful poet of *A Week* what the mockingbird is to the "outsetting bard" in Whitman's "Out of the Cradle, Endlessly Rocking," a projection in birdlike form of a companionable muse. Thoreau addresses this muse in the third epigraph of *A Week* as "the only permanent shore, / The cape never rounded, nor wandered o'er," and thus an inhabitant of a far "tropical" shore toward which bittern, two herons, and persona aspire. In a sense, too, as in Whitman's "Cradle," the bird replicates a "dead brother" as the beckoning muse to which Thoreau consigns himself in the first epigraph of *A Week*. Similarly in a poem written in 1843, "Brother Where Dost Thou Dwell," Thoreau versified his brother's spirit as a bird, and a bird of the shore as well:

> Dost thou still haunt the brink
> Of yonder river's tide?
> And may I ever think
> That thou art at my side?
>
> What bird wilt thou employ
> To bring me word of thee?
> For it would give them joy,
> 'Twould give them liberty,
> To serve their former lord
> With wing and minstrelsy.
> (CP, p. 151, ll. 21-30)

Publication of the Princeton edition of Thoreau's *Journal* (volumes I and II at this date) reveals that the bittern passage in *A Week* evolved through at least three journal versions: A) that of June 11, 1840 (PJ, I, 126); B) that of September 12, 1842 (PJ, II, 10); C) an undated passage from the period 1842-44 (PJ, II, 71-72). Versions A and B characterize the bittern's study of the "rocks and sandy capes" as an attempt to wrest "the whole of her secret from nature." In version C, as in *A Week*, the bittern is referred to as "the genius of the shore," though a bird "of the oldest Thalesian school" who "believes in the priority of water to the other elements," thus underscoring both the law of currents and the possibility of a law of the land discernible by a "genius" whose study is in "rocks and sandy capes." In version C, written almost surely after the death of his brother, Thoreau refers to the bird as "my kindred after all then—and I have a lingering respect for my unreclaimed brother." That this version does not survive in *A Week* may well be due to the allusion to his "unreclaimed brother," which at some stage of revision would clearly have reminded Thoreau of his painful personal loss.

That the bittern affected Thoreau is clear: from the first he wondered, because of "that dull yellowish green" eye, whether his own soul was not "a bright invisible green" (PJ, I, 126). If Walden Pond would come to seem a reflection of his soul, as he suggests in "The Ponds," might not the "bright green weed" (Wa, 179) at the profoundest depths of "Earth's eye" correspond to the "bright invisible green" (Wk, 236) of his own soul upon looking into the eye of the bittern? Through color alone, Thoreau's response to the bittern is expressive of the faint deep stirrings of the law of vegetation to which he would respond in life by cultivating, getting to know his beans at Walden Pond.

In form as well, the bittern suggested the burgeoning law of vegetation. In *A Week,* though in none of the journal passages, Thoreau describes the bittern in detail as it probes for food: "the whole head being concealed, while the neck and body formed an arch above the water" (Wk, 236). In the interval between the C version and the publication of *A Week,* Thoreau had lived at Walden Pond, and come to know beans by long experience. The similitude between a germinating bean seed thrusting its roots into the soil while arching its stem into the air prior to the eruption of its radical leaves and a bittern thrusting its neck into the sand while making its body form an arch over its concealed head must have struck Thoreau at some level of consciousness, even though Jonathan Bishop could find "no symbolic overtones to *these* facts."[24] One only needs to have hoed beans to appreciate the resemblance, and to be aware that for Thoreau especially, the book of nature was a more persistent "literary" influence than the publications of mankind. In my estimation, Thoreau, in his treatment of the bittern, amended, however subconsciously, the view he had expressed in the spring of 1841:

What have I to do with plows—I cut another furrow than you see—. . . Is not my sand well clayed—my peat well sanded. . . .

> Plows of new pattern—hoes the same—
> Designed a different soil to tame,
> And sow my seed broadcast in air,
> Full sure to reap my harvest there.
> (PJ, I, 297-98)

For the bittern is a creature not only of the air and water, but of the earth as well, and nature camouflages it as vegetation when it thrusts its head upward to blend in with the growth on the shore, a characteristic Thoreau was well aware of.[25] In Thoreau's imagination, the bittern's connection with the earth and its resemblance to growing things are illuminated by his description of it in flight as "sluggishly . . . plowing the air with the coulter of his breast-bone" (J, IV, 233), and by an image that recalls the weary farmer in the first stanza of Thomas Gray's "Elegy Written in a Country Churchyard," for "*plodding* home over the meadows at evening," the bittern comes to a perch where it stands, "just like a stake, or the point of a stump or root" (J, IV, 334). The peculiar call of the bittern, which resembles halfway the pumping of water, halfway the driving of a stake (J, V, 193), provoked such nicknames as "stake-driver" and "pump-er-goŕ" (J, XI, 251), the latter of Thoreau's own coinage. Thus by its color, by its form, by its habits, and by its call, the bittern conveyed an affinity for the earth as well as for water.

In his strange fascination with the bittern, Thoreau sensed, particularly in its green eye, that his own imagination needed to take root in order to soar, and in the soil underfoot he had begun to seek, with the bittern, a common ground for expression. Nudged earthward, he wrote in "Friday" as if to approve the pull of gravity and the need to take root,

> All things are current found
> On earthly ground,
> Spirits and elements
> Have their descents.
> (Wk, 389)

Thus, though *A Week* is governed by a genius of hypaethral and fluvial currents, a genius or muse of vegetation is beginning to stir. In "Thursday" Thoreau declared that "a worm is as good a traveler as a grasshopper or a cricket, and a much wiser settler" (Wk, 304), and belatedly confessed in "Friday" that it is "but thin soil where we stand; I have felt my roots in a richer ere this" (Wk, 383). Near journey's end he confesses to having caught glimpses of a vegetal harvest "behind the sheaves, and under the sod," which held promise of "a ripe fruit, which the reapers have not gathered, the true harvest of the year, which it bears for ever . . ." (Wk, 378-79). Such seeds may in fact have been present at the launching out, as evidenced by the weeds at the bottom of the stream, "shaken by the watery wind [but] still planted where their seeds had sunk" (Wk, 13). Listening to the sound of his plying oars as "a sort of rudimental music," Thoreau grew intent on leading "a *purely* sensuous life" (Wk, 382) so that his own organic development would ensue, his present senses being "but the rudiments of what they are destined to become" (Wk, 382). Even the operative word (and image) sown in *A Week*—*lapse*—contained the rudiments, in its radicle letters *l* and *p,* of what it would become in the chapter "Spring" in *Walden*—*lobe.*

If Thoreau had his seeds ready in *A Week,* they were too watery—like the cranberries he mentions as he draws to an end—and as yet unconcentrated. Resting under the shade of a tree in "Monday," the two sojourners contemplated the "lapse of the river and of human life" (Wk, 124) while eating a melon and carelessly casting its seeds into the stream. The moment looks back to Genesis—as Van Anglen notes, "melon" derives from

Greek *melon* or apple[26]—but forward as well to the redemption Thoreau will work out in his beanfield. Thoreau ruminates,

> He who eats the fruit, should at least plant the seed; aye, if possible, a better seed than that whose fruit he has enjoyed. Seeds! there are seeds enough which need only to be stirred in with the soil where they lie, by an inspired voice or pen, to bear fruit of a divine flavor. (Wk, 125)

If in his first book Thoreau's pen had been too like an oar, his style steeped too exclusively in the law of currents, his seeds too watery, in his next work, already germinating, it would be very like the hoe he wielded while standing in the broad margins of a field where he would shift ground to involve the law of vegetation with the law of currents, to make a terrene expression—to make the earth say "beans," or what it would. For *Walden,* he would have his seeds ready, and this time they would be concentrated and hardened.

III

Half Way That of Vegetation

5

Johnswort: The Roots of *Walden*

Some upland pasture—where the John's wort grew—
PJ, I, 352; J, I, 304

IN LATE MARCH 1845, Thoreau, as he puts it in *Walden*, "borrowed an axe and went down to the woods by Walden Pond, nearest to where I intended to build my house, and began to cut down some tall arrowy white pines, still in their youth, for timber" (Wa, 40). Settled in his cabin by August on land owned by Emerson, his first bean crop flourishing and his work on *A Week* before him, he recalled an unforgettable visit to the pond with his family when he was five years old, when the landscape had seemed the "oriental asiatic valley of my world" (PJ, II, 173-74; J, I, 381). With his flute he tried to fetch back that primal scene, musing that but a single generation of pines had fallen in the interval, the roots of some having cooked his supper. "Almost the same johnswort springs from the same perennial root in this pasture.—Even I have at length helped to clothe that fabulous landscape of my imagination—and one result of my presence and influence is seen in the bean leaves. . . ." Some years later in the first surviving worksheets of the sand foliage paragraphs in "Spring," he wondered, "Between the inert bean and this luxuriant vegetation, what interval is there?"[1]

Aside from that of literal space—his beanfield was a scant quarter mile from the Deep Cut—there was an interval of imaginative space as well, between first impression and the flowering of truth that would come of meditated and mediated expression. In his life and in the pages of his journal, Thoreau became tireless in his efforts to daily "go out and re-ally" himself with nature, as he summed up his habits in 1856. "We must make root, send out some little fibre at least, even every winter day" (J, IX, 200). And so he had. By confounding knowing and growing into a similitude of what I. A. Richards called "growledge," Thoreau sent out a veritable network of roots in his journal that obeyed at least halfway the law of vegetation.[2] In 1859 he would look back to this period of the genesis of

Walden with an understanding that "it is only when we forget all our learning that we begin to know. . . . If you would make acquaintance with the ferns you must forget your botany. You must get rid of what is commonly called *knowledge* of them" (J, XII, 371). When he moved to the pond, however, and even as late as 1850, Thoreau did not have the rudiments of botanical and philological knowledge that he must thereafter "forget" in order that *Walden* might "grow."

*

Despite his deserved reputation as an amateur naturalist, not till the early 1850s did Thoreau become an avid student of botany, one of those "*Miscellaneous* Botanophilists" (J, III, 309) as he described himself in his journal. In an entry of late 1856 he recalled a time twenty years earlier when—finishing at Harvard, starting his journal, and making use of field trips in his stint as a teacher—he had first confined himself to "Bigelow's 'Plants of Boston and Vicinity,'" but forgot the plant names almost immediately. Then, about 1850, he found himself "again attending to plants with more method, looking out the name of each one and remembering it" (J, IX, 156-67). In late 1851 he wrote a thumbnail summary of the key figures he had become acquainted with in the literature of botany:

> What shall we say of the comparative intellectual vigor of the ancients and moderns, when we read of Theophrastus, the father of botany, that he composed more than two hundred treatises in the third century before Christ and the seventeenth before printing, about twenty of which remain. . . . Among the last are two works on natural history and the generation of plants. What a stimulus to a literary man to read his works! They *were opera,* not an essay or two, which you can carry between your thumb and finger.
>
> Dioscorides . . . who lived in the first century after Christ . . the first to inquire into the medical properties of plants, "the literary father of the *materia medica*." . . . next . . . Pliny the Elder . . . "his natural history is a compilation from about twenty-five hundred (?) different authors." Conrad Gesner, of the Sixteenth Century, the first botanist of note among the moderns; also a naturalist generally. In this century botany first "became a regular academical study." (J, III, 118)

While he complained two months later that there was "no good introduction to the study of the natural system" (J, III, 252), he was at work learning the meaning of botanical terms through a careful scrutiny of the *Philosophia Botanica* of the Swedish botanist Carolus Linnaeus (1707-78), the excellent plates of which he found more instructive than a whole "volume of explanations or glossaries" (J, III, 347).[3]

At the time, an enthusiasm for Linnaeus, father of taxonomy, was only beginning to wane: in the third quarter of the eighteenth century a small army of naturalists had ranged out from the Linnaean camp in northern

Europe, scouting newly discovered areas of the globe and naming, describing (often by superb painterly means), and classifying their fauna and flora. One of the Linnaean disciples in America was Peter Kalm (1715-79), whom Thoreau was reading in 1851 (J, II, 463). By the third decade of the nineteenth century, shortly before young Charles Darwin embarked on his momentous voyage on the *Beagle* (Thoreau read about that voyage in late spring, 1851), the Linnaean penchant for systematizing had been subjected to caricature in America with James Fenimore Cooper's *The Prairie* (1827).[4] In Dr. Obed Battius, a nearsighted "disciple of Linnaeus," Cooper attacked a dead-language systematizer whose blindness to the vital processes of nature was reinforced by a Latin cognomen—Dr. Bat.

But by their work in the classification and division of species, the eighteenth- and early nineteenth-century taxonomists had provided the basis for the Darwinian leap in the ordering of natural species from a logical to a chronological system. The work of the Linnaean naturalists inevitably provoked musings about the morphology of nature, for no scientist could long ignore the apparent resemblances of species in major as well as minor details. In the skeletal structures of different species of contemporaries—an alligator, a lynx, and a man, for instance—the analogies detected readily suggested that the different species might at least be conceived as descendants in a chronological scheme. The less "perfect" form would then appear not as a deviation from a perfect archetype (a notion sustained by the myth of the Fall of man and an attendant lapse in nature), but as a prototype from which more complex forms derive. The early "dictionaries" of nature, intent upon defining, had simply ignored the time factor.

Despite his enthusiasm for Linnaeus and his reading of Darwin, Thoreau feared his scientific studies might dry up his imagination. In the summer of 1851 he wrote of

> this habit of close observation,—in Humboldt, Darwin, and others. Is it to be kept up long, this science? Do not tread on the heels of your experience. Be impressed without making a minute of it. Poetry puts an interval between the impression and the expression—waits till the seed germinates naturally. (J, II, 341)

Two years later he feared that to look at Nature directly, or not to look "through and beyond her," was as "fatal as to look at the head of Medusa. It turns the man of science to stone" (J, V, 45). Indeed, "a slight, dry headache as the result of all this observing" suggested that the petrification might already have begun. Standing "in the midst of all this dust and filings," he cried out, "O for a little Lethe!"—and as much for a draught of forgetfulness as for a reflux of the waters of imagination: "O for a little Lethe! To crown all, lichens, which are so thin, are described in the *dry* state, as they are most commonly, not most truly, seen. Truly, they are *dryly* described." And what follows is a paragraph on his claim to have "a civil right in the river." His attraction to the vital, aqueous humor is likewise evident in an undated 1851 journal passage copied from C. C. Felton's translation of Arnold Guyot's *The Earth and Man*: "Compared with the Old World, the New World is the humid side of our planet, the *oceanic, vegetative* world, the passive element awaiting the excitement of a livelier impulse from without" (J, II, 148).

Thoreau found one such impulse in Asa Gray's *Manual of Botany,* a "dry" work at first glance, but one that nonetheless inspired Thoreau's "humid" or "passive element" into elaborating "a perfect analogy between the life of the human being and that of the vegetable, both of the body and the mind." While Joel Porte finds Thoreau's four-page commentary on Gray (J, II, 201-5) in the entry of May 20, 1851, a "tedious attempt at proving" the perfect analogy—he calls it Thoreau's "longest exercise in Transcendental writing"—Thoreau is there less intent on proving than he is in putting an interval between his "dry" source and his own moist and fanciful, if not yet poetic, thoughts.[5] As an exercise in Transcendental writing, it is an especially crucial one, the roots of which are soiled in the nourishing, humid side of Thoreau's planet, waiting "till the seed germinates naturally" (J, II, 341). In his long commentary Thoreau, especially alert for analogies between "roots" in the vegetal and in the human conditions, alternates direct quotations from Gray with his own fanciful, but persistently searching, reflections. Thus to Gray's remark that "the first point of the stem preexists in the embryo (*i.e.*, in the rudimentary plantlet contained within the seed): it is here called the radicle," Thoreau responds, "Such is the rudiment of mind, already partially developed, more than a bud, but pale, having never been exposed to the light . . . packed away in the seed, unfolded" (J, II, 202). To Gray's "the plant . . . develops from the first in two opposite directions . . . upwards [to expand in the light and air] . . . and downwards [avoiding the light] to form the root," Thoreau responds that the mind develops similarly, "upwards to expand in the light and air; and downwards avoiding the light to form the root. One half is aerial, the other subterranean" (J, II, 202-3; the bracketed portions are Thoreau's interpolations). Thoreau finds "the mere logician, the mere reasoner, who weaves his arguments as a tree its branches in the sky,—nothing equally developed in the roots,—is overthrown by the first wind." Gray notes the roots may spring from any part of the stem when the conditions are favorable, "that is to say in darkness and moisture." This evokes Thoreau's comment that

> the most clear and ethereal ideas (Antaeus-like) readily ally themselves to the earth, to the primal womb of things. They put forth roots as soon as branches; they

are eager to be *soiled.* No thought soars so high that it sunders these apron strings of its mother. The thought that comes to light, that pierces the empyrean on the other side, is wombed and rooted in darkness,—its roots in Hades like the tree of life. . . . Wherever there is an air-and-light-seeking bud about to expand, it may become in the earth a darkness-seeking root. (J, II, 204; see Appendix A for the whole of the passage.)

However mechanical Thoreau's interpolations might seem to some, they mark a stage in the evolution of his radical tendencies that gave root to his imagination, enabling it to grow like "the tree of life," a figure of increasing generative vigor in Thoreau's expression.[6]

Three months later Thoreau was drawing nourishment from Bronson Alcott's copy of *Rei Rusticae,* which contained the classical agriculturists—Cato, Varro, Columella, and Palladius. While Ethel Seybold contends that Thoreau's reading in the Roman husbandry writers satisfied his need to "send downward new roots to ally [himself] to the earth," it was only symptomatic of a general earthward tendency, for reading a farm report by some husbandmen of Middlesex made him feel as if he had "got my foot down on to the solid and sunny earth, the basis of all philosophy, and poetry, and religion even" (J, III, 327). Robert D. Richardson, Jr., is surely right in viewing Thoreau's reading of the Roman agricultural writers during this period as a sign of his belief "that the cultivation of one's self has a good deal in common with the cultivation of the soil."[7]

By 1853, his sympathy with plant roots having become habitual, Thoreau on the morning of a particularly fine Indian summer day in November walked out from his home with a rake, cryptically noting his purpose: "To river, to examine roots" (J, V, 527). He devotes nearly the whole of the "A.M." entry to the roots he examined there, particularly those of the white and the great yellow lily. On the way home from such moist radicalizing, he noticed, by way of contrast, the "withered grasses and sedges" that lined the riverbank. And he sought a humid character not only in nature, but in books on nature, finding in John Evelyn (1620-1706) an expression more deliquescent than that in the dry Gray. Following a lengthy comment on the last few "*washing* days" when the breeze made all the vegetation "wave," even if the "liquid-velvety" grass was becoming "bosky," Thoreau dealt appreciatively with *Sylva, or a Discourse of Forest Trees.* He noted especially Evelyn's comments on the alder, which lies under water, and the "oziers or aquatic salix," especially good for "fish-weirs, and to support the banks of impetuous rivers: In fine, for all wicker and *twiggy* works." Evelyn's "meldews," Thoreau wonders—is it the source of "mildews"? In many of Evelyn's words he finds a moist, "poetic genius," among them "a *sobbing* rain" and a "dewie *sperge* or brush," which Evelyn recommended instead of a watering-pot, which "gluts" the earth

(J, IV, 83-87). Two years later Thoreau complained that Nuttall's *North American Sylva* was insufficiently humid, "sapless, if not leafless," its fine plates "greener and higher-colored than the words" (J, VI, 265). In another extended comment upon Evelyn's verdant style, Thoreau reveals his attraction to an expression that confounds arboreal with verbal life:

> Evelyn and others wrote when the language was in a tender, nascent state and could be moulded to express the shades of meaning; when sesquipedalian words, long since cut and apparently dried and drawn to mill,—not yet to the dictionary lumber-yard,—put forth a fringe of green sprouts here and there along in the angles of their rugged bark, their very bulk insuring some sap remaining; some florid suckers they sustain at least. Which words, split into shingles and laths, will supply poets for ages to come. (J, V, 43)

Thoreau's distaste for the dry naturalists, his fanciful elaboration on the passage from Gray's *Botany* where he inclined scientific botany to the "oceanic" and poetic, his study of fluvial roots, his perceptive comments about Evelyn's "moist" diction (as contrasted with the "sapless" diction of *North American Sylva)*—all are signs of a disinclination for dry scientific botanizing and an attentiveness to moist imaginative probing into philological as well as botanical roots. In Thoreau's imagination, it seemed as if the moist roots of plants and of words drew their nourishment from a common uterine soil.

*

As with botany, philology in the nineteenth century had only begun to take account of the impact of time upon its subject matter. The English dictionary, which was originally little more than a glossary or hard word list, was a comparatively recent arrival; Dr. Samuel Johnson's groundbreaking *Dictionary* (1755) was less than a hundred years old at the time *Walden* was published. There Dr. Johnson had intended to fix his native language in its pristine state, at the wellsprings of English undefiled; but he grudgingly came to realize that language does change, seems to have a life of its own, and the etymologies he supplied for some words provided the hint later taken up as a principle in formulating the *New English Dictionary* (N.E.D.). As more information about a variety of languages came to light, word cognates and other richly suggestive analogies provided a firmer basis for speculation about the morphology, and thus about the chronological dimension, of language.[8]

In his lifetime an amateur student of languages, Thoreau in *A Week* had mentioned Germany's "philological industry . . . indirectly serving the cause of philosophy and poetry" (Wk, 142-43), though at the time he knew scarcely more of that industry than of the botanical. But he had "a philological side" in his writing that "needs to be thoughtfully considered," as his frequent walking companion William Ellery Channing noted.[9] Examples abound, as in his remark that he liked "the name pansy—or pensèe, best of any," its use being "for thoughts" (PJ, I, 233, 235; J, I, 178, 180); or that "our fields" are "but *felds* or *felled* woods. They bear a more recent name than the woods, suggesting that previously the earth was covered with woods" (J, IV, 482-83). Even when etymologically sound, to a twentieth-century philologist such juggling with words might seem impertinent—a sideshow to divert attention from the ring where nomenclature, description, and function of language clamor for attention. But playful as Thoreau might be with language, he believed "the analogies of words are never whimsical and meaningless, but stand for real likenesses" (J, I, 99). Indeed, he was cognizant of the best-known writers on the subject. One of them was John Horne Tooke (1736-1812), English politician and philologist, whose *Diversions of Purley* (1786; expanded 1798) supplies a point of departure for nearly every subsequent musing about the mother tongue. In a college essay Thoreau showed enough familiarity with *Diversions* to realize that its title was misleading ("Titles of Books," EEM, 91-92). A decade later, during his Walden Pond sojourn, Thoreau signaled an intention to begin philological studies by noting "Johnson and Tooke, for a criticism of words" (J, I, 398).[10] And though he seems never to have labored systematically in this area, over the years he managed to amass a small library of dictionaries, brought together "A List of Indian Words" that was appended to *The Maine Woods* (MW, 320-25), and speculated in a richly suggestive way about word origins.

In early 1853, Thoreau was delighted to discover *On the Study of Words* (1851), a small volume by the English divine Richard Chenevix Trench (1807-86). Trench, who acknowledged his own debt to Horne Tooke, had proposed to the London Philological Society in 1829 a scheme that eventuated in the *New English Dictionary,* the equivalent in its field of Darwin's work in natural history. Over Trench's learned discussions of words Thoreau could not contain his exuberance. He relished the reserved meanings in such words as "transport, rapture, ravishment, ecstasy. These are the words I want. . . . I am rapt away . . . out of myself. These are truly poetical words. I am inspired, elevated, expanded. I am on the mount" (J, IV, 466-67). What one finds here is a witty response to Trench's fetching philology that actively reinforces the sense of life dis-covered in words.[11] It also reveals Thoreau's inclination to frolic in the mainstream of language activity, thereby dramatizing the play of words rather than merely recording them from the bankside. His mimicry demonstrates, sometimes to the consternation of his readers, that words do get out of line, without apparent intention, to convey an unanticipated truth, sometimes in an extraordinarily radiant way.[12] Thus, Thoreau favorably notes Trench's definition of the primary sense of "rivals" as "those who dwell on the banks of the same stream"; extending the idea, he then punningly localizes to those rivals who happened to live on the banks of the Concord, "which flows . . . without a rapid or a brawl" (J, IV, 467-68). Caught up in this spirit of philological frolic, he laments that in the writings of Thomas Carlyle one finds "no *double entendre*" (EEM, 241).

A few months after his extended commentary on Gray's *Botany,* Thoreau was delving into the moist, productive soil of a book by J. J. G. Wilkinson (1797-1875) where he found "what I have dreamed of,—a return to the primitive analogical and derivative senses of words. His ability to trace analogies often leads him to a truer word than more remarkable writers have found . . ." (J, II, 462). In Wilkinson, Thoreau discerned a faith in "old and current expressions as having sprung from an instinct wiser than science," for unlike the man of science, Wilkinson found "a *home* for the imagination, and it is no longer outcast and homeless. All perception of truth is the detection of an analogy; we reason from our hands to our head" (J, II, 463). By "descent and analogy" Thoreau had similarly sought out the "inner sense" (J, I, 172) of words, as in such Old World works as *Purchas his Pilgrimes,* which had "a certain fertility, an Ohio soil, as if they were making a humus for new literatures to spring in. . . . Decayed literature makes the richest of all soils" (J, III, 353). In the works of Francis Quarles and Sir Walter Raleigh he found equally pleasing crabbed and earthy expressions, and pursued them in writing that "the word is well naturalized or rooted that can be traced back to a Celtic original. It is like getting out stumps and fat pine roots" (J, III, 232-33). He did just that in musing that "the rose owes its preeminence in great measure to its color. It is said to be from the Celtic *rhos,* red . . . nature's most precious color" (J, IV, 217-18).[13]

If Greek mythology derived from a humus "much more fertile," the Old World soil that nourished it was now exhausted, as Thoreau believed; but he likewise believed that "the nature which inspired mythology still flourishes" in a fertile West that was "preparing to add its fables to those of the East" (J, II, 145). In January 1854, he came across a passage from Varro that his fancy seized to plant in his "Bean Field" chapter in order to make a transcendental language of agriculture, a step in preparing his own Western fable:

> The grain, *granum,* is a *gerendo,* for this is the object of planting, that this may be borne. "But the *spica* (or ear), which the rustics call *speca,* as they have received it from their forefathers, seems to be named from *spes* (hope), since they plant because they *hope* that *this* will be hereafter (*eam enim quod sperant fore*)." (J, VI, 82)

Elsewhere, too, his radical readings in the classical languages tend to merge the botanical and the philological, as when he remarks that in Grecian mythology Phaeton's sister Lampetie "*subitâ radice retenta est.* All the sisters were changed to trees while they were in vain beseeching their mother not to break their branches. *Cortex in verba novissima venit*" (J, II, 145). This last sentence echoes the opening of the Gospel of St. John (St. John's Word) with a startling naturalistic twist; and David Greene, who in *A Frail Duration* analyzes the first chapters of *Walden* with particular effectiveness, states:

> Insistence on the written word . . . provides a key to Thoreau's method of composition. For him *in principio verbum est*; as a practitioner of the organic method he erects his literary structure not only *with* words but *on* words—basic symbols that must be grasped in all their far-reaching ramifications if the whole is to be understood. Of this he warns us by reiterating the virtues of the written word: it stands still that we may pause over it, taste it, inspect it, think about it, and gradually absorb its full freight of meaning, rather than let it flash by as a mere communicatory counter as it does in speech. . . . Thoreau never ceases to remind us that practically no one takes the time or has the patience to attend to words, *especially in his own tongue*.[14]

Greene's italicized terminal remark reminds us how thoroughly involved Thoreau's tongue was with words ("As if languages were especially of the tongue" [PJ, II, 178; J, I, 386]). Speculating on the arrival of the written word in Latin and Greek, in 1845 Thoreau wrote that a word "is the most perfect work of human art, and as it may be breathed and taken on our lips and as it were become the product of our physical organs as its sense is of our intellectual—it is the nearest to life itself" (PJ, II, 164; J, I, 370). In 1851 Thoreau found himself gazing—in a manner grazing—on words with the terminal Latin root *-cious,* which he felt were particularly succulent, and reflected on the physical organs they set to work:

> These *lipped* words, which, like the lips of moose and browsing creatures, gather in the herbage and twigs with a certain greed. This termination *cious* adds force to a word, like the lips of browsing creatures, which greedily collect what the jaw holds; as in the word "tenacious" the first half represents the kind of jaw which holds, the last the lips which collect. It can only be pronounced by a certain opening and protruding of the lips; so "avaricious." These words express the sense of their simple roots with the addition, as it were, of a certain lip greediness. . . . When these expressive words are used, the hearer gets something to chew upon. . . . What is *luscious is especially enjoyed by the lips. . . . To be edacious and voracious is to be not nibbling and swallowing merely, but eating and swallowing while the lips are greedily collecting more food.* (J, II, 443)

Such unusual radical browsing discloses a Thoreau ruminant, not groveling, intent on communing sympathetically with the roots of a word, "the simplest and purest channel by which a revelation may be transmitted from age to age" (PJ, II, 164; J, I, 370). In delving into the ground where they were rooted, he was inevitably plummeting toward a hard bottom and rocks—would they be sterile?—in place. In less verdant seasons he was taken by the same desire to go behind the "dissertations—on language" to reach the "tongue" of nature, the "language that is—that is really universal—the inexpressible meaning that is in all things & every where" (PJ, II, 178; J, I, 386); and, analogously, he would ponder "the cracks in the ice showing a white cleavage. What is their law? Somewhat like foliage, but too rectangular, like the characters of some Oriental language. I feel as if I could get grammar and dictionary and go into it" (J, III, 175). And so he tried.

But to avail himself of such a law, he must first learn the ABC's in nature's elementally formulated grammar and dictionary, based on "the natural and broader pedestal of the living rock" (PJ, II, 119; J, I, 480). His New England neighbors might seemingly master rock in monuments and mortuary verse, beneath which they attempted to preserve human "remains." But Thoreau, disturbed that "all the stone a nation hammers goes towards its tomb only" (J, IV, 153), could not abide the dead language of cemeteries or statues, and found comfort in nature's way, where old bones were knocked about by every beast until, in a post- humus condition, they were returned to the cycle of life. He found rock "crude and inaccessible" to his nature; still, the influence of a particularly warm sun could melt his "stoniness a little" (J, III, 136). Rather than dwell on death as an absolute, or on the mortuary significance of rock, he gravitated to rock "translated" by the symbiotic process into soil, the basis for vital organization. After the death of his brother John in early 1842, and of little Waldo Emerson but a few days later, Thoreau wrote of "the sad memory of departed friends . . . soon incrusted over with sublime & pleasing thoughts—as their monuments are overgrown with moss." And then he traced Nature's healing powers in "the mediation of a thousand little mosses and fungi," which make "the most unsightly objects become radiant of beauty." He went on to say that

> there seem to be two sides to this world . . . as we see things in growth or dissolution—in life or death— For seen with the eye of a poet—as God sees them, all are alive and beautiful, but seen with the historical eye, or the eye of the memory, they are dead and offensive. (PJ, I, 372; J, I, 328)

Fixing his poetic eye on the living rock as the point d'appui of Nature's language, he discerned in its clefts an alphabet—mosses, fungi, lichens—a hopeful expression from the side of the sentence contiguous only to the gods.

In the years immediately before the publication of *Walden,* Thoreau was preoccupied with the lichen, as if it contained the secret of the grammar of nature, or served as its alphabet. At the beginning of a four-year period when he paid particular heed to mosses, fungi, and lichens, in late 1850 he wrote that whoever "would study lichens must go into a new country where the rocks have not been burned" (J, II, 88). In 1852 he listed the names of all the lichens he had identified during the previous winter (J, IV, 112-13) when he was "studying lichens" (J, III, 336). His habit of examining them microscopically had kept him from seeing much else; he even took a cosmological view, analogizing that the sky was a kind of thallus, "cerulean, which scatters its infinite sporules of light," and he found "the shield (or rather the apothecium) of a lichen disproportionately large . . ." (J, III, 337). Recalling this period still later, he wrote in 1859 of how when he saw "the sulphur lichens on the rails brightening with the moisture," he felt "like studying them again as a relisher or tonic. . . . To study lichens is to get a taste of earth and health, to go gnawing the rails and rocks" (J, XI, 439-40).

But the lichen seemed nearly intractable to extended imaginative development; as Thoreau represents him, Channing was soon weary of it: "It was so thin, and there was so little of man in it! Why, the whole of it wasn't more than an inch thick" (J, III, 184); and when Thoreau imbibed the "fertilizing influence" of a January rainstorm, he thought "the part of you that is wettest is fullest of life, like the lichens" (J, X, 262). In fair weather the thin dry lichen only suggested the myth of Cadmus; it needed the context of the "moist, humid" words to express nature's language. Only when he had on his seven-league (sesquipedalian) word boots was Thoreau able to read through "the book" of nature to its radical origins and ends.

He did so by communing with the soil underfoot, for were not the roots of words and of vegetation "soiled" in a common life principle? And were not the roots of nature and of language somehow contained in one radical expression? conveyed in one word? Was *radical* the word made light? Or was *radical* the word affected by the light? into life? Was it the word that signified the inexpressible from which language and nature alike proceeded, drawn from the earth by the sun, the word made light? Surely for Thoreau, as for Gerard Manley Hopkins, the world *was* charged with the grandeur of God. And underfoot was a holy land toward which radical man might plummet, and within which he could renew himself. Man's journey toward *that* holy land could be conceived in terms of growth, not mere travel, like that of a root toward (or from) a bedrock holy land of the imagination. These were the speculations haunting Thoreau in late autumn and early spring of the 1850s as he pondered the sacred "wort," the "inner sense" beneath the superficial appearance of the radicals projecting from his own and nature's journals. In *A Week* he had noted that "*religion*" was derived from "ligature" (Wk, 64, 78), although

> in most men's religion, the ligature, which should be its umbilical cord connecting them with divinity, is rather like that thread which the accomplices of Cylon held in their hands when they went abroad from the temple of Minerva, the other end being attached to the statue of the goddess. But frequently, as in their case, the thread breaks, being stretched, and they are left without an asylum. (Wk, 78)

In the early 1850s, Thoreau was tugging at the ligature and finding it a tough root, attached to no stone statue of a goddess, but to the living rock itself.

*

In journalizing over the seasonal lapse of life, Thoreau wrested transcendent meaning out of favored plants or trees—the skunk-cabbage, the saxifrage, the goldenrod, the shrub oak, the rose, the water lily, the swamp pyrus. He seemed especially intent on their testimony of persistent life, or on their function in forming a soil that might nourish vegetation. He noted the "saxifrage, well named ['stone-breaking'], budded but not risen," growing "in the seams of the rocks, where is no earth apparent" (J, III, 424). Then there was the skunk-cabbage, to which Nature had assigned a "conspicuous place . . . first flower to show itself above the bare ground! What occult relation is implied between this plant and man?" (J, III, 437).[15] And the goldenrod, later in the year, which he regarded as the fruit of the sun (J, V, 403-4), and which in midsummer "already . . . preaches of the lapse of time" (J, IV, 225). He prized the shrub oak for retaining its leaves throughout the long New England winter with a tenacious grip on life: "You might say of a very old and withered man or woman that they hung on like a shrub oak leaf, almost to a second spring. There was still a little life in the heel of the leaf-stalk" (J, II, 139).

In late winter 1852, "a backward season" with him, Thoreau observed that the frost in the ground had thawed, though he saw no new growth in open field plants, "but if I should explore carefully about their roots, I should find some expanding buds and even new-rising shoots" (J, III, 363). By year's end, vigilant for radical leaves as mounting evidence of the continuity of life, Thoreau noted how the frost formed around the pinweed and surmised that it was not because of the plant's form, but "may have something to do with the life of the root, which I noticed was putting forth shoots *beneath.* Perhaps the growth generates heat and so steam" (J,

IV, 428-29). In November 1853, his annual vigil over the dying year in progress, he thought it "time to observe the radical leaves of many plants, which put forth with springlike vigor and are so unlike the others with which we are familiar that it is sometimes difficult to identify them" (J, V, 476). A few days later he had observed enough radical leaves to generalize "that many plants about this season of the year or earlier, after they have died down at top, put forth fresh and conspicuous radical leaves against another spring." And then, as he had done in response to Asa Gray's *Manual of Botany,* he analogized:

> So some human beings in the November of their days exhibit some fresh radical greenness, which though the frosts may soon nip it, indicates and confirms their essential vitality. When their summer leaves have faded and fallen, they put forth fresh radical leaves which sustain the life in their root still, against a new spring. (J, V, 508-9)

As *Walden* was being readied for publication at the approach of spring 1854, Thoreau, most alert for the signs of life and growth in radical leaves, queried, "Has not the johnswort two lives, in winter sending out radical shoots which creep flat on the ground under the snow, in the summer shooting upward and blossoming?" (J, VI, 152). The next day the "radical leaves of the pinweeds . . . like the johnswort" seemed "unaffected by frost. The radical leaves of the crowfoot everywhere are the commonest green, as soon as the snow goes off. You can hardly tell when it begins to spring" (J, VI, 157). Three days later his examination of the radical leaves of the shepherd's purse prompted him to generalize that "the vegetable kingdom showed the influence of the spring as much in the air as in the water,—that is, in the flowing of the sap, the skunk-cabbage buds, and the swelling of the willow catkins" (J, VI, 160). In early April he noticed a brightness in the radical leaves of some plants—the shepherd's purse and the skunk-cabbage, and "a little yellow lily in the ditch and sweet flag *starting* in the brook" (J, VI, 182). In such vernal reflections, Thoreau seems to advance the backward season in himself by sympathy with a holy land the johnswort (a plant known also as St.-John's-wort, literally St. John's word) had been in touch with in its reflective winter season.[16]

Indeed, Thoreau found particular plants numinous with scriptural meanings. One of these in addition to the johnswort was the life-everlasting, which he described in detail on November 11, 1850; the "minute young fragrant life-everlasting, with only four or five flat-lying leaves and thread-like roots" spotted the pasture, and at each center was "a little pellet of cotton or down . . . ready for an early start in the spring" (J, II, 93). Some time later he noted that the "sweet-scented life-everlasting has not lost its scent yet, but smells like the balm of the fields" (J, II, 100). The next summer he was alert for the budding of this fragrant flower (J, II, 305) and a year later rhapsodized: " 'The dry, pearly, and almost incorruptible heads of the Life Everlasting.' Ah! this is a truly elysian flower now, beyond change and decay, not lusty but immortal. . ." (J, IV, 307). The next spring he again took note of the "fragrant life-everlasting," which together with the ribwort seemed an innocent "born in a cloud. . . . Better learn this strange character which nature speaks to-day than the Sanscrit. Books in the brooks" (J, V, 28).

That Emerson was aware of the high value Thoreau found in this plant is clear from his eulogy, where it serves as the terminal symbol:

> There is a flower known to botanists, one of the same genus with our summer plant called "Life-Everlasting," a *Gnaphalium* like that, which grows on the most inaccessible cliffs of the Tyrolese mountains, where the chamois dare hardly venture, and which the hunter, tempted by its beauty, and by his love (for it is immensely valued by the Swiss maidens), climbs the cliffs to gather, and is sometimes found dead at the foot, with the flower in his hand. It is called by botanists the *Gnaphalium leontopodium,* but by the Swiss *Edelweisse,* which signifies *Noble Purity.* (EW, X, 484-85)

Emerson's perception is so nearly on the mark that one can imagine as Thoreau's prickly rejoinder that he dwelt at a Walden Pond in a New World, not in a Waldensian Valley in the Old, though the struggle for religious freedom that had been waged in that high alpine valley in Milton's day went on near Walden Pond's low shore; and that the flower he sought was of native growth, the cliffs he must climb to pluck it being no more and no less precipitous than those at Fairhaven.[17]

As early as 1841, Thoreau projected himself into the hidden source of life expressed by the life-everlasting in writing in his journal: "I have some notion what the John's-wort and life-everlasting may be thinking about when the sun shines on me as on them and turns my prompt thought into just such a seething shimmer. . . . I am evaporating and ascending into the sun" (J, I, 203-4; PJ, I, 256). But it was in the golden blossomed johnswort that the combination of vegetal and linguistic meanings ran deepest for Thoreau. The first syllable of "johnswort" suggests a "profane" version of the writer of the gospel of light, St. John; the second, a form both of "root" and of "word." Thus "johnswort" is a punning version of the words of the Evangelist who introduces the New Testament with "In the beginning was the word." In Thoreau's search for the signs of growth about the radical leaves of plants in the dead of winter, he attempted to read *to* the beginning of the plant "wort," to delve with deliberation to the *sainte terre* that soiled it, and of which it was a "New Testament."

In the winter of 1853, on the face of Fairhaven Cliff, Thoreau pulled up a johnswort, and was "surprised to see the signs of unceasing growth about the roots,—fresh shoots two inches long, white with red leafets, and all the radical part quite green" (J, IV, 460). And while he diverts his glance to the crowfoot, the johnswort remains near at hand:

> The leaves of the crowfoot, also, are quite green, and carry me forward to spring. I dig one up with a stick, and, pulling it to pieces, I find deep in the centre of the plant, just beneath the ground, surrounded by all the tender leaves that are to precede it, the blossom-bud, about half as big as the head of a pin, perfectly white. There it patiently sits, or slumbers, how full of faith, informed of a spring which the world has never seen, the promise and prophecy of it shaped somewhat like some Eastern temple, in which a bud-shaped dome o'ertops the whole. It affected me, this tender dome-like bud, within the bosom of the earth, like a temple upon the earth, resounding with the worship of votaries. Methought I saw the flamens in yellow robes within it. The crowfoot buds—and how many beside!—lie unexpanded just beneath the surface. May I lead my life the following year as innocently as they! May it be as fair and smell as sweet! I anticipate nature. Destined to become a fair yellow flower above the surface to delight the eyes of children and its Maker. It offered to my mind a little temple into which to enter and worship. It will go forth in April, this vestal now cherishing her fire, to be married to the sun. How innocent are Nature's purposes! How unambitious! Her elections are not Presidential. The springing and blossoming of this flower do not depend on the votes of men. (J, IV, 460-61)

In a journal entry for December 30, 1841, Thoreau versified the symbolic, translating powers of the johnswort:

> I have remembered when the winter came,
> High in my chamber in the frosty nights,
> How in the summer past some
> Unrecorded beam slanted across
> Some upland pasture where the Johnswort grew,
> Or heard, amidst the verdure of my mind, the bee's
> long-smothered hum,
> So by the cheap economy of God made rich to go upon
> my wintry work again.
>
> (J, I, 304; PJ, I, 351-52)[18]

In this high ground, this upland New England pasture, this high interval of the imagination, cultivated by the "cheap economy of God," New Adam conjoined with Old in an Edenic remembering of a "wort" whose expression obeyed halfway the law of vegetation.

6

Walden: A Radical Myth

Why has man rooted himself thus firmly in the earth,
but that he may rise in the same proportion
into the heavens above?
Wa, 15

IN 1841, when the prospects of living a retired life were already appealing, Thoreau pondered the contrast between art, which "cannot afford concealed wealth," and nature, which "contents us still by the assurance of a certain generosity at the roots" (J, I, 271). A "certain generosity at the roots" of *Walden*, evident to the reflective reader, is itself a product of Thoreau's radical reflections. And though "Civil Disobedience" was undoubtedly the most influential radical document for the student coming of age in America in the late 1960s and early 1970s, that essay is only one manifestation of a deep radical bent in the man of Concord. In many ways *Walden* is the more thoroughly radical work, for not only does it offer to alienated youth, of whatever age, the archetypal experience of withdrawal, it is also shot through with pronouncements that attack the conventions of every age: "I have lived some thirty years on this planet," Thoreau writes, "and I have yet to hear the first syllable of valuable or even earnest advice from my seniors" (Wa, 9); and, "if I repent of anything, it is very likely to be my good behavior" (Wa, 10). Such statements—especially abundant in the framing chapters, "Economy" and "Conclusions"—are radical in being extreme departures from opinions prevailing in his time: they are opinions "carried to the farthest limit; extreme; sweeping."[1]

One of Thoreau's attainments in moving to the pond was a condition, however temporary, of interior concord, of integrity, of at-one-ment. Before moving to the site of his experiment, he had written that the brave man was a moral illustration of mathematical integrity: "this is to be an integer, and not a fraction. Be even for all virtuous ends, but odd for all vice. Be a perfect power, so that any of your roots multiplied into itself may give the whole again" (PJ, I, 236; J, I, 181). And since he attempted to become one by reflecting the deep, unfractioned self mirrored in Walden Pond, his act of integration in the magic circle of his own mathematically conceived wanderings is the equivalent of squaring the circle, impossible in the discipline though tantalizing to the upright and square man.

However subtle the radical mathematics of *Walden,* the subject of the opening and longest chapter is radical economics. In "Economy" Thoreau is apparently concerned about dollars and cents, incomes and outgoes, and the various essentials of life—food, clothing, shelter, and fuel; but he is there challenging the conventional system of economy, claiming that it is a young man's "*mis*fortune . . . to have inherited farms, houses, barns"; and asserting, in "Where I Lived and What I Lived For," that "a man is rich in proportion to the number of things which he can afford to *let alone*" (Wa, 5, 82; emphasis added). Such remarks suggest Thoreau's economy is more radical—"arising from or going to a root or source" (AHD)—than that prevailing with his countrymen who put their faith in Benjamin Franklin's nagging gospel: "Remember That TIME is Money. He that can earn Ten Shillings a Day by his Labour, and goes abroad, or sits idle one half of the Day . . . has really spent or rather thrown away Five Shillings besides."[2] But Thoreau, who in his journal once wrote that Poor Richard did not speak to our condition "on the subject of getting an honest living" (J, II, 164), regarded money as a mere counter for time. The basis of his economy is underscored by a definition of cost as "the amount of what I will call life which is required to be exchanged for [a thing], immediately or in the long run" (Wa, 31). Franklin's economic quiz is "How much did you spend for your whistle?"; Thoreau's, "How do you spend your life?"[3]

To illustrate his cost principle, Thoreau frequently draws upon the notion of travel, as when he shows that a man must spend more of his capital of life in riding the railroad to Fitchburg than in walking there, since he would first need to spend a day's life earning the fare of ninety cents before he could even mount the platform. For Thoreau, time is that precious, irrecoverable commodity measured out to each mortal man, the sole capital from which he can draw for his specifically *human* acts. And walking is thus an exercise in radical economics, a conservation of human life. But if at first glance Thoreau's radical economy seems merely conservative, a closer look discloses it to be an exercise of human life as well; for a creative principle is at work in his resorting to "travel" as an illustration of cost. In "travel," as in a number of terms with a similar meaning, Thoreau employed the radical—"of or designating a word root" (AHD)—to illustrate his values. In a letter to Isaac Hecker, he wrote that "*far* travel, very *far* travel, or travail, comes near to the worth of staying at home" (C, 71).[4] Similarly, he discerned that *journey* was formed from the radical *jour,* day.

The term *journeyman,* current for one who had a certain craft skill, formerly signified one who had put in either a day's work or a day's travel. And thus *journeyman* implied both *traveler* and *travailler;* and he thought of himself as a journeyman embarked neither to Fitchburg nor to Europe, but within, to an unknown Interior West, "white on the chart," in order that he might become an expert in "home-cosmography" (Wa, 320-21). As William Drake remarks, the very structure of *Walden* is "an elaborate metaphor . . . of the traveller who, instead of leaving home, explores the very ground he lives on."[5]

By focusing on radicals in various terms that signify travel, Thoreau implies that walking is a symbol of life itself, and that life is itself a walk, a pilgrimage. His favorite word in this connection was *saunterer.* On the face of it, superficially, the term indicates an aimless walk; but Thoreau's radical eye, falling on the word, detected in its roots—*sainte* and *terre*—a spiritual destination, a "holy land." He once wrote of seeing "an advertisement for able-bodied seamen, when I was a boy, sauntering in my native port, and as soon as I came of age I embarked" (W, IV, 460). Near the end of his posthumous essay "Walking," he offers what may be considered his valediction: "So we saunter toward the Holy Land, till one day the sun shall shine more brightly than ever he has done, . . . and light up our whole lives with a great awakening light. . ." (W, V, 247-48). Elsewhere in the essay after noting that there is in man "something akin to the migratory instincts" that compels him to walk, especially in the spring of the year, he implies a quasi-spiritual destination by quoting from the "General Prologue" of Chaucer's *Canterbury Tales:* "Than [in spring] longen folk to gon on pilgrimages, / And palmeres for to seken strange strondes" (W, V, 219). Consistently, Thoreau's version of himself as traveler expresses an inward pilgrimage: "I have travelled a good deal in Concord," which is nearly the equivalent of calling himself a "saunterer," a "Holy-Lander," since "Concord" retains a great deal of the religious significance of "Sainte Terre," or of "Canterbury," the holy destination of Chaucer's pilgrims, saunterers.[6]

But Thoreau professed himself a Concord trader as well as traveler; he went to live at Walden Pond in 1845 "to transact some private business with the fewest obstacles," he tells us, not waiting "to acquire the usual capital" to start his trade (Wa, 19-20). While in part his private business there was the writing of his first book, *A Week,*[7] in part it was conducting a peculiar commodity trade through the port city of Salem. "If your trade is with the Celestial Empire, then some small counting house on the coast, in some Salem harbor, will be fixture enough" (Wa, 20). "Salem" is, of course, the name of a literal port some thirty odd miles from Concord, from which clipper ships plied their lucrative trade with China, the Celestial Empire, as it was called; "Salem" is also a shortened form of "Jerusalem," the richly symbolic port for trade with the heavenly city. In "Sounds," Thoreau discriminates between earthly and heavenly trade in his description of two "trains." One of these belongs to the Fitchburg Railroad, whose line makes the Deep Cut near the west bank of Walden Pond. Conveying its material products, this "petty train of cars . . . hugs the earth in its journey"; but while the superficial train makes its journey to Boston, a "train of clouds" from its engine is "rising higher and higher, going to heaven" (Wa, 116-17). By "travel," "journeyman," "sauntering," "train," and the like, Thoreau illustrates the basis of the economic system in New England as well as that in his own interior New England.

Not only did Thoreau suggest that he was a local journeyman—a Concord traveler and trader—but also that he was a local journeyman, a Concord worker. His literal occupation at Concord was surveying, while living at Walden Pond, raising beans. Having once noted that many people read the *Times* though few bother to read the Eternities, Thoreau took up residence by the pond in order to survey and read the Eternities, trying even to catch the nick of time and notch it upon his stick. It was a task that required losing his superficial life. As he writes in "The Village": "Not till we are lost, in other words, not till we have lost the world, do we begin to find ourselves, and realize where we are and the infinite extent of our relations" (Wa, 171). Over beans, too, he cultivated the eternities; but finding that "it is not necessary that a man should earn his living by the sweat of his brow, unless he sweats easier than I do" (Wa, 71), he turned to the more difficult task of reading well, "that is, to read true books in a true spirit," which "is a noble exercise, and one that will task the reader more than any exercise which the customs of the day esteem" (Wa, 101).

Paradoxically, Thoreau's travail over words rather than stumps and beans does move him, making him a traveler, even while he remains at home. Toiling over words, the Concord worker becomes the Concord traveler. Like the train of clouds, the movement of Thoreau's vicarious travel is vertical and spiritual rather than horizontal and superficial, and is effected by verbal, rather than mechanical, conveyances—by trains of words, sentences, rather than trains of cars. And the responsive reader of *Walden* is invited to board the volatile word with the mental traveler of Concord, to journey to the region that is holy land. In the concluding chapter of *Walden,* Thoreau projects further travels for whoever would "be a Columbus to whole new continents and worlds within you, opening new channels, not of trade, but of thought" (Wa, 321).

Through such verbal means, Thoreau translates his responsive reader on mental and spiritual journeys. Consider his climactic insistence on this point in a celebrated passage in the "Conclusion" chapter:

> I fear chiefly lest my expression may not be *extra- vagant* enough, may not wander far enough beyond the narrow limits of my daily experience, so as to be adequate to the truth of which I have been convinced. *Extra vagance*! It depends on how you are yarded. . . . I desire to speak somewhere *without* bounds; like a man in a waking moment, to men in their waking moments; . . . in this part of the world it is considered a ground for complaint if a man's writings admit of more than one interpretation. (Wa, 324-25)

In this dramatization of his radicalism, Thoreau, by italics and division, first isolates the roots of the word "extravagance," then supplies a definition for each root ("wander" for vagant; "far enough" for extra) in order to convey a radical (original) meaning for the word. Elsewhere, a more subtle radical extravagance is at work in this passage:

> Let us rise early and fast, or break fast, gently and without perturbation; let company come and let company go, let the bells ring and the children cry,—determined to make a day of it. Why should we knock under and go with the stream? Let us not be upset and overwhelmed in that terrible rapid and whirlpool called a dinner, situated in the meridian shallows. (Wa, 97)

In this passage a radical meaning of "dinner" (noise-maker, one who makes a din, or a situation in which noise occurs) is conjured up without italics, and not so much by word division (as is the case with "break fast") as by a context in which such words as "break," "gently," "without perturbation," and the like suggest a radical meaning of "dinner," one not apparent on the face of the word, "in the meridian shallows." By means of his radical pun on "dinner," he suggests a preference for a local *sainte terre,* a deep and quiet Concord, even in the midst of civilization's ritual "dinner."

Many readers with an historical or a sociological bent find Thoreau's frontier living at Walden Pond not only extravagant but quixotic because in the 1840s the actual American frontier was far to the west. Thoreau's experiment seems more like the retreat of a primitivist who is playing Indian than the advance of a real pioneer to an actual frontier. So considered, Thoreau seems a backwoodsman, not a frontiersman.[8] But while Thoreau's life at Walden Pond may be thought of as a sociological experiment, *Walden* is itself a literary experiment, and its frontier is philological, a boundary line of words and sentences that delineates the expressed from the unexpressed, perhaps the inexpressible.

In the account he gives of the beginning of his experiment, Thoreau confesses that he momentarily succumbed to the lure of superficial journeying by reading "one or two shallow books of travel . . . till that employment made me ashamed of myself" (Wa, 100). In the remainder of "Reading," where this confession occurs, he evokes a symbol to suggest a deepening spiritual journey. Once again it is a radical (or now, "radicle")—"The part of the plant embryo that develops into the primary root" (OED).[9] In this symbol, Thoreau involves both the principle of local, vertical travel (explore yourself, travel a good deal in Concord) and the principle of organic growth that critics have rightly found so central to the meaning and art of *Walden*. In the midst of "Economy," seemingly devoted to the reduction of the so-called essentials of life, Thoreau announces his radicle symbol of the affirmation of life:

> When a man is warmed by the several modes which I have described, what does he want next? Surely not more warmth of the same kind, as more and richer food, larger and more splendid houses, finer and more abundant clothing, more numerous incessant and hotter fires, and the like. When he has obtained those things which are necessary to life, there is another alternative than to obtain the superfluities; and that is, to adventure on life now, his vacation from humbler toil having commenced. The soil, it appears, is suited to the seed, for it has sent its *radicle* downward, and it may now send its shoot upward also with confidence. Why has man rooted himself thus firmly in the earth, but that he may rise in the same proportion into the heavens above? (Wa, 15; emphasis added)

A few pages later, Thoreau expands the image to consider man as a tree:

> We don garment after garment, as if we grew like exogenous plants by addition without. Our outside and often thin and fanciful clothes are our epidermis or false skin, which partakes not of our life, and may be stripped off here and there without fatal injury; our thicker garments, constantly worn, are our cellular integument, or cortex; but our shirts are our liber or true bark, which cannot be removed without girdling and so destroying the man. (Wa, 24)

Though this passage suggests that Thoreau was taking a tree for a man, Perry Miller felt that Thoreau came dangerously near to taking a tree for a woman, and was especially bothered by his journal entry, "I love and could embrace the shrub oak with its scanty garments of leaves rising above the snow, lowly whispering to me." In Miller's estimation such "spasms" of language are "highly erotic," and he viewed with modulated alarm Thoreau's remark, "I fell in love with a shrub oak." But Thoreau was not here unintentionally revealing by metaphor a subconscious craving for some woodland nymph. He was no anonymous voyeur, no Peeping Tom staring into the woods instead of out from them, even though he could rhapsodize about "Blond nymphs"—yellow birch in "undress"—and stood in some doubt "about a birch whose vest was buttoned . . . till I came nearer and saw the yellow gleaming through, or where a button was off" (J, IV, 448-49). Ultimately, Miller put down his suspicions by remarking, "Were these the diaries of any other writer, we would say that he was having a series of 'affairs' " (LJ, 205).

One of Thoreau's preliminary affairs in going to the woods was to search for a place of residence, a seat or "*sedes*," as he punningly called it, from where the landscape might radiate out (Wa, 81). In "Where I Lived and What I Lived For," he tells of how, in going to Walden Pond, he had his own seeds ready; moreover, he had read Cato's "De Re Rusticâ," which he considered his "Cultivator." There Cato recommends that before purchasing a farm one should survey it carefully by going around it a number of times. Fresh from his real estate speculations on the Hollowell farm, Thoreau comments, "I think I shall not buy greedily, but go round and round it as long as I live, and be buried in it first, that it may please me the more at last" (Wa, 84). He is here suggesting that the seed he is about to sow is himself, and he ends the chapter with various metaphors of rooting, making of his head a radical burrowing instrument: "My head is hands and feet" (Wa, 98).[10]

After the seeding, there are frequent, scattered reports of the crop's progress. In "Sounds," Thoreau seems to divert the reader's attention to the more literal money crop in writing that "I did not read books the first summer; I hoed beans" (Wa, 111). But in raising beans he was also cultivating his radical spirit. Once after observing that a gentle rain is a beneficent influence to his crop, Thoreau goes on to describe how "an early twilight ushered in a long evening in which many thoughts had time to take root and unfold themselves" (Wa, 132). A few pages later he asks, rhetorically, "Shall I not have intelligence with the earth? Am I not partly leaves and vegetable mould myself?" (Wa, 138). And indeed, under the influence of a gentle rain and a long evening's reflection, Thoreau's seeds of contemplation were beginning to germinate.

In "The Bean Field," a focal chapter in *Walden,* Thoreau seems to revert from radical to superficial economics, itemizing his money crop, providing a ledger of incomes ($23.44) and outgoes ($14.72 1/2), seemingly engaged fully in the battle to sustain his vital heat, his animal life. If his tips to farmers on how to grow beans appear to be completely utilitarian, the moral allegory is nonetheless plainly stated: "I will not plant beans and corn with so much industry another summer, but such seeds, if the seed is not lost, as sincerity, truth, simplicity, faith, innocence, and the like" (Wa, 163-64). Aside from the moral exercise of cultivating virtues and eradicating vices, hoeing encourages the roots of the beans to penetrate more deeply into the soil. At his task of cultivation, Thoreau puzzles over his work in an obvious rhetorical stance:

> What was the meaning of this so steady and self-respecting, this small Herculean labor, I knew not. I came to love my rows, my beans, though so many more than I wanted. They attached me to the earth, and so I got strength like Antaeus. But why should I raise them? Only Heaven knows. (Wa, 155)

His confession of ignorance notwithstanding, Thoreau's agriculture is clearly a metaphor for self-culture. And as he labors over his beans, he unites the notions of travel and growth: as this hoer of beans (*travailler*) cultivates his crop of seeds whose radicles are shooting (traveling), Thoreau and beans become one in a holy task, together forming a single journeyman. Trance–like, Thoreau confounds human and vegetal conditions: "It was no longer beans that I hoed, nor I that hoed beans" (Wa, 159).

Concerned about the results of his labor, Thoreau at chapter's end summarizes the principal monetary results of his cultivation, then shows a special concern for the "results" of "beans . . . not harvested by me. Do they not go for woodchucks partly?" (Wa, 166). This is his way of reporting that part of the literal bean crop was lost to his brute neighbors, thereby escaping his superficial economic system. He then shifts to radical economics: "Why concern ourselves so much about our beans for seed, and not be concerned at all about a new generation of men?" (Wa, 164). Then he strains for an extravagant, radical meaning by imaginatively converting the crop raised from "beans" to "wheat" in order to avail himself of a pun based on the radical in the Latin term for wheat: "The ear of wheat, (in Latin *spica,* obsoletely *speca,* from *spe,* hope,) should not be the only hope of the husbandman; its kernel or grain (*granum,* from *gerendo,* bearing,) is not all that it bears. How, then, can our harvest fail?" (Wa, 166). Thus his cash crop, beans, converts to a radical harvest of hope won by his cultivation in the beanfield, where he was at work "removing the weeds, putting fresh soil about the bean stems, and encouraging this weed which I had sown, making the yellow soil express its summer thought in bean leaves and blossoms . . . making the earth say beans instead of grass . . ." (Wa, 156-57). These beans, not harvested for economy's sake, went "for the sake of tropes and expression, to serve a parable-maker one day" (Wa, 162). *Walden* is that parable.

The report of Thoreau's harvest at the conclusion of "The Bean Field" is a climactic moment in *Walden,* considered as a radical myth. In the next chapters one hears little about seeds or roots, though there is a passing remark about the difficulty of cultivating such an unpromising seed as an Irishman. Watching John Field flailing in the muck, Thoreau remarks with dismay that "the culture of an Irishman is an enterprise to be undertaken with a sort of moral bog hoe" (Wa, 205-6). More positively, he observes in "Higher Laws" that man's "generative energy" (Wa, 219) might produce such fruits as "Genius, Heroism, Holiness" (Wa, 220), if he has within "the seeds of a better life" (Wa, 213).

In chapter 13, as the vital heat of the year flickers ever lower—it is October—Thoreau tells of discovering and gathering two homely radicles: the "ground-nut" (Wa, 239), which furnishes a humble food much like a potato; and the "fat pine roots" (Wa, 252), a humble fuel for his hearth. These roots help Thoreau sustain the vital heat that is almost the equivalent of animal life, and they remind us that his place of residence, built where a woodchuck had once burrowed, was the equivalent of a root cellar: he had there dug his cellar cabin "down through sumach and blackberry roots . . . to a fine sand where potatoes would not freeze in any winter," for "in almost all latitudes men dig into the earth for an equable temperature" (Wa, 44). The whole of the chapter, significantly titled "House-Warming," records the adventures of these homely radicles united in their attempt to survive the general freeze. Thoreau observes, "It was I and Fire that lived there" (Wa, 253). Outside his cabin as the sun dips lower toward the southern horizon, a general freeze sets in, locking Walden Pond in the vise of winter. The question of the condition of nature then turns inevitably to a question about radical man, the divine seed crop in nature. What is to become of this seed, this root, this radical? Is the banked interior fire to be snuffed out? Is the radical, man, to be frozen and destroyed? Is man's seed of hope, *speca,* gathered by his moral efforts in life's beanfield, only a mordant harvest? Or can such hope somehow survive the great annual catastrophe of nature?

The answer to such questions is directly tied to another: has the seed been planted below the frost line? Sent down its roots beyond that line to a vital, protective depth? In "Where I Lived and What I Lived For," Thoreau urged that we

> wedge our feet downward through the mud and slush of opinion, and prejudice, and tradition, and delusion, and appearance, that alluvion which covers the globe, through Paris and London, through New York and Boston and Concord, through church and state, through poetry and philosophy and religion, till we come to a hard bottom and rocks in place, which we can call *reality,* and say, This is, and no mistake; and then begin, having a *point d'appui,* below freshet and frost and fire. . . . (Wa, 97-98)

Man's capacity to survive is thus put to the test in agricultural terms: has he rooted himself below this frost-line? It is this question Thoreau ruminates as he gazes across Walden Pond, now a solid sheet of ice in the dead of winter.

A negative response is first implied in "The Pond in Winter" by the arrival of the ice harvesters, a horde of "a hundred men of Hyperborean extraction [who] swoop down on to our pond one morning, with many car-loads of ungainly-looking farming tools, sleds, ploughs, drill-barrows, turf-knives, spades, saws, rakes. . ." (Wa, 294). First imagining that they are there to "skim the land," Thoreau watches these grotesque "farmers" go about their work ploughing, harrowing, rolling, furrowing; . . . I was looking sharp to see what kind of seed they dropped into the furrow, [when] a gang of fellows by my side suddenly began to hook up the virgin mould itself, with a peculiar jerk, clean down to the sand, or rather the water,—for it was a very springy soil, . . . and haul it away on sleds. . . . (Wa, 295)

The description of the ice harvest as a reaping of the very land itself not only realizes the pun value of the harvesters being men of "Hyper*bore*an extraction," it is an ominous portent for the seed beneath. But some days later, the brutal harvesters having vanished, Thoreau looks out on the melting pond, which has become a pure "sea-green," and is reminded of the parable of the sower (Wa, 297). The pond, the metaphorical land, stands perdurable, imperishable. Spring is perennial.

Yet again the question: what of the seed, the root? Was it planted, did it take root, below the frost line? The answer is again indicated metaphorically, in the passage describing the thawing bank of clay in the Deep Cut. As the bank of clay thaws, its trickling rivulets trace in the bankside the figure of a leaf. Soon not only seed and root are apparently "growing," but even the very clay itself. And from the appearance of growth sketched into the thawing bankside, Thoreau turns to gaze on the signs of nature's germination in the pond and on the hillsides about him. After an extended lyrical passage in which he describes the renewal of the earth, Thoreau turns abruptly to man as the focal point in his vigil of renewal to remark, "What is man but a mass of thawing clay?" (Wa, 307). To the elaborate description of the thawing bank of clay from which the appearances of foliage are emerging, Thoreau brings his own gloss: "The symbol of perpetual youth, the grass-blade, like a long green ribbon, streams from the sod into the summer, checked indeed by the frost, but anon pushing on again, lifting its spear of last year's hay with the fresh life below" (Wa, 311). And with an utter simplicity that renders the bare statement persuasive, Thoreau concludes, "So our human life but dies down to its root, and still puts forth its green blade to eternity."

In the concluding pages of "Economy," Thoreau complained that in the garden of the world

there are a thousand hacking at the branches of evil to one who is striking at the root, and it may be that he who bestows the largest amount of time and money on the needy is doing the most by his mode of life to produce that misery which he strives in vain to relieve. (Wa, 75-76)

To Thoreau these philanthropists seemed to be "plants of whose greenness withered we make herb tea for the sick" (Wa, 77). He wanted none of their "cast-off griefs," for he believed "we should impart our courage, and not our despair, our health and ease, and not our disease, and take care that this does not spread by contagion." But he did want to make his sense of new life contagious, and in "Spring" crowed elaborately over the regeneration of radical man, the fulfillment of the promise of hope ("*speca*") garnered in the first harvest of his beanfield, where he had gone to "cultivate poverty like a garden herb, like sage" (Wa, 328), as he wryly punned. That regeneration is the fulfillment, in botanical terms, of his statement in "Economy" that "men remain in their present low and primitive condition; but if they should feel the influence of the spring of springs arousing them, they would of necessity rise to a higher and more ethereal life" (Wa, 41).

7

Springs to Remember

Shall not a man have his spring as well as the plants?
J, II, 34

Remember thy Creator in the days of thy youth!
J, II, 330

IN HIS *Divine Comedy*, Dante Alighieri placed himself imaginatively at midpoint in man's allotted threescore and ten, in the dark wood, about to pass beneath an arch that proclaimed the loss of hope to all who entered, but that instead gave entry to a passage ultimately leading to a heavenly vision of redemption. Thoreau left the woods of Walden shortly after his thirtieth birthday, having caught glimpses of his inner self in a landscape less sullen and forbidding than that in Dante's poem, and glimpses of an arch that proclaimed the discovery of hope, not its abandonment. He had not yet found himself: further reflection, speculation, and a struggle to articulate what he saw would be his means of doing so. On the threshold of his thirty-fifth year he sensed such an "interval between my ideal and the actual . . . that I may say I am unborn" (J, II, 316), for his life seemed "in the germ" only, "almost wholly unexpanded." But as the "year of observation" came to a close, it seemed to Thoreau, now "in the fulness of life," that nature "rushes to make her report. To the full heart she is all but a figure of speech" (J, IV, 174). Having hitherto felt "differently timed" (J, II, 316) than the seasons, on the brink of spring 1852, he seemed full of expectations: "I go forth to make new demands on life. . . . I pray that the life of this spring and summer may ever lie fair in my memory" (J, III, 351). By April the incongruity between the cycles of the seasons and of his own life had so far diminished that he could write: "For the first time I perceive this spring that the year is a circle. I see distinctly the spring arc thus far" (J, III, 438). And his passage beneath this arc is attended by a radical reshaping of the *Walden* manuscript, a process beginning in late January 1852, as critics generally agree.[1]

A month before this creative renewal, Thoreau, on Christmas Day, 1851, seems to have been haunted by the warning of Ecclesiastes in writing,

Remember your Creator in the days of your youth and justify His ways to man, that the end of life may not be its amusement, speak—though your thought presupposes the non-existence of your hearers—thoughts that transcend life and death. (J, III, 157-58)[2]

And as he began a major reshaping of *Walden* as an organic work, he linked authorial self to a mythic spring by means of radical imagery:

If thou art a writer, write as if thy time were short, for it is indeed short at the longest. Improve each occasion when thy soul is reached. Drain the cup of inspiration to its last dregs. Fear no intemperance in that, for the years will come when otherwise thou wilt regret opportunities unimproved. The spring will not last forever. These fertile and expanding seasons of thy life, when the rain reaches thy root, when thy vigor shoots, when thy flower is budding, shall be fewer and farther between. Again I say, Remember thy Creator in the days of thy youth. (J, III, 221-22)

At the beginning of the period of such "rememberings," Thoreau's journal discloses a genesis of several important meanings of "spring" that will inform *Walden*: (1) a season of the year (and of the day), (2) a welling up of waters, and (3) a rapid growth, a leap—all of which shape *Walden* as a spring of springs.

*

Standing vigil over the workings of Thaw on the frost in the Deep Cut, Thoreau in 1852 remarked that "the element of water prevails" (J, III, 437), thereby suggesting an aqueous "spring of the year." On the last day of 1851 he had found a low mist suffusing the woods, making an "exhibition of lichens at Forest Hall," and wrote approvingly: "True, as Thales said, the world was made out of water. That is the principle of all things" (J, III, 167). Some fifteen years earlier he had entertained an etymological basis for Thales' true principle by copying into his first notebook a passage from "Gebelin—Monde Primitif—Dictionnaire Etymol. Francoise":

From the primitive word, Ver, signifying water . . . is derived the word verite; for as water, by reason of its transparency and limpidness, is the mirror of bodies—of physical etres, so also is truth equally the mirror of ideas—of intellectual etres, representing them in a manner as faithful and and [*sic*] clear, as the water does a physical body.[3]

Thus in Thoreau's mind "Ver" seemed at once significant of Spring, the vernal season, and of water, the "true" element that mirrored and reflected nature.

To be sure the watery element had long prevailed in Thoreau's imagination, at least from the time he journalized in 1838 under the heading "Resource" that while some were "constantly dinging in my ears their fair theories and plausible solutions of the universe," he would "return again to my shoreless—islandless ocean, and fathom unceasingly for a bottom that will hold an anchor, that it may not drag" (PJ, I, 51; J, I, 54). During expeditions to Cape Cod in 1849 and 1850, Thoreau not only visited "Ocean," but attempted to interpret the powerfully voiced expression of Thales' element, which seemed the utterance of a "Reverend Polyphloisboios Thalassa," as he phonetically sounded the Greek for this "loud-roaring" and "infinite smiling" ocean (CC, 51- 52).

His ear was better attuned to fluvial preachments—those of the Concord (and its branches, the Sudbury and Assabet), of the Merrimack, and of the turbulent rivers of the Maine woods. But even after publication of *A Week,* he had not yet put the foot of his mind into the true element so as to be influenced by it, to flow with it. In the summer of 1851, he felt he could not "get wet through," even with repeated bathing in the river. So when he came to a river in his walks, he would remove his clothes, carrying them on his head. "I would fain take rivers in my walks endwise" (J, II, 335). So compulsive did his immersive tendencies become that the next summer he did indeed begin such "endwise" walks, on July 10 making "quite an excursion up and down [the Assabet] in the water, a fluvial, a water, walk. It seemed the properest highway for this weather" (J, IV, 212). Two days later he took another fluvial walk, and a fortnight thereafter, on a day too cool for such a pilgrimage, wrote at length about the virtues of such holy exercises (J, IV, 220, 260). When he came across Richard Chenevix Trench's *On the Study of Words* early in 1853, he found, in a discussion of "rivals," philological support for radical, if paradoxical, meanings in the Concord River:

Trench says that " 'rivals,' in the primary sense of the word, are those who dwell on the banks of the same stream" or "on opposite banks," but as he says, in many words, since the use of water-rights is a fruitful source of contention between such neighbors, the word has acquired this secondary sense. My friends are my rivals on the Concord, in the primitive sense of the word. There is no strife between us respecting the use of the stream. The Concord offers many privileges, but none to quarrel about. It is a peaceful, not a brawling, stream. It has not made rivals out of neighbors that lived on its banks, but friends. My friends are my rivals; we dwell on opposite banks of the stream, but that stream is the Concord, which flows without a ripple or a murmur, without a rapid or a brawl, and offers no petty privileges to quarrel about. (J, IV, 467-68)

Such fluvial and etymological saunterings show the degree to which Thoreau, situated on the banks of the Concord, was influenced to think of himself as a hydrostatic paradox. Moreover, he interiorized, almost surely with a pun on his name, his preference to be "a channel or *thorough*fare . . . of the mountain springs, and not the town sewers,—the Parnassian streams" (J, II, 289-90; emphasis added).

But the essential factor in his etymological interiorizing and radicalizing was not stasis, but movement, a sense of flowing. A river was "superior to a lake in its liberating influence," he would write in 1858, for it has "motion and indefinite length. A river touching the back of a town is like a wing. . . . With its rapid current it is a slightly fluttering wing. River towns are winged towns" (J, XI, 4-5). In 1850 he wrote in sympathy with a river on the rise: "The life in us is like the water in the river; it may rise this year higher than ever it was known to before and flood the uplands—even this may be the eventful year . . ." (J, II, 33). A few days later he queried, "Does not the stream still rise to its fountain-head in you?" (J, II, 44). On the very eve of his thirty-fifth birthday, with the Concord River running low, he commented that "the shrunken stream of life overflows its banks, makes and fertilizes broad intervals," and these flooded and fecund "intervals" are enough to sustain generations. "If we have not dissipated the vital, the divine, fluids, there is, then, a circulation of vitality beyond our bodies" (J, IV, 219).

When the stream in the prevailing figure shifts from shrunken and static to boisterous and living, its "circulation of vitality" is attributed to the elevation of its source or wellspring above any other point on the river's course. When the stream's inclination is most emphatic and pronounced, the plane of its movement tending from the horizontal to the vertical, its utterance is most lavish, vocal, gleeful. Thoreau sensed "something more than association at the bottom of the excitement which the roar of a cataract produces." There seemed to be a boisterous stream in the veins as well:

We have a waterfall which corresponds even to Niagara somewhere within us. It is astonishing what a rush and tumult a slight inclination will produce in a swollen brook. How it proclaims its glee, its boisterousness, rushing headlong in its prodigal course as if it would exhaust itself in half an hour!

Then, bending his ear, he seemed to catch what the flowing water expressed: "I would say to the orator and poet, Flow freely and *lavishly* as a brook that is full,—without stint. Perchance I have stumbled upon the origin of the word 'lavish' " (J, II, 155-56).[4]

In 1851, his "watershed year" according to Lewis Leary, the flow of his thought seemed without stint, his journal a lavish, loving concordance. And in 1857, another year of high water, he wrote of an autumnal "rise of the waters [that] must affect every thought and deed in the town. It qualifies my sentence and life." He hoped there might be some perceptible influence in his journal, "some flow, some gradual filling of the springs and raising of the streams, that the accumulating grists may be ground" (J, X, 126). In learning to "express adequately only the thought which I *love* to express" (J, II, 291), Thoreau suggests a lavish confluence of outer and inner streams in an expression of truth, *verite,* especially pronounced in Spring (*Ver*).

But it was to Walden Pond that Thoreau turned in 1845-47 for an expression of spring. He found its surface a continual fascination, a "field of water [which] betrays the spirit that is in the air" (J, II, 57). Here was a "pool of Bethsaida [*sic*] which must be stilled and become smooth before we can enter to be healed" (J, V, 454). When subject and object shared a reflective mood, the still surface of this water became a tabula rasa upon which the aerial spirit breathed a sentence that on land could be discerned only by the most sensitive brow. Perhaps Walden Pond presented such a brow, a temple sur-face better able than the brow of man to sense the least movement of spirit. In the late spring of 1854, a few months before the publication of *Walden,* Thoreau wrote in his journal of how dead the earth would appear

> if it were not for these water surfaces! We are slow to realize water,—the beauty and magic of it. It is interestingly strange to us forever. Immortal water, alive even in the superficies, restlessly heaving now and tossing me and my boat, and sparkling with life! I look round with a thrill on this bright fluctuating surface on which no man can walk, whereon is no trace of footstep. . . . (J, VI, 246)

But Walden Pond presented a reflecting mirror of deeper realities as well. Gazing into the "bottomless" pond was like looking to the backing of a magic mirror wherein one could not only see a reflection of the animal (or animated) self, but also catch a glimpse of an image or shadow divine, a similitude of the "ungraspable phantom of life" Melville's Ishmael sought in his watery reflections. And this glimpsed if ungraspable reflection becomes a kind of revelation uniting man and pond in a universal, aqueous expression. As he gazes upon its reflecting surface, Thoreau seems to merge his personality with that of the pond, just as the pond—returning his gaze from an "iris" (Wa, 176) deep in "earth's eye" (Wa, 186)—assumes a personality and even "licks its chaps" (Wa, 181) as if about to speak. The water seems to be lapping its lips, its shoreline, boundary of the literal, from which its beard, its trees, have been "*shorn*" (Wa, 181). Except for John Field's well, and perhaps Flint's Pond, the bodies of water that figure in the pages of *Walden* serve as vital links with the springs below. For Thoreau the very sight of a spring seemed an expression of the divine. Going out of his way to pass Boiling Spring, he exclaimed: "What a treasure is such a spring! Who *divined* it?" (J, IV, 104). And in *Walden* he would complain that the "devilish Iron Horse . . . has muddied the Boiling Spring with his foot" (Wa, 192). For him the sealing up of a well was a funereal ceremony forestalling the pilgrimage of water from its radical springs to its celestial destination, and if we would "go in search of the springs of life," Thoreau believed, we would "get exercise enough" (J, II, 472).[5]

Walden Pond was such a spring, having no inlet except from springs below, no outlet except to the overarching heavens. In a journal poem of 1838, Thoreau had provokingly suggested a dialogue with the ebullient spring, even as he discounted that literal possibility:

> True, our converse a stranger is to speech;
> Only the practiced ear can catch the surging words
> That break and die upon thy pebbled lips.
> Thy flow of thought is noiseless as the lapse of thy own
> waters,
> Wafted as is the morning mist up from thy surface,
> So that the passive Soul doth breathe it in,
> And is infected with the truth thou wouldst express.
> (J, I, 50; PJ, I, 47)

By the early 1850s, Thoreau's ear had grown so practiced in listening to nature that in the living waters of Walden Pond his "passive Soul" could detect the articulations of a perennial "flow of thought." The "noiseless . . . lapse" from "these lips of the lake, on which no beard grows"—had they become a littoral expression of a paradoxical "sound silence" he had come to hear? Might he now be able to express, from the shores of his Walden spring, the very silence over which *A Week* had closed?

But the deepest, as well as the most lavish, expressions of spring were subject to the stilling tyranny of nature's frost, which might seal to silence the deep springs of the text of Walden Pond. In 1853, as summer's flame began to gutter, Thoreau mused upon the names of those months for the period of frost's tyrannic grip. With kinesthetic extravagance he noted,

September is at hand; the first month (after the summer heat) with a *burr* to it, month of early frosts; but December will be tenfold rougher. January relents for a season at the time of its thaw, and hence that liquid *r* in its name. (J, V, 400)

Of special pertinence in unfolding a sense in his remarks about these "ber" months is that Thoreau had a speech "defect" that gave a peculiar sort of "burr" sound to the letter *r*, thus the terminal syllable of each "-ber" month would elicit an equivalent shiver from him.[6] That winter, Thoreau enlarged on the relationship between the names of the months and the freezing and thawing they signified:

But the last part of January and all February thus far have been alternate thaw and freeze and snow. It [February] has more thaws, even as the running 'r' (root of ῥέω) occurs twice in it and but once in January. I do not know but the more light and warmth plainly accounts for the difference. . . . We begin to have days precursors of spring. (J, VI, 127-28)

His verbal radicalism here suggests that the seasonal thaw converts a frozen (radical) *r* of the "-ber" months to a running liquid *r* in January, and as with a more intensive or repetitive thaw, to a double liquid *r* in February. If one could weather January, "the hardest month" for Thoreau, he would be "into the gulfstream of winter, nearer the shores of spring" (J, VI, 91).

In the spring of 1852, at a time when he was reading Sir John Richardson's account of a polar expedition, Thoreau had tried to dig some parsnip roots out of the half-frozen ground and wrote that "the Greek word ἔαρ [Spring] runs in my head in connection with the season and Richardson's Book" (J, III, 363; my brackets); but "though the frost is nearly out of the ground, the winter has not broken up in me".[7] Two days later he found in the thoughts and sentences of William Gilpin's *Forest Scenery* a frost-free expression, as if "some of the cool wind of the copses converted into grammatical and graceful sentences, without heat" (J, III, 370). That day he walked along the railroad causeway near the pond, where the laborers had "dug around the sleepers [railway ties] that the sun may thaw the ground and let them down" (J, III, 371). From this place of vantage he could see the "cheering," open waters of the Great Sudbury Meadows (J, III, 372). Still, and despite hearing the "*spring* note of the chickadee from over the ice" at Walden Pond, his thoughts went "back at once some weeks toward winter, and a chill comes over them" (J, III, 370). Flint's Pond, still nearly frozen over, seemed "that Icy Sea of which I have been reading in Sir J. Richardson's book" (J, III, 372), an "opaque dumb pond . . . unexpectedly dumb and poor," a "dull, white ice" doubtless all

Greek, a riddling, frost-encrusted blankness. But beneath the frost, as December gave way to January with one thaw, to February with two, Thoreau sensed an impending spring that would release the "living waters" in the stream of nature as in language, even as the burr in the first syllable of his last name, *Thor,* thawed to express *-eau,* water. By such radical expressions, Thoreau's verbal artistry paralleled that of the primal artist laboring in the Deep Cut near the shores of a woodland "spring." There Thoreau studied the tracing of leaves and fossil words in the thawing bankside, and there the fluid, lapsing sounds of running water filled the ear of one now practiced to "catch the surging words / That break and die upon [Walden's] pebbled lips" (J, I, 50; PJ, I, 47).

In a moving journal entry for February 7, 1841, Thoreau had anticipated frost's subsiding to the breath of spring and the flow of waters, capturing in sibilants and liquids the affecting results of a midwinter thaw:

> The eaves are running on the south side of the house; the titmouse lisps in the poplar; the bells are ringing for church; while the sun presides over all and makes his simple warmth more obvious than all else. What shall I do with this hour, so like time and yet so fit for eternity? Where in me are these russet patches of ground, and scattered logs and chips in the yard? I do not feel cluttered. I have some notion what the John's-wort and life-everlasting may be thinking about when the sun shines on me as on them and turns my prompt thought into just such a seething shimmer. I lie out indistinct as a heath at noonday. I am evaporating and ascending into the sun. (J, I, 203-4; PJ, I, 256)

Though he might not know what to do with the hour in 1841, he would store it in his journal for the day in which he might fulfill his injunction of July 21, 1851, at the threshold of his thirty-fifth year, to "remember thy Creator in the days of thy youth; *i.e.*, lay up a store of natural influences. Sing while you may, before the evil days come. He that hath ears, let him hear" (J, II, 330). And when he came to sing of Walden Pond as his spring of natural influences, he found that "A thousand rills which have their rise in the sources of thought burst forth and fertilize my brain" (J, II, 405). He had stopped short of such sources in *A Week*; now he was prepared to go on.

*

What inspired Thoreau's wonder about the thoughts of the "John's-wort" and "life-everlasting" four years before taking up residence at Walden Pond, thirteen years before the publication of *Walden*? Was he merely attempting to drive a wedge into *sainte terre* by cheap wordplay? upon the Gospel of St. John (John's "wort") and the promise of immortality (life-everlasting) in St. Paul? Or was he so elementally soiled that he likewise anticipated a lavish, liquid call to life, engendered by the vernal sun, by which the germs and radicals that endured the winter would spring into life? One sign of the latter is the emergence of "spring" as a verbal in the pages of his journal, as when he speculates that "perhaps after the thawing of the trees their buds universally swell before they can be said to spring" (J, III, 366). Pulling up a lily by the roots that summer, he closely considered "how it sends its buds upward to the light and air to expand and flower in another element. How interesting the bud's progress from the water to the air!" (J, IV, 162). The next spring, looking for signs of the vitalizing fluid in plants, he reported on March 13 that "no sap flows yet from my hole in the white maple by the bridge" (J, V, 19); a week later, however, he "rejoiced to see the sap falling in large, clear drops from the wound" (J, V, 31). The flow of sap running in vertical rivers in the cambium layer or liber of trees prophesied leaf, flower, and fruit; and the sight of a load of rock maples transported from the north country on the Fitchburg Railroad on May 8, 1852, prompted him to write that "their buds have not yet started, while ours are leaved out. . . . A tree, with all its roots, which has not felt the influence of spring is a most startling evidence of winter . . ." (J, IV, 38). The next spring it was still more evident that Thoreau conceived vegetation as an organic consequence of the flow of living waters through a root system: "Now, when the sap of the trees is probably beginning to flow, the sap of the earth, the river, overflows and bursts its icy fetters" (J, V, 11). Within plant systems, rivers flowed vertically to become lavish expressions, flowed into flowers and leaves, even as Thoreau's interior stream flowed into "flowers of thought, and . . . leaves of thought; most of our thoughts [being] merely leaves, to which the thread of thought is the stem" (J, II, 441).[8]

Thoreau had witnessed a dry run of the bud's progress from the water to the air in 1842 by watching corn popping on his hearth, which he considered "a more rapid blossoming of the seed" that nonetheless observed the same "law by which flowers unfold their petals." In the rapid, dry "blossoming" of the popcorn into white flowers, not only was the element of water, the law of currents, absent; but the "blossom," an expression of the law of vegetation, was merely fanciful: "By my warm hearth sprang these cerealious blossoms . . ." (J, I, 311-12; PJ, I, 357). A somewhat less rapid patterning of vegetation was the frost on his window, which Thoreau had witnessed in 1837 as another formulation of nature's springing. A few months before the publication of *Walden,* he again reflected upon the formation of ice foliage, this time outside his window: "I saw some crystals beginning to shoot on the pools between the tussocks, shaped like feathers or fan-coral,—the most delicate I ever saw." So, too, did the ice begin "with crystal leaves, and birds' feathers and wings are leaves, and trees and rivers with intervening earth are vast leaves" (J, VI, 154).

*

With fire effecting a similitude of rapid blossoming in popcorn, and the formation of ice a swift and delicate growth of vegetation, the influence of an actual spring was only somewhat less urgent in advancing the bud's progress. As Thoreau wrote in May, 1853: "How rapidly the young twigs shoot . . . as if they had acquired a head by being repressed so long. . . . Many do most of their growing for the year in a week or two at this season. They *shoot*—they *spring* . . ." (J, V, 189). His excited passage—the emphasis is his—only finds relief from an intense struggle for expression in the verb "spring." And when *Walden* was all but complete, Thoreau, sitting on a rail over a brook in which there was "the least possible springing yet," caught sight of "a little yellow lily in the ditch and sweet flag *starting* in the brook" (J, VI, 182; again Thoreau's emphasis), whereupon he heard "something which reminded me of the song of the robin in rainy days in past springs. Why is it that not the note itself," he mused, "but something which reminds me of it, should affect me most?—the ideal instead of the actual" (J, VI, 182). And to this outward sound of spring he started, for it seemed a confirmation of spring—sweet flag, robin, and Thoreau springing in consort with the yellow lily in the ditch. And it seemed a remembrance as well—of a dreamlike vision on a day in his youth when he had first visited the pond that would become his own spring of springs.

Finally, Thoreau's style of writing, no less than his vision, has a spring to it. Like the mythic Antaeus, his expression, never "long absent from the ground," found its basis on "the spring floor of our life." His were sentences with "little resiliencies" of meaning, having "a distinct fruit and kernel . . . , springing from terra firma" (J, III, 107). In a cattail he examined in the spring of 1853, he found a natural exemplar of such sentences: "Apparently there is a spring to the fine elastic threads which compose the down, which, after having been so closely packed, on being the least relieved at the base, spring open apace into the form of parachutes to convey the seed afar" (J, V, 44). His own manner of walking was of a kind: his Harvard classmates noticed a kind of Indian elasticity in his gait, and his friend Channing once "kept up an incessant strain of wit, banter, about my legs, which were so springy and unweariable," declaring "I had got my double legs on . . . not cork but steel" (J, III, 96).

Thoreau's manner of walking provided the physiological base for a writing style that has been called walked; moreover, he confounded walking and writing in brilliantly characterizing Bronson Alcott's poetic style as "sublimo slip-shod" (J, III, 118). To Emerson, Thoreau's style seemed somewhat military; Thoreau himself wrote of there being

> a true march to the sentence, as if a man or a body of men were actually making progress there step by step, and these are not the mere *disjecta membra*, the dispersed and mutilated members though it were of heroes, which can no longer walk and join themselves to their comrades. They are not perfect nor liberated pieces of art for the galleries, yet they stand on the natural and broad pedestal of the living rock, but have a principle of life and growth in them still, as has that human nature from which they spring. (J, I, 480; PJ, II, 118-19)

By cultivating beans at Walden Pond, Thoreau ran the risk of the money farmer, who soon "lost his elasticity" (J, II, 160), became stiff-jointed, and could neither run nor jump. He sensed that "at a very early age the mind of man, perhaps at the same time with his body, ceases to be elastic. . . ." No longer expansive in his thinking, as in "his growing days," one's movements would contract and harden. "What was flexible sap hardens into heart-wood, and there is no further change" (J, III, 203). In youth one's spring came without thought, he could then "run and leap; he has not learned exactly how far, he knows no limits" (J, III, 204). With some notable exceptions, however, Thoreau would maintain his spring walk throughout life, sometime with extravagant bounding, in a way to sympathize with the plant's aspirations to spring.[9] In his approach for the spring, however, Thoreau had his eye not so much on the height to which he aspired as on the ground from which he would spring. In his downward thrust for the leap, he compared himself to the leaves that fall "at the first earnest touch of autumn's wand. They stoop to rise, to mount higher in coming years . . ." (J, V, 444). Unlike most of the Transcendentalists—and especially Emerson, who found promise in many a youth, only to be disappointed later—he was wary of the premature spring that was warned of in the parable of the sower (Wa, 297), a spring that would quickly exhaust the resources of the root system and conclude in a fruitless fall, hope unfulfilled.[10] What counted was the harvest, not early growth merely; so he checked the impulse to leap before his roots were planted:

> When introduced to high life I cannot help perceiving how it is as a thing jumped at, and I find that I do not get on in my enjoyment of the fine arts which adorn it, because my attention is wholly occupied with the jump, remembering that the greatest genuine leap on record, due to human muscles alone, is that of certain wandering Arabs who cleared twenty-five feet on level ground. The first question which I am tempted to put to the proprietor of such great impropriety is, "Who boosts you?" (J, II, 230)

While his testy friend Channing would not "stoop to rise" (J, III, 108), Thoreau, because the only real booster was the "spring floor of life," relished delving to a sound base for his leap:

> Better dive like a muskrat into the mud, and pile up a few weeds to sit on during the floods, a foundation of your own laying, a house of your own building, however cold and cheerless.
>
> Methinks the hawk that soars so loftily and circles so steadily and apparently without effort has earned this power by faithfully creeping on the ground as a reptile in a former state of existence. You must creep before you can run; you must run before you can fly. Better one effective bound upward with elastic limbs from the valley than a jumping from the mountain-tops in the attempt to fly. The observatories are not built high but deep; the foundation is equal to the superstructure. It is more important to a distinct vision that it be steady than that it be from an elevated point of view. (J, III, 108)

Thoreau once questioned Alex Therien, that finest expression of mere animal vitality in the pages of *Walden,* to find out "if he was satisfied with himself. I was trying to get a point d'appui within him, a shelf to spring an arch from, to suggest some employment and aim for life" (J, VI, 35-36). The implied architectural image, another form of "springing," is explicit in Thoreau's noting that the mason requires "but a narrow shelf to spring his brick from; man requires only an infinitely narrower one to spring the arch of faith from." He then remarks that "the only ledge I can spring the arch of friendship from is the ground of infinite faith" (J, III, 259). Sometimes the spring "arch of faith" was in the form of the rainbow, a "faint vision of God's face" (J, IV, 128) transcendentally suggesting an "infinite faith." His claim to have once stood in the light at the end of the rainbow arch has been disputed earnestly by critics whose concern for objective truth is frustrated by Thoreau's willfully extravagant, fabulous truth. What he may have meant was that he was standing on *sainte terre,* a sacred point d'appui from which every "arch of faith" must be sprung, especially the arch of faith that is the sign of the covenant sprung in the heavens by the divine architect, perhaps Thoreau's ideal friend. On the spring floor of that arch Thoreau basked in the "faint vision of God's face," and "lived like a dolphin" (Wa, 202) in a light that, refracted, made a rainbow arch.[11]

But it was in vegetation, chiefly, that Thoreau found his spring "arch of faith." At Flint's Pond in late summer 1851, he found in the swamp loose-strife, a "willow-like" formulation:

> It grows up two feet from a large woody horizontal root, and droops over to the sand again, meeting which, it puts out a myriad rootlets from the side of its stem, fastens itself, and curves upward again to the air, thus spanning or looping itself

along. The bark just above the ground thickens into a singular cellular or spongy substance, which at length appears to crack nearer the earth, giving that part of the plant a winged and somewhat four-sided appearance. (J, II, 501-2)

Many of the spring arches come together in Thoreau's observation of "the firm earth mingled with the sky, like the spray of the sea tossed up." In such an arch, as he saw it, is there not always "a latent reference to its beauty? The arch supports itself, like the stars, by gravity,—by always falling never falls (*semper cadendo nunquam cadit*)" (J, IV, 152). The most nearly perfect expression of such arches, however, was in poetry. "Methinks there are few specimens of architecture so perfect as a verse of poetry," Thoreau wrote. "Architectural remains are beautiful not intrinsically and absolutely, but from association" (J, IV, 153). And the poet, "he who generates poems," was affected by his work so that "by continence he rises to creation on a higher level, a supernatural level" (J, III, 191).[12]

The level to which Thoreau rose was proportional to the resilience of his "understanding." In the early spring of 1853, he wrote of his open-soled communion with the earth, which struck him

as a wonderful piece of chemistry, that the very grass we trample on and esteem so cheap should be thus wonderfully nourished, that this spring greenness was not produced by coarse and cheap means, but in sod, out of sight, the most delicate and magical processes are going on. The half is not shown. The very sod is replete with mechanism far finer than that of a watch, and yet it is cast under our feet to be trampled on. (J, V, 69)

He thought the process that goes on "in the sod and the dark, about the minute fibres of the grass,—the chemistry and the mechanics,—before a single green blade can appear above the withered herbage," if adequately described, "would supplant all other revelations." And he went on to suggest his brief contact with the fine organization on the other side of nature's sentence: "We are acquainted with but one side of the sod. I brought home some tufts of the grass in my pocket, but when I took it out I could not at first find those pearly white fibres and thought that they were lost, for they were shrunk to dry brown threads"; and when he examined the "still finer gossamer . . . with few exceptions they were absolutely undiscoverable,—they no longer stood out around the core,—so fine and delicate was their organization" (J, V, 69).

The apex of the spring arc is implicit in Thoreau's lengthy description of the flight of the hawk in paragraph 22 of "Spring" ("On the 29th of April . . ."), which had appeared, almost verbatim, in the first version of *Walden* in 1847.[13] A number of journal analogues point up the impression made upon Thoreau by such stirring flights, though no single journal source survives. On March 27, 1842, Thoreau was observing two little hawks overhead when suddenly a new bird, flying in over Fairhaven Cliffs, joined them with stunning abruptness. It was "probably an eagle, quite above me, laboring with the wind not more than forty rods off." The "largest bird of the falcon kind" he had ever seen, he "was never so impressed by any flight" (J, I, 351; PJ, I, 393-94). Four days later he was still fascinated by "the majesty of that bird at the Cliff. . . . It was a great presence, as of the master of river and forest" (J, I, 356; PJ, I, 398). On December 20, 1851, he was impressed by the flight of what appeared to be a large hawk, rising above him and circling, and showing

> with beautiful distinctness its wings against the sky,—primaries and secondaries, and the rich tracery of the outline of the latter (?), its inner wings, or wing-linings, within the outer,—like a great moth seen against the sky. A will-o'-the-wind. Following its path, as it were through the vortices of the air. The poetry of motion. (J, III, 143)

And after a journal aside, Thoreau underscored his awe: "What made the hawk mount? Did you perceive the manoeuvre? Did he fill himself with air? Before you were aware of it, he had mounted by his spiral path into the heavens" (J, III, 145). With his own heart "on the mount" (J, IV, 467) in sympathetic aspiration, Thoreau was answering his complaint of 1850 that "we hug the earth. How rarely we mount! . . . Shall not a man have his spring as well as the plants?" (J, II, 34). And when he related the flight of the bird to the spring of the plant, he drew himself into a pattern of natural spring arches that he stood within, understood. In *Walden* he would work these impressions into "sentences in which there is no strain," sentences without "a fluttering and inconstant and *quasi* inspiration, and ever memorable Icarian fall, in which your helpless wings are expanded merely by your swift descent into the *pelagos* beneath" (J, III, 108).

"What made the hawk mount?" It was a question he posed in the first version of *Walden*: "Where was the parent that hatched it [the bird], its kindred, and its father in the heavens?"[14] As Thoreau pushed the cause of its mounting back from leaf, to bud, to radicals, and finally to the spring floor of life, the answer was emerging as nature's revelation. In a journal entry for April 2, 1852, Thoreau described how, a few weeks before the birds actually returned to Concord,

> there came to my mind in the night the twittering sound of birds in the early dawn of a spring morning, a semiprophecy of it, and last night I attended mentally as if I heard the spray-like dreaming sound of the midsummer frog and realized how glorious and full of revelations it was. Expectation may amount to prophecy. (J, III, 377)

By summer he had mentally reversed the "bud's progress from the water to the air," seeing in the lily root, which "sends its buds upward in the light and air to expand and flower in another element," a rudimentary expression of the same principle. In his search for the radical cause of the bud's progress, his eye was turning to the Deep Cut, where nature seemed to be tracing its vernal fable—in Greek (ἔαρ), in Latin (*Ver, Verite*), and finally, in Thoreau's native tongue—*Spring.*

*

In his classic mid-life pilgrimage, Dante begins in a wooded maze of the spirit to pass beneath the arch of despair and the Fall; in his pilgrimage to his classic, Thoreau, recovering from the dashed hopes or lapsing dreams of *A Week,* passes beneath the arch of hope and spring in his thirty-fifth year. Like Dante, he may have been on his way to a fabulous "mountain in the easterly part of our town (where no high hill actually is) which once or twice I had ascended, and often allowed my thoughts alone to climb" (J, X, 141). But if his "way up used to lie through a dark and unfrequented wood at its base," as he reports in 1857, he paid little attention to the wood, and soon "lost [himself] quite in the upper air and clouds." Even this late the thoughts Thoreau entertains about these mountains are in a formative stage, as the phrasings and interlineations suggest:

> It chances, now I think of it, that it [the mountain] rises in my mind where lies the Burying-Hill. You might go through its gate to enter the dark wood, but that hill and its grave are so concealed and obliterated by the awful mountain that I never thought of them as underlying it. (J, X, 142-43)

For Thoreau, who had a positive phobia about graveyards, the Dantean passageway through the arch of death in order to ascend the mountain seems rarely to have entered his mind:

> There are ever two ways up: one is through the dark wood, the other through the sunny pasture. That is, I reach and discover the mountain only through the dark wood, but I see to my surprise, when I look off between the mists from its summit, how it is ever adjacent to my native fields, nay, imminent over them, and accessible through a sunny pasture. Why is it that in the lives of men we hear more of the dark wood than of the sunny pasture?[15]

In *Walden* he would briefly attend to such dark wood sounds, singling out the call of the hooting owl as "the most melancholy sound in Nature . . . some poor weak relic of mortality . . . yet with human sobs, on entering the dark valley . . ." (Wa, 125). Without a Virgil—as a fellow saunterer

Channing filled the bill only peevishly and inconstantly—a solitary Thoreau would reject the Dantean note of despair, as exemplified in the hooting owl, to recover a lapsed hope beneath a spring arch. Emerging in an upland "sunny pasture," Thoreau pushed aside the medicinal cup of Hygeia and communed with the laws of currents and vegetation by drinking deeply from the cup of Hebe (Spring), "cupbearer to Jupiter, who was the daughter of Juno and wild lettuce, and who had the power of restoring gods and men to the vigor of youth." And he continued with what is again almost surely a pun on his own name: "She was probably the only *thoroughly* sound-conditioned, healthy, and robust young lady that ever walked the globe, and wherever she came it was spring" (Wa, 139; emphasis added). Indeed, she was its personification, a spring to remember. But a spring to re-member as well, and make of a two-year sojourn at Walden Pond a fitting, organic response to the admonition "Remember thy Creator in the days of thy youth" (J, II, 330), a response that was a spring of springs.

8

Walden: A Spring of Springs

. . . to read every letter received, and write or read every letter sent. . . .

Wa, 20

The radicals of lobe are *lb*. . . .

Wa, 306

WHEN THOREAU made his deliberate *volte face* from the village to the woods in order "to transact some private business," he intended to supervise all details in person, to get his accounts "audited," and "to read every letter received, and write or read every letter sent. . ." (Wa, 18-20). No doubt this involved letters from his publisher, Munroe and Company, but it also involved whatever letters might come his way from another publisher, Nature, as well. That he was ill-prepared to conduct the latter "correspondence" is suggested by his confession in "Where I Lived and What I Lived For" that he did not know "the first letter of the alphabet" (Wa, 98). But so far did he improve in literacy that by the chapter "Sounds" he could imitate the articulation of despair in the "gurgling melodiousness" of hooting owls by "beginning with the letters gl . . . expressive of a mind which has reached the gelatinous mildewy stage in the mortification of all healthy and courageous thought" (Wa, 125). Did not these letters initiate a note of dejection in Nature that found its counterpart in the despondency that saddens the reformer and makes the hymnbook "resound with a melodious cursing of God," in a way that "rather consoled the fears than confirmed the hopes of man"? Thoreau's antidote for such joyless "faith" was simple: "Let this be righted, let the spring come . . ." (Wa, 78). And when in "The Pond in Winter" he tells of awakening from a "still winter night" with the impression that some question had been put to him that he is now prepared to deal with, his "answered question, to Nature and daylight" (Wa, 282), is the next chapter, "Spring," in which he reads and translates some of Nature's radical letters and expresses an extravagant hope that his readers might in turn "read every letter received"—or sent.

In this chapter Thoreau fastens upon the thawing, lapsing bankside of the Deep Cut of the railroad, and delves, burrows, roots into the sand foliage until he can read and translate the articulations of Nature emergent in two letters of a redeeming word—"lobe." Nowhere is the radicalism of *Walden* more intricately elaborated than in these passages. Here nature's lapsarian condition, an analogue of the Fall of man and the hooting, despairing owl, translates into a natural resurrection, "a spring of springs" (Wa, 41) proclaimed by a crow of the spirit and bathed in such a light "as would have waked the dead" (Wa, 317).

*

At midpoint in "Economy," reflecting upon the "pleasant spring days, in which the winter of man's discontent was thawing as well as the earth," Thoreau reports seeing a "striped snake run into the water" where it remained for at least a quarter of an hour. He likened its torpor to the "present low and primitive condition" of men who, "if they should feel the influence of the spring of springs arousing them . . . would of necessity rise to a higher and more ethereal life" (Wa, 41). His use of the present tense in the next chapter dramatizes the urgency of his quest: "I think that the richest vein is somewhere hereabouts; so by the divining rod and thin rising vapors I judge; and here I will begin to mine" (Wa, 98). Literally a forked hazel or willow stick used to locate well sites and springs, the divining-rod has been taken as a pun for Thoreau's search for God.[1] But if *divining* suggests the object of the search, *rod* may well suggest the searching subject. *Webster's New International Dictionary* illustrates one meaning of *radical* thus: "a straight and slender stick, as one cut fresh from a tree; hence, stock; race; tribe, as of the *rod* of Jesse." In *Walden* the divining "rod" suggests the radical or root man, or a generation of men attracted to, yearning for, having a love of the "spring of springs," the perennial source of life.

"To divine" is a process of discovering what has been revealed, but it is also the process of revelation. To the orthodox Christian, "rod of Jesse" implies a particular religious divination: Jesus Christ is the fruit of the womb of Mary, herself the flower of the generation of the House of David, son of Jesse. *O Radix Jesse*! In this view, Christ is the culmination of a process of divination reaching back in the Old Testament to Abraham. To such a view, Christ is the "divine-ing" god-man, the culmination of a divine generation. Another viewpoint is that of Emerson who, in his "Divinity School Address," discounts the divination of the historical god-man, Christ, in order to attend the divining of a god within each man, and in

"Self-Reliance" presents his fullest statement of a relationship with the divine Self in every man. The orthodox position emphasizes God's activity in the process, that of Emerson, man's. But if there be any truth in divination, the process necessarily involves man and God. For it concerns God's becoming man, an Incarnation, and man's becoming God, made divinely "becoming," beatified. As Francis Bacon wrote in a statement attributed to King Solomon, "The glory of God is to conceal a thing, the glory of a king is to find it out."[2]

In *Walden,* what is the role of God—or the gods—in the process of divination that the book seems to dramatize? Playfully devious, Thoreau suggests that God used a divining rod to create Walden Pond. In "Solitude" he mentions "an old settler and original proprietor, who is reported to have dug Walden Pond" (Wa, 137). In "The Ponds," he again refers to this "ancient settler . . . who remembers so well when he first came here with his divining rod, saw a thin vapor rising from the sward, and the hazel pointed steadily downward, and he concluded to dig a well here" (Wa, 182). Similarly, Thoreau's discovery of Walden Pond was through his use of such a divining rod: "By the divining rod and thin rising vapors I judge; and here I will begin to mine" (Wa, 98). Thus both God and man employ the divining rod, are divining rods, though man is only divining what God has already divined—created or revealed. Both parties are brought into sympathy at Walden Pond by use of the divining rod, but they are looking at revelation from different sides of one sentence, different sides of a reflecting surface.

In *Walden,* the object of divination is Walden Pond itself—a "gem of the first water" (Wa, 179), "God's Drop" (Wa, 194), a "spring of springs" (Wa, 41), a "perennial source of our life" (Wa, 133). And having located this wellspring, Thoreau brings himself into sympathy with it by taking up his residence, his *sedes,* near its shore, then sending his roots down below the level of freshet and frost line to that of this spring of springs. By this means he is *influenced,* whereupon the living waters rise within, higher than they ever have before. But the climactic divination in Thoreau's radical myth occurs in "Spring," which is really about a number of extraordinary, transcendent, extravagant springs—a "spring of springs" in search for which Thoreau impels the reader to become a divining rod of the book's meaning.

In the first place, the chapter is about spring, the season when the sun makes its annual return from an apparent defection southwards to shine again, vigorously, on a cold, sterile earth, a dead earth. But the focus is upon a superlative spring, a "spring of springs," an ideal, fabulous season whose supremely brilliant sun compels all that was dead to rise again. In this season when the sun reigns and re-creates as the God Thaw, Thoreau views his vertumnuous domain at Walden Pond as a transcendent season: "There needs no stronger proof of immortality. All things must live in such a light" (Wa, 317).

In the second place, the chapter is about Walden Pond, a spring-fed body of water, a "perennial spring in the midst of pine and oak woods, without any visible inlet or outlet except by the clouds and evaporation" (Wa, 175). Flowing beneath the superfluities of life, below freshet and frost and fire, Walden Pond is in touch with the wellsprings of life, for at its bottom, in a "perennial waveless serenity" (Wa, 283), grows a "bright green weed" (Wa, 179), even in the midst of winter. At this well Thoreau drank long and deep, elaborating his punning figure that "it makes no odds at what well you drink, provided it be a well-head" (J, II, 170). In drinking in the pond, he gazed into the depths of what seemed at once "earth's eye" (Wa, 186) and "God's Drop" (Wa, 194), reflecting that "Heaven is under our feet as well as over our heads" (Wa, 283). Walden Pond is thus the second superlative "spring of springs."

In a way to emphasize the liquidity in the season of spring, Thoreau seems to draw on a meaning of "radical" common in medieval philosophy: "Radical humidity, humor, moisture, sap . . . the humor or moisture naturally inherent in all plants and animals, its presence being a necessary condition of their vitality" (OED). Thoreau loved to quote the opening lines of Chaucer's "General Prologue" to the *Canterbury Tales,* which furnishes our literature's aptest illustration of the moist humour in spring:

> Whan that Aprille with his shoures soote
> The droghte of March hath perced to the roote
> And bathed every veyne in swich liquor
> Of which vertue engendred is the flour.

Near the shores of Walden Pond, Thoreau roots himself down into such a moist humour, a spring of springs where his dry root or seed is permeated to its very "liber" (Wa, 24) or life by the vitalizing influence. And a consequence is a third "spring of springs": an extravagant, extraordinary leap or spring into the air by radical man, expressed in terms of vegetal germination. Thoreau anticipates this condition with his statement that if men "should feel the influence of the spring of springs arousing them, they would of necessity rise to a higher and more ethereal life" (Wa 41).

As stated earlier, Perry Miller rightly believed that Thoreau brought *Walden* "to its climax in a slime of sand" (LJ, 126); and it is precisely in the passages describing the thawing bankside—paragraphs 6 through 9 in "Spring"—that the radical myth of *Walden* is most intricately wrought.[3] At his vigil over the thawing sand and clay, Thoreau here sees the warm sun eliciting a stream of clayey sand that "obeys half way the law of currents, and half way that of vegetation" (Wa, 305). The "hybrid product" of these two laws takes the shape of a leaf, traced on the bankside by the rivulets, first forming "sappy leaves of vines . . . resembling . . . the laciniated lobed and imbricated thalluses of some lichens." He soon fastens on *lobe* as the term best expressing the natural phenomena over which he keeps watch. This Greek derivative refers to the "lobe of the ear, of the liver, capsule or pod of leguminous plants" (OED); botanically, it is "a pod, capsule, or fruit-case," with the obsolete meaning "a rounded projection or division of a leaf (sometimes of other organs) of a plant." As one illustration, the OED cites the *Gardiner's Dictionary* (1753): "A Pea or Bean committed to the Ground is first found to cleave into two parts, which are, as it were, two Leaves or Lobes of the Placenta."

Thoreau's description of the thawing bankside points up its resemblance to the actual germination in a lobe or seed. When the embryonic leaf within a lobe or seed emerges from its seed case, the moist interior lobe erupts into a flatter and broader exterior leaf. Analogously, the appearance traced in the thawing bankside first suggests an interior, thick, moist lobe, but only until its "separate streams" lose their "semicylindrical form" and flatten and broaden to trace the pattern of a leaf. In both instances, the pattern "lapses" from that of the lobe to that of the leaf. Thoreau finds "in the very sands an anticipation of the vegetable leaf. No wonder that the earth expresses itself outwardly in leaves, it so labors with the idea inwardly" (Wa, 306).

The results of earth's labor to express this pattern are everywhere evident: "The Maker of this earth but patented a leaf" (Wa, 308). From an actual leaf overhanging the clay bank, Thoreau shifts attention to an imagined prototypical leaf within the bank, which he conceives as a "moist thick *lobe*" (Wa, 306). He then suggests that the whole earth expresses itself in leaves, from lobes. But because the earth is "capacious," or sizable, the articulation of "lobe" is rendered as *globe*: "In globe, *glb,* the guttural *g* adds to the meaning the capacity of the throat." By further remarking that the prototypical leaf or lobe exists "*internally* . . . in the globe or animal body" (Wa, 306), Thoreau indicates that the clay bank can be thought of indifferently as macrocosm (earth) or microcosm (animal body, including man's), vessels of clay containing prototypical lobes.

In the actual germination process, the interior lobe is expressed (dispatched) in part because of the influence of liquid.[4] The seed case is first swollen with moisture, whereupon the radical lobes "spring" from the seed case to form leaves. Similarly on the thawing bankside, the influence of liquid first formulates the appearance of a lobe, soon thereafter, of a leaf. Thoreau writes: "What makes this sand foliage remarkable is its *springing* into existence thus suddenly" (Wa, 306). And man likewise gives bodily expression to the lobe principle by moist thick lobes within (pulpy lobes in the form of lungs, brains, liver, even "leaves" of fat, or leaf lard), and dry thin leaves without (ears, hands, and feet).

At this stage Thoreau points up his radical tendencies more sharply by calling attention to the expression of "lobe" in its printed or written form: "The radicals of *lobe* are *lb*," he writes, here calling attention to radical as "(a) an original unchanged letter (so also radical sound); (b) a letter belonging to the root of a word" (OED). His implication is that *l* and *b* are permanent letters, radicals in a word whose vowels (non-radical, more or less transient letters) can shift to transform the word *lobe* to many variations, a point to which I shall return.

At his vigil over the sand foliage, Thoreau finds radical confirmation of the aqueous "spring of springs" he had been seeking in his move to Walden Pond. As he ponders nature's articulation in the bankside, the first stage of which is expressed by the law of currents, Thoreau muses over the written word *lobe* as if it were a stream of speech frozen into a form that is sound only *in potentia.* The revitalization of the word as sound is analogous to the phenomena in the bankside, for a liquid "l" is the radical sound that begins the process of *thawing,* or expressing, the word "lobe" in its audible components. Similarly in "Reading," he had speculated on the word as a verbal Pygmalion "carved out of the breath of life itself," which could "not only be read but actually breathed from all human lips," and thus it was "the work of art nearest to life itself" (Wa, 102), needing an "inspired" reader to reanimate.

Thoreau found an expression of the vegetal "spring of springs" in the second radical letter of *lobe.* In appearance the written or printed *b* resembles a vegetal lobe, a monocotyledon when lower case, a dicotyledon when capitalized: "the *b* (single lobed, or B, double lobed,). . . ." Doubtless Thoreau was familiar with the fascinating philology in "the single sign beta [which] means a letter among the Greeks but a vegetable among the Latins."[5] If the prototypical lobe is *frozen* into the bankside, so, too, is the second radical letter *frozen* into the written word *lobe* and needs a minister other than the Reverend Mr. Frost to release its spirit from the "text" in the bankside. But as "lobe" is pronounced, the influence of a flowing, liquid "l" dispatches the explosive second radical, "b," making it spring forth as sound in a similitude of Thoreau's observation that "what makes this sand foliage remarkable is its springing into existence thus suddenly" (Wa, 306). Thoreau's own words are most clear: "The radicals of lobe are *lb,* the soft mass of the *b* (single lobed, or B, double lobed,), with a liquid *l* behind it pressing it forward." In expressing the word "lobe" with a feel for its inner shape, the reader-speaker may detect in the radical consonants something of the liquid and vegetal radicals, for in its radical components "lobe," too, obeys halfway the law of currents, halfway the law of vegetation.

In the actual seed or lobe, similarly, two kinds of embryonic radicals find expression. One of these is the embryonic root, which in the process of germination moves downward to seek the dark and moist; the other is the embryonic leaf, which moves upward to seek the light and air. The first is a natural equivalent of the radical (liquid) *l,* the second, of the radical (vegetal) *b.* Both oral and vegetal expressions of lobe, therefore, conform to the pattern that obeys halfway the law of currents, halfway that of vegetation, and these in turn are extensions of Thoreau's quest for the aqueous and the vegetal "spring of springs," discernible in the early pages of his journal, and in his life adventures that are the basis of his two published books.

Ultimately the physical reality underpinning these myths derives from the sun, the light of the world.[6] When the light illuminates the macrocosmic globe or microcosmic lobe, seminal life stirs to express itself, whereupon lobe or globe converts to leaf, lavishly. "The Maker of this earth but patented a leaf" (Wa, 308). The conversion of lobe into leaf that occurs in nature finds its parallel in a hypothetical conversion of the word *lobe* into the word *leaf.* When these two words are considered as stages of a continuum of oral expression—"lobe" gliding to "leaf"—the liquid *l* is a radical, permanent letter, abiding through the change. But as "lobe" or "lobes" may be conjectured as gliding to "leaf" or "leaves," the radical *b* shifts to *f* and to *v* respectively. Thus it would appear that the *b* is not a radical at all in this process, for it does not abide. Nonetheless, there is a relationship among the *b, f,* and *v* (and the *p* as well). The *b* in "lobe" is a voiced explosive sound; the stop preceding the explosion is made at the lips. When the explosive *b* glides, or lapses, to an *f* or *v,* it is because that stoppage of air at the lips has become incomplete, and the air rubs (L. *fricare*) its way through the lips, creating the sound of *f,* voiceless, or *v,* voiced labiodental, both fricative sounds closely related to the explosive *b.* An extravagant and gratuitous analysis? Not in the least, for Thoreau's own words are deliberate and transparent:

> *Internally,* whether in the globe or animal body, it [the lobe principle] is a moist thick *lobe,* a word especially applicable to the liver and lungs and the *leaves* of fat, (λείβω, *labor, lapsus,* to flow or slip downward, a lapsing; λοβος, *globus,* lobe, globe; also lap, flap, and many other words,) *externally,* a dry thin *leaf,* even as the *f* and *v* are a pressed and dried *b.* (Wa, 306)

Such additional examples as "*lapsus,*" "slip," "lapsing," "lap," and "flap" imply that the explosive *p* is in the same pattern with that of the *b. f,* and *v.*

Thus the radical letters *l* and *b* (or such variations of the latter as *f, v,* and *p*) persist in these words.[7]

In the paragraphs of the sand foliage section of "Spring," the unfolding of organic expression is conveyed by a succession of operative terms that retain the radical consonants of *lobe,* and in an order that accords with the dominant themes and images of successive paragraphs: "lava," "labor," "lapse," "lobe," "globe," "leaf," "leaves," "life," "living." Thus in paragraph 6, where the term "lava" occurs, the earth struggles toward expression, is in its "labor" pains, disgorges its exuviae, its *dejecta,* lapses. In paragraph 7, as the term *lobe* insistently emerges, the earth is attempting to formulate "lobe" as both natural and written utterance. In paragraph 8 the emphasis turns to oral expression: while the first half describes Nature's attempts to write in the thawing sand with "a drop-like Point, like the ball of the finger," the second half emphasizes Nature's speaking apparatus: "The lip (*labium,* from *labor* (?)) laps or lapses from the sides of the cavernous mouth." Nature seems capable only of drooling speech, and written and spoken words of Nature are paralleled by frequent mention of expanding leaves. In paragraph 9 the attention is first upon leaves, the "hieroglyphic" (-*glyph*ic) of Nature, then upon Nature's own life: "There is nothing inorganic"; "The earth is not a mere fragment of dead history . . . but living poetry like the leaves of a tree . . . not a fossil earth, but a living earth." In this paragraph the operative terms are "life" and "living," metamorphosized *lobes* that retain the radical consonants.

Near the end of Thoreau's vigil at the lapsing and fabulating bankside, he seems to shift attention from vegetal growth to the flights of birds and butterflies. It is no shift at all. Rather, it is a further projection or expression of the lobe, transcending, transmuting, and translating itself from conditions vegetal, to animal, to spiritual. In the wings of the bird and butterfly Thoreau sees the lobe expressed more ethereally than in the leaf: "The feathers and wings of birds are still drier and thinner leaves. Thus, also, you pass from the lumpish grub in the earth to the airy and fluttering butterfly." These wings are the loftiest visible expression of the lobe principle, and of the radical *b.* Moreover, the liquid *l* attends metaphorically, for the liquid notes of the "song sparrow singing from the bushes on the shore" are "helping to crack" the ice of Walden Pond (Wa, 311), releasing its spirit from the frost in melodious concert with the expression of "lobe."

To what upland heights the lumpish grub or lobe can aspire is conveyed later in the chapter, in the description of the flight of a hawk:

On the 29th of April, as I was fishing . . . I heard a singular rattling sound . . . when, looking up, I observed a very slight and graceful hawk, like a nighthawk, alternately soaring like a ripple and tumbling a rod or two over and over, showing the underside of its wings, which gleamed like a satin ribbon in the sun, or like the pearly inside of a shell. . . . It was the most ethereal flight I had ever witnessed. It did not simply flutter like a butterfly, nor soar like the larger hawks, but it sported with proud reliance in the fields of air; mounting again and again with its strange chuckle, it repeated its free and beautiful fall, turning over and over like a kite, and then recovering from its lofty tumbling, as if it had never set its foot on *terra firma*. It appeared to have no companion in the universe,—sporting there alone,—and to need none but the morning and the ether with which it played. It was not lonely, but made all the earth lonely beneath it. Where was the parent which hatched it, its kindred, and its father in the heavens? The tenant of the air, it seemed related to the earth but by an egg hatched some time in the crevice of a crag. . . . (Wa, 316-17)

In one paragraph of "Spring," Thoreau lightly touches the vibrating chords of each of the referents of that superlative and manifold spring he sought in *Walden*. This occurs when radical man—the divining rod, lobe, or cognate seed—witnesses, in the flight of the sun-tipped hawk, the culmination of the seed's expression into fields of air. Stirred by a bird, he stands apart from the hawk while retaining a vision of springing, the hawk's flight being the outward sign and assurance of the commencement of his own spring of springs. Having taken up residence and put down his roots to draw from the influence of the spring of springs he had wished to dwell near, he now turns his attention from the illuminated hawk to look about him. And what he sees is the old scene, but transfigured by his recent vision of radical man's spring into the heavens that was realized by an affinity with the spring of springs. "Ah!" he exclaims,

I have penetrated to those meadows on the morning of many a spring day, jumping from hummock to hummock, from willow root to willow root, when the wild river valley and the woods were bathed in so pure and bright a light as would have waked the dead, if they had been slumbering in their graves, as some suppose. (Wa, 317)

In this transcendent moment, radical man, springing so lightly upon the vernal earth, still retains an affinity with the soaring hawk. Both are tenants of the air, related to the earth "by an egg hatched some time in the crevice of a crag." That the hatched egg—not unfairly a hatched lobe, an incarnate lobe?—is fathered by the sun and becomes sunlike in its generating ascendancy seems confirmed in the scant lines: "There needs no stronger proof of immortality. All things must live in such a light. O Death, where was thy sting? O grave, where was thy victory, then?" Thus in "Spring" the seed is the word, and the word is made light in an upland pasture, where the johnswort grew.[8]

In the term *lobe,* Thoreau has contained something of the notion of a vegetable redeemer that converts Nature's fall to its resurrection.[9] Germinated by the living waters elicited from the frozen bankside by the Great God Thaw, these eternal seeds or lobes spring into life as leaves, and then as finer leaves soar toward the sun as to the source of life itself. In the lapsing clay bank, the revelatory sentences of Nature's God and one man's divination of its Word conjoin, nearly, to validate Thoreau's observation, so lightly tossed off in "Where I Lived and What I Lived For," that "God himself culminates in the present moment, and will never be more divine in the *lapse* of all the ages" (Wa, 97; emphasis added). In the "lapse" of the soaring hawk as well, in its "repeated . . . free and beautiful fall," followed by its effortless resurrection, its "recovering from its lofty tumbling," one sees an ethereal expression of the lobe principle, springing from neither a beanfield nor a clay bank, but "the fields of air" where it sported with "proud reliance," soaring "as if it had never set its foot on *terra firma*." The proud reliance of the hawk is an expression in the language of Nature of a hope matured to faith and possession, a transcendent, transmuted life in an immortal condition that springs from the lobe incarnate.

Explicitly and didactically, the spokesman of *Walden* invokes comparison of himself with Chanticleer crowing in the day's natural sabbath to wake his neighbors up. With the hawk soaring in the year's natural sabbath (April 29), the comparison is implicit and tropical. Moreover, the hawk has its radical counterpart in the loon of Walden Pond; the hawk's flight is, as it were, playfully *grounded* in the diving loon who is alone on the pond, in "springy" (Wa, 295) soil, remote from and laughing at a profane world that would try to catch it—an apt symbol *for the spokesman of Walden* and the "springy" mystery he articulates. From its spring, Thoreau's loon utters joyous, looning cries to its wild god. Those sounds, peculiar to the loon, may haunt whoever turns the leaves of *Walden* and walks upon the "shores of spring" (J, VI, 91). Similarly, it may be, the radical myth of *Walden* exerts its haunting influence on those readers whose intimations of higher laws have persuaded them of a truth that is fabulous. In presenting his radical fable as a truth deliberately attenuated from relentless pursuit of such higher laws as those he discerned in currents and vegetation, Thoreau remarks that "shams and delusions are esteemed for soundest truths, while reality is fabulous" (Wa, 95). If that is not altogether clear, it may be because the soundest human truths can only be come upon indirectly, by fable. One might prefer the more direct statement of Thoreau in "Economy":

> There is a certain class of unbelievers who sometimes ask me such questions as, if I think that I can live on vegetable food alone; and to strike at the root of the matter at once,—for the root is faith,—I am accustomed to answer such, that I can live on board nails. If they cannot understand that, they cannot understand much that I have to say. (Wa, 65)

IV

Leavings from the Deep Cut

9

Concentration: The Bank Untangled

For the hardening of the seed is the crisis.
J, V, 210

AS THE PAGES of his journal suggest, Thoreau's pursuit of the law of currents and the law of vegetation in the dimension of time shaped a resurrection myth in and through words, at one point becoming so concentrated as to inform a single word, *lobe,* to win from silence a metamorphsis of the "lapse" over which he had broodingly concluded *A Week on the Concord and Merrimack Rivers.* In the dimension of space as well—that of the whole text of *Walden*—his pursuit concentrated to an emergent "lobe" in a few paragraphs of "Spring" (see Appendix B for statistical evidence of this concentration). In pursuit of the genius by which the two laws were expressed, Thoreau might temporarily have taken a false trail or come to a dead set, but he acted on the premise he declared in "Higher Laws" that "no man ever followed his genius till it misled him" (Wa, 216). Following his most deliberately, he nonetheless left many clues on the trail of his passing that provide extraordinary insights to the creative process.

In his so-called "Lost Journal" for December 1840, when he was suffering through a period of despondency over disease and corruption and "filfth"—which he spelled in a way to suggest a gathering to the tip of the tongue of what is bitter or distasteful in order that it be spit out—he wrote: "Shall we not be judged rather by what we leave behind us, than what we bring into the world? The guest is known by his leavings" (LJ, 189).[1] Philip Wheelwright, though decrying the blanket linguistic explanations for nearly every myth as expounded by the nineteenth-century philologist Friedrich Max Muller, believed, nonetheless, that "much can be learned from exploring such etymological factors in myths when (as happens all too rarely) a sufficient knowledge of the relevant early language developments is available."[2] He was doubtless referring to cultural developments of a collective nature; but his parenthetical remark should alert us to the "leavings" of Thoreau—the journals and working papers—as remarkably generous evidence of "early language developments" in a particular instance, and these provide an insight to "the linguistic approach to myth" that, in Wheelwright's opinion, "should be examined."[3]

Any such examination should first take into account the genetic studies of *Walden,* which reveal something of the artistic concentration whereby Thoreau's "transcript of an adventure in primitive living" became, as Perry Miller indicated, "a highly schematized pattern of words, product of a hundred revisions, designed not so much to make a sociological point as to become a thing of beauty, to translate facts into form" (LJ, 27). In *The Making of* Walden, J. Lyndon Shanley not only provided the whole of the first manuscript version of *Walden,* but also described the progressive growth of that work through seven long manuscript "groups" and two short ones. He demonstrated that the revisions to the second half of Walden, more extensive than those to the first half, began to stress the cycle of the year, in part by compressing Thoreau's two years' experience into one.[4] But Shanley's reading, reiterated in his "Historical Introduction" in the CEAA (Center for Editions of American Authors) edition of *Walden* (Princeton, 1971), tends to slight the mythic "fable of the renewal of life" that Sherman Paul and others have discerned in the book's configuration.[5]

A decade after Shanley's ground-breaking study, Ronald Clapper, in "The Development of *Walden*: A Genetic Text" (Ph.D. diss., Univ. of California, Los Angeles, 1967), confirmed the growth of a cyclical pattern through the stages of the *Walden* manuscripts. He found the B and C versions of the late 1840s "little more than a polishing and recopying of version A," but detected a "vague yearning" in Thoreau by 1850 that peaked on January 22, 1852, as the moment of his creative rebirth. Thereafter, a symbolizing process was underway in which "the pond itself became more and more the center of focus," even before the chapters of *Walden* were delineated to reflect the cycle of the year and point up the climax of "Spring." Thus the spring that is Walden Pond, a spring-fed lake welling up in the woods, and the spring that is the focal point in the cycle of the season, though present as fact in the early manuscript versions, are made increasingly significant, are circumscribed and concentrated to symbol in the genetic growth of *Walden*; they are not so from the outset.[6]

Other evidence shows that the process of concentrating to mythic configuration may be at work in the first versions of a paragraph that, with revisions, will become paragraph twenty of "Economy":

When a man is warmed by the several modes I have described, what more does he want? Not surely more warmth of the same kind, or more and richer food, larger and more splendid houses, finer and more abundant clothing, more numerous, incessant, and hotter fires, and the like, but to adventure on life now, his vacation having commenced. The soil, it seems, is suited to the seed, and it may germinate at length. Why has he rooted himself thus firmly in the earth but that he may rise in the same proportion into the heavens above, for the nobler plants bear their fruits at last into the air and light, far from the ground, and are not like the humbler esculents, continually cut down at top that they may make more root.[7]

Four versions of paragraph 13 of "Spring" that Shanley conveniently assembles (see Appendix C) reveal that a similar concentration on the radical process is underway. The telegraphic style of version one, the journal passage, is articulated into three short paragraphs in version two. In version three (Shanley's "V"), an organic relationship between and among the birds, the brooks, and the grass in spring is suggested in a single paragraph. In each successive version, the apparent subject of nature is effectually displaced by the real subject, man, in a sentence that increasingly becomes the focal point in the paragraph: "So our human life but dies down to its root, and still puts forth its green blade to eternity" (Wa, 311). Shanley sees Thoreau's revisions in the paragraph as the eliminating of "superfluous materials" and attaining of the right order and rhythm to arrive at "a sense of an ever increasing flow of life." Shanley's "flow of life" fittingly describes the genetic progression as well: the successive versions exert a mounting tension between water and fire as to what image will dominate. The earth sends forth an "inward green heat and the grass flames up on the warm hill sides like a green fire" in the journal version, even as the grass blade is "streaming from the sod . . . as steady a growth as the rill which leaks out of the ground." Only with "V" is the conflict resolved by means of the radical image that occurs in the focusing statement that survives, unchanged, in the *Walden* text: "So our human life but dies down to its root, and still puts forth its green blade [rather than "fire"] to eternity." Thus, when Thoreau substituted, as Shanley shows, the "fine and accurate image 'dies down to its root' for the vague 'to the surface of nature,' " was he merely remembering George Herbert's "Thy root is ever in its grave," as Shanley contends? Perhaps so, but with the telling difference that Thoreau's root is soiled in life, Herbert's in death. The end result of the genetic growth of paragraph 13 of "Spring" is not so much a cancellation of fire or water images as an integration of them to dramatize those common vital influences arousing not only birds, brooks, and grass, but radical man as well.[8]

In Shanley's judgment, the sand foliage paragraphs (paragraphs 6 through 9) are the most prominent major addition to "Spring" after the first manuscript version, in which there had been only "a few lines on sand foliage" in a single sentence of one paragraph, the italicized words representing Thoreau's interlineation as he worked over the first version:

As I go back and forth over the rail-road through the deep cut I have seen where the clayey sand *like lava* had flowed down when it thawed and as it streamed it assumed the forms of vegetation, of vines and stout pulpy leaves—unaccountably interesting and beautiful—which methinks I have seen imitated somewhere in bronze—as if its course were so to speak a diagonal between fluids & solids—and it were hesitating whether to stream in to a river, or into vegetation—for vegetation too is such a stream as a river, only of a slower current.[9]

Not only were the principles—currents and vegetation—somewhat uncertainly positioned, but in the interlineation the radicals of *lobe* were emerging, in *l*a*v*a. Clapper finds the sand foliage passages a late addition, introduced as substantially new material in the F and G manuscript versions, 1853-54. Philip Van Doren Stern takes note of the difficulty Thoreau had in phrasing paragraph 6 of "Spring." With the publication of the second volume of the Princeton edition of Thoreau's journals, we have additional evidence in some four pages of Thoreau's extensive revising and ordering of material on the sand foliage (PJ, II, 576-79).[10]

Such artistic "leavings," or shavings from the artist's workbench, are telltale signs of the struggle for concentration and the movement from fact to form in the composition of *Walden.* But the most arresting "leavings" are in *Walden* itself, where the incorrigible Concord punster asserted that all nature is patterned on a leaf, and thereby intimated that we may all be "leavings" or expressions of life, organically rendered, rather than the mere residue thereof. Thus in *Walden,* Thoreau's organically styled "leaving" is an invitation to the reader to enter the higher life its progenitor has shown glimpses of, after the lower life has died down to its roots. Perhaps this is what Thoreau had in mind when, on March 11, 1859, he wrote that "what we do best or most perfectly is what we have most thoroughly learned by the longest practice, and at length it falls from us without our notice, as a leaf from a tree. It is the *last* time we shall do it,—our unconscious leavings" (J, XII, 39).

*

Within the leaves of *Walden,* critical commentary has concentrated so insistently upon the sand foliage passages as to furnish ample material for a casebook study. To partially compensate for this lack, the following essay—in effect an annotated bibliographical essay—is offered as an indication of this critical concentration, with sources cited parenthetically for convenience. In the main, the critical commentary on the passages seems to have divided into the camps of the psychological and of the literary critics. In the former is Raymond D. Gozzi, "Some Aspects of Thoreau's Personality" (in *Henry David Thoreau: A Profile,* ed. Walter Harding [New York: Hill and Wang, 1971], pp. 150-71), who finds evidence for "thinking of Thoreau as an obsessional personality" because he "shows elements of unconscious libidinal regression to what is termed the 'anal-sadistic' level" (p. 165). Gozzi's chief evidence for this conclusion is Thoreau's "interest in and literary descriptions of sand-and-clay banks having an excrementitious appearance."

At a conference in the spring of 1978 titled "Psychology and the Literary Artist: A Case Study of Henry David Thoreau" (since published as *Thoreau's Psychology,* ed. Raymond D. Gozzi [Lanham, Md.: University Press of America, 1983]), scholars discussed the results of their siftings through what Carl Bode has called "The Half-Hidden Thoreau," in order to further our understanding of the Concord Saunterer, and perhaps—as "and" in the conference title left open—to reveal a hitherto concealed source of his creativity.[11] What emerged were the outlines of a man in flight from a dark and obsessive past, with its disturbing infantile memories, sibling rivalries, amatory "affairs" with a surrogate Mother (Nature), and murderous thoughts about a father and other authority figures, including the state. Terms such as "guilt feelings" (p. 156), "unconscious libidinal regression" (p. 6), "anality" (p. 173), and "psychological moratorium" (p. 19) advanced a case that Thoreau had an "identity crisis" (p. 28), possibly involving his sexual identity, and acted out his obsessions through fear and retirement—from woman, from society, from the threat of disease, perhaps from life itself. From such obessions and repressions—so tended the argument—Thoreau the artist emerged.

As illuminating as the conference may have been about Thoreau the man—and perhaps more so about his critics in the latter half of the twentieth century—what remained in shadow, as Professor Norman Holland pointed out in a trenchant and high-spirited summation, was a convincing accounting for the uniqueness of his artistry. Two key papers that used depth psychology to explain Thoreau's identity were characterized by Holland as deterministic—Raymond Gozzi's offering a "hard determinism" (Freudian), Richard Lebeaux's a "soft" or "foggy determinism" (Eriksonian).[12] Defining "foggy determinism" as a common sense speculation subsequently "promoted into history or at least psychohistory" (p. 170) as fact, Holland quoted the first two sentences of Erik Erikson's *Young Man Luther* as an example:

> It is probable that in all historical periods some—and by no means the least gifted—young people do not survive their moratorium; they seek death or oblivion, or die in spirit. Martin [Luther] must have seen such death of mind and spirit in some of his brethren, and came to feel close to it more than once. (P. 170)

Holland further detected the same tactic of elevating the speculative to the determined in the paper by Lebeaux, a former student of Erikson and author of *Young Man Thoreau* (Amherst: Univ. of Massachusetts Press, 1977). It may be that Walter Harding's "Thoreau and Eros," which sifted the evidence for homosexuality in Thoreau, is vulnerable to the same charge, for despite a judicious and cautious assessment that the evidence is inconclusive, Harding wondered whether Thoreau was "forced by society" (p. 156) to sublimate his homoerotic tendencies "by turning to his love of nature," and finally speculated whether "it is not possible that at least a portion of the generating force for Thoreau's creativity . . . grew out of his feelings over *his homosexuality and his efforts to combat it*" (p. 157; emphasis added). Aside from balking at such strategies to promote a case for Thoreau's artistry as determined, Holland wondered whether any attempt "to explain the 'great man' by experiences"—sublimation, repression, obsession—"he shares with others who are not at all great" (p. 166) can satisfactorily account for his unique genius.

As an alternate, nondeterministic way of discerning the creative "identity" of Thoreau without advancing causes, Holland proposed a "characterology" based on the "theme-and-variations" (p. 178) scheme of Heinz Lichtenstein, which would focus on Thoreau's expression rather than on what biographers can reconstruct of his life.[13] In proposing this method, Holland admitted his *a priori* assumption of an "essentialistic strategy" that there is a "kind of unity to people," or at least "it is useful to look at people as though they have a kind of unity" (p. 186). In the acts of Thoreau, especially his verbal acts, Holland thought one might discover "a theme that will interrelate all the myriad details of [his] thoughts, words, and actions into a coherent pattern." To this end he advised that we ponder Thoreau's own phrases "like 'shapes of mud and sand,' or details of his life, like 'lockjaw,'" rather than such imposed psychological terms as "anality" or "identification" (p. 173). Persuaded that Thoreau "talks a lot about dirt and earth and soil," and about the theme of reversal as well, Holland wondered whether "a concept of dirt *or* reversal" (emphasis added) might lead anywhere, and if so, "follow it up and see where it goes" (p. 86).

Quite predictably, the pleasure Thoreau took "in the shapes and textures of mud and sand as excrements of natural processes" (p. 168) attracted the notice of conference participants, some of whom saw it as an affirmation of his decidedly "anal character." And since the conference Richard Bridgman, in a highly selective stylistic study of Thoreau (*Dark Thoreau* [Lincoln: Univ. of Nebraska Press, 1982]) that sketches a portrait of the artist darker far, and certainly more driven than any limned by conference participants, devotes some ten pages (pp. 140-49) to an attempt to sound the obsessive character of those passages in the "Spring" chapter of *Walden* dealing with dirt *and* reversal. But Bridgman dismisses the reversal from excrement to vegetation as a deceptive manipulation, a lie, and sees in Thoreau's reversal of names, from David Henry to Henry David, a similar deception. In doing so, he extends the line of inquiry into the man behind the persona, which was the thrust of Raymond Gozzi's benchmark dissertation, "Tropes and Figures: A Psychological Study of David Henry Thoreau."[14] In an offhand remark at the end of the conference, Holland himself wondered whether this reversal of names might be an example in life of Thoreau's penchant for thematic reversal, apparently regarding the name-switch as an expression, rather than a rejection or denial (p. 186).

In his summation, Holland seemed to slight the theme of generativity in Lebeaux's paper, later published as " 'Sugar Maple Man': Middle-aged Thoreau's Generativity Crisis," in *Studies in the American Renaissance, 1981*, ed. Joel Myerson (Boston: Twayne, 1981), pp. 359-77. In *Thoreau's Seasons* (Amherst: Univ. of Massachusetts Press, 1984), Lebeaux further extended his Eriksonian analysis of generativity to cover the years from Thoreau's move to Walden Pond in 1845 until his death in 1862. In this book, as Roderick W. Harvey points out ("Thoreau: Psychology," *Canadian Review of American Studies* 17 [1986]: 211- 12), Lebeaux derives from Daniel J. Levinson's pioneer study *The Seasons of a Man's Life* (New York: Ballantine Books, 1978) not only his title, but the metaphor of the changing seasons as a means to depict the stages of adult development in Thoreau.[15] But while Lebeaux seems to sense that the Deep Cut experience was central to Thoreau's developing artistry, he retreats from that tack to read the thawing bankside in "Spring" as an instance of a passage or stage in Thoreau's psychic development, and persists in a deterministic Thoreau in writing, "Out of the Deep Cut, out of the wounds he had suffered and endured, was emerging, however haltingly, his 'creative moment' " (p. 150).

But was the Deep Cut a projection of Thoreau's wounded self, a place of vantage from which he witnessed, in the felling of a pine tree, the "unkindest cut of all," as Lebeaux lamentably puns (p. 149)? Or was it the locale of the *kind*-est, the *like*-liest, cut of all, as suggested by Richard C. Trench's observation that "we like what is like"?[16] Had Thoreau been drawn ineluctably to a place he had scarcely noticed during his actual stay at Walden Pond because Nature there gave him a reflecting configuration of his own psychic wounds? Or did burgeoning Nature there impel him to attention so that with eye and ear on point he tried to catch what it was that she would say? From the perspective I have developed, the Deep Cut passage provided not so much the place and the moment of Thoreau's lying, as Bridgman and Perry Miller imply, but of Nature's lying-in—a passage for Nature's deliverance that involved Thoreau as midwife in the process of converting to language what Nature of herself could only struggle to articulate.[17] In the Deep Cut passage, Thoreau served as a procreator by teasing to rich meaning the expression in the bankside. The passages that derive from the bankside at the railroad passage have a long genesis, and Thoreau's *Journal* furnishes a truly astonishing revelation of the process of procreation that Emerson described so theoretically and abstractly in "The Poet":

> The path of things is silent. Will they suffer a speaker to go with them? A spy they will not suffer; a lover, a poet, is the transcendency of their own nature,—him they will suffer. The condition of true naming, on the poet's part, is his resigning himself to the divine *aura* which breathes through forms, and accompanying that. (CW, III, 15)

When Raymond Gozzi seconded what Lebeaux proposed at the conference as the "most pressing and difficult 'historical' question . . . how the 'unconscious' interacted with the conscious" (p. 70) in Thoreau, he failed to notice that the door had already been left enticingly ajar for viewing the Deep Cut passages as the focal creative moment of a poet's "resigning himself to the divine *aura*" at a place of contact, or of close proximity, between the unconscious and the conscious, a place of passage or, as Emerson put it, a "path of the creator to his work" (JMN, IX, 71; CW, III, 22). Emerson furnishes a further hint for locating this place of interaction in writing, in the spring of 1840, in a way to suggest meanings in the unconscious that are apocalyptic rather than excremental:

> There is an important *equivoqué* in our use of the word Unconscious, a word which is much displayed upon in the psychology of the present day. We say that our virtue & genius are unconscious, that they are the influx of God, & the like. The objector replies that to represent the Divine Being as an unconscious somewhat, is abhorrent, &c. But the unconsciousness we spake of was merely relative to *us*; we speak, we act from we know not what higher principle, and we describe its circumambient quality by confessing the subjection of our perception to it, we cannot overtop, oversee it,—not see at all its channel into us. But in saying this, we predicate nothing of its consciousness or unconsciousness in relation to itself. We see at once that we have no language subtle enough for distinctions in that inaccessible region. That air is too rare for the wings of words. We cannot say God is self conscious, or not self- conscious; for the moment we cast our eye on that dread nature, we see that it is the wisdom of wisdom, the love of love, the power of power, & soars infinitely out of all definition & dazzles all inquest. (JMN, VII, 344)

But if Emerson found "no language subtle enough" to delineate the consciousness from the unconsciousness, Thoreau suggested a merging of the teleological and eschatological in writing, "The unconsciousness of man—is the consciousness of God—the end of the world" (PJ, I, 109; J, I, 119).

In their notice of the Deep Cut passages, Gozzi, Bridgman, and Lebeaux join a growing army of Thoreau scholars who, following the lead of Perry Miller, have centered upon Thoreau's telling expressions of the Deep Cut. But to read those passages as revelations of an obsessive and repressive personality only is something paradoxical, as is a book, Bridgman's, whose title—*Dark Thoreau*—is almost completely alien to the spirit of a masterpiece that crows with the tone of Chanticleer, comes to full circle with "Spring," celebrates an entomological resurrection from the wood of an apple tree, and closes upon the rising of the sun, not the going down thereof. Still again, the pull of paradox *is* well-nigh irrepressible on anyone soundly assessing the style of a man who, while he once listed as a fault his propensity for the paradox (J, VII, 7), also wrote, early in his journal, that "Truth is always paradoxical" (PJ, I, 143; J, I, 153). Holland is by no means the first to notice that "Thoreau often talks as though he gets what he wants by being the opposite" (p. 178)—a trait that finally exasperated neighbor Emerson; and he is hardly alone in surmising that "in the words Thoreau used to make the transition between opposites," one can "trace the roots" (p. 179) of his creative achievement.

Richard Poirier, in *A World Elsewhere: The Place of Style in American Literature* (New York: Oxford Univ. Press, 1966), pp. 88- 89, while suggestively touching upon the "excremental activity that occurs in . . . 'Spring,' " finds Thoreau's attempts to relieve the "polarity" stylistically ingenious, but unconvincing—the inventiveness of an "artist-as-show-off." Bridgman in *Dark Thoreau* sees there "associations of the passing of excrement and . . . fantasies of wounding" (p. 143). And while he senses that Thoreau was "genuinely affected by the sand bank," he considers Thoreau's efforts to "transform it into a sacrament of earth" in vain (p. 147), his writings on the lobe only "dubious imaginative exercises" (p. 145).

Many critics have prospected in the sand foliage passages for a literary, rather than psychological, source of Thoreau's leaf metaphor, more often than not to credit Goethe. James McIntosh, *Thoreau as Romantic Naturalist: His Shifting Stance Toward Nature* (Ithaca: Cornell Univ. Press, 1974), p. 245, finds that "Thoreau's instincts led him back to experience Goethe's original intuition for himself"; and although he does not examine the sand foliage passages in detail, he finds, with Perry Miller, something suspect in the climax in "Spring" (p. 246). Charles Anderson, *The Magic Circle of* Walden (New York: Holt, Rinehart & Winston, 1968), believes Thoreau's reading of Goethe's *Metamorphosis of Plants* supplied the leaf metaphor, but he finds Thoreau's "metaphoric embodiment" of the leaf "entirely original," as are the "punning etymologies" (pp. 243-45). Gordon E. Bigelow, "Thoreau's Melting Sandbank: Birth of a Symbol," *International Journal of Symbology* 2 (1971): 7-13, traces the genesis of the leaf symbol as it unfolds in "Spring," but without examining the journals of Thoreau. He asserts that Thoreau's "leaf symbol" shares "the organicism of Goethe and Coleridge, the occultism of the French Symbolists, and the idea of imagination later exploited by Wallace Stevens" (p. 7). Jeffrey L. Duncan, "The Logic of Metamorphosis in Thoreau," *The Missouri Review* 3 (Winter 1980): 90-102, finds that in the sand foliage passages "the motifs and metaphors [are] patented, we should understand, not by nature, but by poetry," and cites Goethe's "aboriginal leaf." But in recognizing that for Thoreau "the sliding sand . . . obeys two 'laws,' that of currents and that of the leaf," he is closer to reading the radically organic, unconscious basis of Thoreau's artistry. In an otherwise sound analysis of the interrelationship of nature and the human consciousness, Duncan nonetheless believes that Thoreau, in his analysis of "lobe," "mixes up letters and sounds, writing and speaking, and the result is not synthesis but confusion" (p. 92)!

Robert D. Richardson, Jr., *Myth and Literature in the American Renaissance* (Bloomington: Indiana Univ. Press, 1978), p. 135, finds that Thoreau "relies heavily on Ovid's *Metamorphoses*" as well as "on the concept of metamorphosis put forward by Goethe," but points out (p. 253 n. 99) that the Goethean hint may have come from Emerson since only an inadequate English translation of the *Metamorphosen* was available. Richardson is surely right in finding that "Spring" finally depends, however, "not on Goethe or Ovid, but on Thoreau's own observation" (p. 135); yet in describing Thoreau's efforts with the sand foliage as a process of "myth-linking" rather than myth-making, he slights Thoreau's genius in the process. More recently, in his excellent intellectual biography *Henry Thoreau: A Life of the Mind* (Berkeley: Univ. of California Press, 1986), Richardson reasserts the Goethean influence, tracing it to the fall of 1837 in Thoreau's journal remarks on the frost vegetation (pp. 156-59). But elsewhere (pp. 254-56) he devotes a brief chapter titled "*Lapidae Crescunt*" to Thoreau's reading of Linnaeus's *Philosophia Botanica* as a major stimulus in the foliage paragraphs; and in "The Social Ethics of *Walden*" (in *Critical Essays on Thoreau's* Walden, ed. Joel Myerson [Boston: G. K. Hall, 1988]) he finds in "the great clay-bank scene" the message of "Linnaeus's magisterial dicta" that stones grow, which signifies that our "planet is itself alive" (p. 241). More discerning, from my perspective, is his assertion in *HT: A Life of the Mind* that

> what Thoreau explored in *A Week* was the extent to which the laws of his own nature were akin to the laws governing streams, crystals, and leaves. If one carried the organic theory of art to its logical conclusion, then literary form would follow after and be created by the character of the writer. (P. 157)

Absolutely!

Sherman Paul, in *The Shores of America* (pp. 346-50), comments at length on the rebirth passage as "one of the most brilliant and best sustained analogies in transcendental writing," but does not attempt to unriddle Thoreau's "lobe." Melvin E. Lyon, "Walden Pond as a Symbol," *PMLA* 82 (1967): 290, finds Walden Pond the "moist inner lobe" of the sand foliage passage. John T. Irwin, "The Symbol of the Hieroglyphics in the American Renaissance," *American Quarterly* 26 (1974): 103-26, sees Thoreau himself as the "Champollion" who will "decipher this hieroglyphic for us" (pp. 116-17), but in suggesting that Goethe, Swedenborg, and especially Plato influenced Thoreau's search for "a single form underlying the variety of natural forms," he offers the form of the "lobe or drop" as a variation of the "Platonic sphere" deriving from Plato's *Timaeus*. Perhaps true for Emerson, but doubtful for Thoreau, who in the first version of *Walden* wrote that Plato's "Dialogues which contain what was immortal to him, lie on the next shelf, and yet I never read them. *I describe my own case here*."[18] In the shape of the letter *b* in *lobe,* Irwin finds "nothing more than the same liquid *l* with a drop or lobe appended to it like the sandy lobes of the bank" (p. 116) and ignores the pervasive hints of the vegetal dimensions of "lobe." Irwin's article appeared subsequently as "Part One" of *American Hieroglyphics: The Symbol of the Egyptian Hieroglyphics in the American Renaissance* (New Haven: Yale Univ. Press, 1980), pp. 3-40.

A hostile view of Thoreau as a transcendental naturalist is presented by Kichung Kim in "Thoreau's Science and Teleology," *ESQ: A Journal of the American Renaissance* 18 (1972): 125-33, which investigates Thoreau's "ambivalence toward the scientists of his day" (p. 125), chiefly Asa Gray and Louis Agassiz. Kim sees both Goethe's "*Urpflanze*" and Thoreau's sand foliage as variant forms of "that immemorial 'unquenchable and irresistible thirst' of man for an explanation of the world he lives in, as alchemy, for instance, was for an earlier time" (p. 131). Both Goethe and Thoreau "saw in nature unity and meaning rather than chance and chaos not so much because there is unity and meaning in nature as because they needed to see them to give a sense of unity and meaning to their own lives. Such has always been the nature of the need for teleology" (p. 132)!

To counter such a withering blast, one need only ponder the concluding paragraph of Charles Darwin's *The Origin of Species,* which speculates on another bankside:

> It is interesting to contemplate a tangled bank, clothed with many plants of many kinds, with birds singing on the bushes, with various insects flitting about, and with worms crawling through the damp earth, and to reflect that these elaborately

constructed forms, so different from each other, and dependent upon each other in so complex a manner, have all been produced by laws acting around us. . . . [F]rom the war of nature, from famine and death, the most exalted object which we are capable of conceiving, namely, the production of the higher animals, directly follows. There is grandeur in this view of life, with its several powers, having been originally breathed by the Creator into a few forms or into one; and that, whilst this planet has gone cycling on according to the fixed law of gravity, from so simple a beginning endless forms most beautiful and most wonderful have been, and are being evolved.[19]

If Newton demanded a muse that found expression in such a poet as Alexander Pope, perhaps the emergent Darwinian view of nature demanded a muse that had its expression in Thoreau, for *Walden* attains its climactic vision over a thawing bankside in a way to anticipate the tangled bank in the concluding teleological and—dare it be said?—transcendent vision in *The Origin of Species,* published five years after *Walden.* A sympathetic view of Thoreau's teleological proclivities is provided by William J. Wolf, *Thoreau: Mystic, Prophet, Ecologist* (Philadelphia: United Church Press, 1974), which points to the use Thoreau made of Asa Gray's *Botany* in "spin[ning] out four pages of analogies between human beings and plants" (p. 148).

Among the soundest analyses on the subject is Michael Orth, "The Prose Style of Henry David Thoreau," *Language and Style: An International Journal* 7 (Winter 1974): 36-52, which differentiates between the symbolic and the scientific theories of language, and examines Thoreau's passages on "clay" to show how the "rational note of science and measurement" with which they open gives way to a scene in which "we are left by ourselves . . . to experience the flux of nature to the full. Throughout the passage Thoreau lets the earth act" (p. 42). Thoreau thus created "a prose style which might truly be called experiential," an organic style in which writing becomes "a psychological act, a process, which must have its own order and nature, and in which the artist is as much caught up as the reader" (p. 40). Though there is some contradiction in Orth's finding almost an embodiment of Ruskin's "pathetic fallacy" in a "tendency toward the sort of elaborate personification Thoreau labored to stitch into his prose" (p. 50), his more emphatic claim is that Thoreau in his "function as a poet-seer is to lead us to see the symbol in the thing by showing us the symbol in the word" (p. 45). Thoreau's "discussion of the pseudo-etymology of the word 'leaf,'" according to Orth, renders "the *langue* . . . an organic and growing flowing" (p. 44).

Stephen Railton, "Thoreau's 'Resurrection of Virtue,'" *American Quarterly* 24 (1972): 210-27, considers Thoreau's "search for a successful metaphor" a "search for a theodicy" (p. 215). Examining the sand foliage material in "Spring" as a candidate, he rejects the expression of the leaf in the bankside as a "conceit, a case of poetic, not natural, transmutation" (p. 221), and finds Thoreau's symbol of natural transmutation in the water lily, which is white and fragrant, not "in spite of the mud, but because of it" (p. 224). Thus Railton finds Thoreau's successful metaphor not in his acknowledged masterpiece, but in a journal passage for June 16, 1854, at the time of *Walden*'s completion, a "found" metaphor he uses at the end of "Slavery in Massachusetts" (RP, 108-9). Leo Marx, in *The Machine in the Garden: Technology and the Pastoral Ideal in America* (New York: Oxford Univ. Press, 1964): pp. 261-62, finds the sand foliage "a blatantly, unequivocally figurative restoration," though it "arouses in Thoreau a delight approaching religious ecstasy." Richardson, in *HT: A Life of the Mind,* persistently denies religious significance to the language of Thoreau, which "emphasizes renewal, reinvigoration, purification. . . . The awakening he seeks is Greek, not Christian . . ." (p. 174). "What he is concerned with is the new typology of the leaf, not the old Christian typology of the history of redemption" (p. 158). The crucial word here, of course, is "history," as it was for Emerson, whose preference was for the god within, and a revelation in the present moment, rather than the history of past revelations.

Claimants for an Eastern influence include James R. Sweeney, "The Cosmic Drama in Thoreau's 'Spring,'" *ESQ: A Journal of the American Renaissance* 24 (Autumn 1961): 3-6, who sees the thawing bankside as a "great metaphor" of a Hindu god, "a magnificent literary example of Shiva's cosmic drama" (p. 5). Similarly, Frank McShane, "Walden and Yoga," *New England Quarterly* 37 (1964): 322-42, finds Eastern influences in the thawing bankside, which "becomes a river like the Ganges which carries along the dead bodies of animals while at the same time providing life for those along its banks" (p. 338).

A Native American influence is advanced by Robert F. Sayre, *Thoreau and the American Indian* (Princeton: Princeton Univ. Press, 1977), pp. 91-100, who finds Thoreau's thawing bankside "not just a sign of spring, it is the act of creation" (p. 92). Yet he somewhat gratuitously wonders whether Thoreau had read an Indian version of the creation story first, and affirms that Thoreau not only "has Indians on the brain" (p. 97), but when he looks at the railroad cut is seeing "Indian red" (p. 99). Eric J. Sundquist, " 'Plowing Homeward': Cultivation and Grafting in Thoreau and the *Week*," in *Home as Found: Authority and Genealogy in Nineteenth-Century American Literature* (Baltimore: Johns Hopkins Univ. Press, 1979), p. 74, suggests that for Thoreau the arrowhead is the "pure figure of

Nature" his plow turns up, as well as "a coin deposited in the sand *bank* he exploits in his commerce with Nature"!

*

Of those who have been particularly fascinated by the language interests of Thoreau, Michael West has pursued the subject most relentlessly. In "Charles Kraitsir's Influence on Thoreau's Theory of Language," *ESQ: A Journal of the American Renaissance* 19 (1973): 262-74; in "*Walden*'s Dirty Language: Thoreau and Walter Whiter's Geocentric Etymological Theories," *Harvard Library Bulletin* 22 (1974): 117-28; and in "Scatology and Eschatology: The Heroic Dimensions of Thoreau's Wordplay," *PMLA* 89 (1974): 1043-64, West successively proposes as particular influences on the sand foliage passages, Charles Kraitsir, Walter Whiter, and James J. G. Wilkinson. But together West's essays undercut a thesis that there is a single literary source for Thoreau's philology and suggest instead a general nineteenth-century fascination with philology that Thoreau steeped himself in. Indeed, West's most recent essay on the subject, "Thoreau and the Language Theories of the French Enlightenment," *ELH* 51 (1984): 747-70, indicates as much. One dimension of his earlier *PMLA* essay is psychobiographical: West interprets the phenomena in the Deep Cut as Thoreau's "own decadent lungs mirrored in the sands," and sees an elaboration of a "doctrine of double personality" in the "Heroic Vitalist" (p. 1060). I am as uneasy with this dimension of West's discussion as I am with the essays of Miller and Gozzi, though it would be unfair to characterize West's complex study as merely psychobiographical. Yet in proposing to deal with both "ends" of man, West in his *PMLA* essay has a penchant for finding the scatological at every turn, while slighting the eschatological, in tone as well as substance. And although he contends that Thoreau's journal records a "preoccupation with his health" (p. 1054)—which could possibly be evidence for his scatological argument—I am struck, rather, by an almost utter absence in his journal of such references: one must go to his letters for these disclosures. Deborah Robbins, "The Ascetic Winter and Excremental Spring of *Walden*," *ESQ: A Journal of the American Renaissance* 24 (1978): 77-82, is similarly uneasy with West on this point (p. 82 n. 8).

Philip F. Gura in three essays sustains West's view of the influence of Kraitsir, especially in "Elizabeth Palmer Peabody and the Philosophy of Language," *ESQ: A Journal of the American Renaissance* 23 (1977): 154-63, and then steers toward the religious significance of Thoreau's philology in "Henry Thoreau and the Wisdom of Words," *New England Quarterly* 52 (1979): 38-54. In the latter he finds that words for Thoreau, unlike Emerson, are "reflections of nothing less than the grand purpose of nature"

(p. 49), and that they "hinted at all we could know of God" (p. 46). In "The Transcendentalists and Language: The Unitarian Exegetical Background," in *Studies in the American Renaissance, 1979,* ed. Joel Myerson (Boston: Twayne, 1979): pp. 1- 16, Gura traces the New England religious tradition out of which this language interest grew. In *The Wisdom of Words: Language, Theology, and Literature in the New England Renaissance* (Middletown, Conn.: Wesleyan Univ. Press, 1981), Gura includes parts of the above mentioned articles and extends his range to study "the cultural context from which discussions of language and symbol originated among certain American romantics" (p. 6). On the other hand, the most recent essay by West on the subject, already cited, ranges into the language theories of the French Enlightenment in tracing a culture's preoccupation with "the relation between language and physical reality" (p. 750). In his examination of a lengthy and broad tradition of speculation to which Thoreau had been exposed in his studies at Harvard, West disassociates himself from his own earlier argument, ungenerously writing that "Gura's claim [in *The Wisdom of Words,* p. 161] for the pivotal importance of Kraitsir's similar work, 126-36, seems implausible" (p. 769n). Though Thoreauvians may never reach consensus on these matters, it is clear that any critical discussion of the whole of *Walden* must inevitably concentrate on the sand foliage passages, and the bibliographical survey here makes no claim to be exhaustive.[20]

*

The direction Gura's criticism has taken is a sign, however, of the spirit of our age, which now seems open to the discovery of sacred meanings in our culture, particularly in our great literature. In *The American Adam: Innocence, Tragedy, and Tradition in the Nineteenth Century* (Chicago: Univ. of Chicago Press, 1955), R. W. B. Lewis astutely observed that the literary artist of early nineteenth-century America repeatedly, if unconsciously, retreated to the biblical period of Adam before the Fall to seek mythic sustenance for his literary creations. And in *Trials of the Word* (New Haven: Yale Univ. Press, 1965), he dwelt on how he was "drawn to testing the energy of the Word within the word—to watching any imaginative attempt to body forth 'the imaged Word,' in Hart Crane's phrase" (p. vii). The very title of his work suggests a return to the creation as depicted in the opening verses of Genesis, or to that moment as poetically summarized in the opening verses of St. John: "In the beginning was the Word. . . ." But Lewis seems reluctant (pp. 98-99) to enter an arena where Randall Stewart, in *American Literature and Christian Doctrine* (Baton Rouge: Louisiana State Univ. Press, 1958), made himself so assailable, and points to the "imaged word" of Hart Crane as if deliberately skirting St. John, even while quoting as somehow relevant Herman Melville's remark, "Take God out of the dictionary, and you would have Him in the Street" (p. viii).

Less skittish about the religious content of literature is Charles Anderson who, in *The Magic Circle of* Walden, entertains notions similar to those expressed by the historian of religion Mircea Eliade, especially as conveyed in the latter's *The Sacred and the Profane* (New York: Harcourt, Brace, 1959). Anderson's title is from Goethe's "The Poet" in *Torquato Tasso,* which Thoreau quotes at length in the third dated entry of his journal, the crucial lines of which are

> In his own magic circle wanders
> The wonderful man, and draws us
> With him to wander, and take part in it. . . .
> (PJ, I, 6; J, I, 4-5)

For Anderson, *Walden* is a poem, masked as autobiography, whose skeleton plot is the "archetypal monomyth of the hero's retreat from society, his initiation and final return," as outlined by Joseph Campbell. The "two laconic bits of autobiographical summary"—Thoreau's reports of his going to Walden Pond in "Where I Lived and What I Lived For," and of his return from it in the last two sentences of "Spring"—simply "frame the transcendent experience that lies between," that of the mythological, wonder-filled man who wanders invitingly within "the magic circle of *Walden*" (pp. 259-60). In his incursion into this magic circle where literature and religion concentrate, Anderson points out that during the genetic process whereby *Walden* shifts from a "factual to a symbolic book," Thoreau in December 1852 noted that his writing is "at present . . . profane, yet in a good sense, and, as it were, sacredly, I may say; for, finding the air of the temple too close, I sat outside" (p. 17).

In his study of myth, Richardson offers the illuminating appraisals that

> the impression is sometimes left by criticism—not just of Thoreau—that myth is a literary ingredient which can be taken up, shrewdly used, and set down again. We are reluctant to believe that a modern writer such as Thoreau could have been religiously committed to myth. It is all very well to use it for metaphor, but to take it seriously seems almost past crediting. But the evidence is that Thoreau did in fact find that certain myths moved him to awe and worship.[21]

And Richardson further asserts that *Walden,* specifically, "gives narrative shape to conceptions that are essentially religious. . ." (p. 136). This is the very claim of Stanley Cavell, who in his influential study *The Senses of Walden* (New York: Viking Press, 1972), p. 26, finds that "what we call spring, and what the writer of *Walden* shows to be an Apocalypse . . . is transformed into a vision of the earth and its dependents in a crisis of foliation; these leaves in turn produce a vision of the world as an open book."

When one considers *Walden*'s genesis as that of a sacred text, Ernst Cassirer's *Language and Myth,* trans. Susanne K. Langer (New York: Dover, 1946), pp. 44-45, is suggestive in pointing to "the supreme position of the Word" in "all mythical cosmogonies." In one text from the Uitoto Indians he finds "a parallel to the opening passage of St. John . . . : 'In the beginning . . . the Word gave the Father his origin.' " Cassirer is quick to caution that

> no one would try to argue from this coincidence to any direct relationship or even an analogy of material content between the primitive creation story and the speculations of St. John. And yet . . . it points to the fact that some indirect relationship must obtain. . . .

And he cannot forbear speculating:

> A more precise insight into the foundations of this relationship can be attained only insofar as we are able to carry back the study of those examples of Word veneration, which the history of religion is always uncovering, from the mere analogy of their respective *contents* to the recognition of their common *form.* There must be some particular, essentially unchanging *function* that endows the Word with this extra-ordinary, religious character, and exalts it ab initio to the religious sphere, the sphere of the "holy."

I contend, nonetheless, that when Thoreau's astonishing midwifery gives linguistic utterance to the natural expression of the sand foliage, one is at the wellsprings of language, the opening verses of Genesis, an analogue in nature of St. John's "In the beginning was the Word. . . ." In *lobe* Thoreau turns—or takes the turn—from a lapse of life into a word of life, expressing thereby the redemptive botanical and philological "Wort" as analogue of that redeeming "Word" as stated by St. John, the theologian of light. Thus Thoreau's redeeming word, with the Word of St. John, is expressive of both Old and New Testament Words. In "Spring" Thoreau not only suggests a natural theology of light to complement the supernatural of St. John, but aptly paraphrases St. Paul, the disciple of resurrection (I Corinthians 15:55), in writing: "There needs no stronger proof of immortality. All things must live in such a light. O Death, where was thy sting? O Grave, where was thy victory, then?" (Wa, 317). Heralded by his search for a vegetal St. John's-wort and a life-everlasting, Thoreau discovered a sacred Wort in "lobe," the expression of a "little vegetable redeemer" (LJ, 206), which interpreted a silence he could neither articulate nor penetrate at the end of *A Week,* though he there concluded with the hope of expressing what "may one day be bread of life to such as dwell by the seashore" (Wk, 393).

Between *A Week* and *Walden,* Thoreau survived a winter of discontent and surmounted a crisis by "the hardening of the seed." A journal entry for February 8, 1857, may be taken as a summary for the concentration that had occurred to Thoreau in expressing both his life and his art:

> By poverty, *i.e.*, simplicity of life and fewness of incidents, I am solidified and crystallized, as a vapor or liquid by cold. It is a singular concentration of strength and energy and flavor. . . . My diffuse and vaporous life becomes as the frost leaves and spiculae radiant as gems on the weeds and stubble in a winter morning. You think that I am impoverishing myself by withdrawing from men, but in my solitude I have woven for myself a silken web or *chrysalis,* and nymph-like, shall ere long burst forth a more perfect creature, fitted for a higher society. By simplicity, commonly called poverty, my life is concentrated and so becomes organized, or a κόσμος, which before was inorganic and lumpish. (J, IX, 246-47)

10

Tree of Life: The Medium and the Message

Only a sweet and virtuous soul,
    Like seasoned timber, never gives;
But though the whole world turn to coal,
    Then chiefly lives.
        George Herbert, "Virtue"

WITH THE comparative deadfall of *A Week* behind him and his *Walden* manuscript shoved aside, Thoreau in late 1850 had felt "no more distinctness or pointedness" in his yearnings "than an expanding bud, which does indeed point to flower and fruit." He felt "ripe for something," without knowing what. "I feel fertile merely," he wrote. "It is seedtime with me. I have lain fallow long enough" (J, II, 101). It was three months later in wondering "how the western Adam in the wilderness will turn out" that he quoted the Puritan view expressed in the *New England Primer*: "In Adam's fall / We sinned all," then added his own "In the new Adam's rise / We shall all reach the skies." Leaning on his pen, he then reached from the tree of the Old Adam to test a limb from that of the New: "perchance the Arbor-Vitae, the tree of life,—is what we want" (J, II, 153). Despite the ambiguities of "want" (lack, need, desire), in the tree of life he hit upon an archetype with which his own genius would vibrate, and upon which the expanding bud of his literary aspirations would flower and bear fruit. For Thoreau, the tree of life would prove to be both the medium and the message, a tree supplanting the tree of the Fall that *A Week* had laid bare, and whose branches would bear the fruit of that tree, half concealed in the leaves of *Walden.* On numerous occasions Emerson had toyed with the notion that trees were imperfect men, and in "The Poet" approvingly quoted both Timaeus's affirmation that a man "is a heavenly tree, growing with his root, which is his head, upward," and George Chapman's characterization of man as a tree "whose nervie root / Springs in his top" (CW, III, 18). But for Thoreau, man was "like a tree which . . . grows as long as it has its root *in the ground*" (PJ, I, 267; J, I, 216; emphasis added). In the winter of 1841 he had wondered why we "go to the woods to cut timber to display our art upon—when here are men as trees walking" (PJ, I, 257; J, I, 204). In his imagination the distinction between man and tree was ever dissolving, and in a series of arboreal trysts he showed himself readier to grasp the limb of an elm tree than of a human. In 1851 he wondered: "Why not see men standing in the sun and casting a shadow, even as trees?" (J, II, 421).

Later that year his eye was drawn insistently to a special tree—a telegraph "tree"—that grew in the Deep Cut through which the iron horse snorted after paring the shores of Walden Pond. Of course such trees "grew" along the entire railroad, but it was at the Deep Cut that Thoreau's ear was attracted, and his eye drawn. One of them grew out of the sand and clay bankside exposed there by man's urgency for internal improvements in transportation and communication (which, by the way, Thoreau regarded as external improvements only), its vibrating branches and leaves—singing wires—becoming a harmonic medium through which the genius of nature was communicated, rearranged, translated. Laying his ear to the heartwood of this vibrating tree, Thoreau cast his eyes negligently toward where it was "rooted" in the lapsing sand and clay, and there discovered the basis of those radical aspirations that ripened his Walden years into a transcendent "fructus"—the "highest use" to which a thing can be put (J, XII, 24).

As happens frequently in his journal, Thoreau's passionate attendance to the phenomena in the Deep Cut has a protracted foreground. In 1840 he had written that "speech is fractional, silence is integral," then elaborated that "in enthusiasm we undulate to the divine spiritus—as the lake to the wind" (LJ, 192-93). A fortnight later he seemed to anticipate his compelling vigil at the Deep Cut in writing: "To discover a gleam in the trenches, and hear a music in the rattling of the tools we work with—is to *have* an *eye* and an *ear*—" (LJ, 201); but perhaps he was also putting to use the title ("The Eye & the Ear") of the fourth lecture in Emerson's 1837-38 series, "Human Culture" (EL, II, 264). In *A Week* Thoreau had written of hearing a "telegraph harp" in Plaistow, Massachusetts (Wk, 176-77); but it was almost exclusively at the Deep Cut, beneath the vibrating tree, that the "fytte" came upon him. Then, when the publication of *Walden* had translated the spirit into another medium, the time of attraction was virtually over.

*

Constructed in the early 1840s, the Fitchburg (later Boston and Maine) Railroad was a prominent feature in Thoreau's Walden Pond experience from 1845 to 1847, and figures in multiple ways in the pages of *Walden*. But Thoreau's initial attitude toward the railroad seems altogether indifferent. In a journal poem of 1850 that eventually found its way into "Sounds," Thoreau wrote:

What's the railroad to me?
I never go to see
Where it ends.
It fills a few hollows,
And makes banks for the swallows;
It sets the sand a-flowing,
And blackberries a-growing.
(J, II, 58-59; Wa, 122)

That November another journal effort flagged at the Deep Cut in the second line of stanza three:

Down in the Deep Cut
. . . .
Where the men lived
Who made the railroad.
(J, II, 117)

Not till the telegraph line was strung in early September 1851 was Thoreau attracted to the Deep Cut, through which he had walked almost daily during his two-year stay at the pond.[1] In his imagination, the telegraph pole seemed almost at once to take on the qualities of a sacred and singing tree. On September 22 he put his ear to one of the newly erected poles there, which seemed "filled with music . . . as if every fibre was affected and being seasoned or timed, rearranged according to a new and more harmonious law." On this occasion his attention turned from the telegraph wires to the pole itself, a "divine tree or wood" that seemed to have been "transmuted" by the musical wires:

What a recipe for preserving wood, perchance,—to keep it from rotting,—to fill its pores with music! . . . [O]n applying my ear I hear the hum within the entrails of the wood,—the oracular tree acquiring, accumulating, the prophetic fury. (J, III, 11)

Putting his ear to this tree the next day, he could "hear it working terribly within," and swelling

into a clear tone, which seems to concentrate in the core of the tree, for all the sound seems to proceed from the wood. It is as if you had entered some world-famous cathedral, resounding to some vast organ. . . . I feel the very ground tremble under my feet as I stand near the post. (J, III, 13)

Here was an expression of the principle of the wood within, rather than without, the tree![2]

On the last day of 1851, Thoreau ventured out to examine the trembling ground beneath his "oracular tree," only to find that a premature thaw made it "too late . . . to see the sand foliage [his first use of the phrase] in the Deep Cut . . . it is now too wet and soft." Except for some nearly "perfect leopards' paws"—the phrase would turn up in "Spring"—the sand seemed excremental: "There is no end to the fine bowels here exhibited,—heaps of liver, lights, and bowels." Thoreau analogized that the poet's creative moment, "when the frost is coming out in the spring," must pass not only through his bowels as feeling, but through his "brain and heart," too, that it might be articulated (J, III, 164-65). Since the moment of his creative rebirth in writing *Walden* was but a few days ahead, the birth metaphor is particularly timely in this, the first of twenty-two entries on the sand foliage.[3]

On January 3 he queried, "Why was it made that man should be thrilled to his inmost being by the vibrating of a wire?" Immediately, by a pun on "boreal" (north wind and tunneling), he linked the telegraph harp with the sand foliage: "Are not inspiration and ecstasy a more rapid vibration of the nerves swept by the inrushing excited spirit, whether zephyral or boreal in its character" (J, III, 175). For several weeks thereafter, he concentrates almost exclusively on the vibrations of the zephyral spirit: with the snowfall of January 18 the telegraph "approached so near an attribute of divinity that music naturally attended it" (J, III, 205). Five days later he could hear no music *except* at the Deep Cut, where "Orpheus is still alive . . . [and] poetry and mythology revive" in the "fine clear tones" coming from the very core and pith of the telegraph pole. He then felt his own chords "tremble so divinely. . . . The latent music of the earth . . . found here a vent. . . . Mr. Morse did not invent this music" (J, III, 219-20). By the next day he had completely reversed his attitude of fourteen months earlier, now declaring his envy for the Irish who lived in the Deep Cut where the telegraph was "approaching to articulation. It sports so with my heart-strings" (J, III, 224).

But even as the harp sounded overhead, he was turning his attention ineluctably to the "boreal" spirit working out from the bankside in the melting and streaming sand and clay at the roots of the telegraph tree. He examined the forms of foliage intently on January 25, and the next day found them still richer in outline. Meanwhile "the harp high overhead" seemed "a new Orpheus modulating, moulding the earth . . . making the sands to follow its strains." The force of "Thaw with his gentle persuasion" here seemed "more powerful than Thor with his hammer" (J, III, 235-36). Four days later a "pure, clear melody" sounded, especially in the Deep

Cut where the "gale is modified, when the favorable conditions occur, and the indescribable coincidence takes place. . . ." The shapes of foliage in the bankside now excited Thoreau as if he were "getting near to life and vegetation." Where the thawing streams broadened "at bottom into mere shallows," the clay and sand seemed to approach articulation, for the fricative and liquid radicals of his key term "lobe" began to emerge in the terms he groped with—"*v*asa, *v*ague sand-bars, *l*ike the mammoth *l*ea*v*es,—makes strands" (J, III, 247-48; emphasis added).

On February 24, thinking he might be too late to observe the workings of the boreal spirit in the Deep Cut, Thoreau contented himself with the sounds of cock-crowings and telegraph harp as prophets of a "natural resurrection, an experience of immortality" (J, III, 319). But on March 9, on the west side of the Cut, "the sight of the moist red sand or subsoil under the edge of the sandy bank" greatly moved him; and when he heard the harp overhead, he felt he "must read the Greek poets"—or did the harp convey a New World sound, the "gods expressing their delight at this invention" (J, III, 342-43)? The next day Thoreau dispensed with all classical allusions in describing the semicylindrical channels made in the bankside by the flow of sand and clay, which formed "a new leafy lobe"—his first use of "lobe" to describe the foliage (J, III, 344). Two days later while watching the sand flowing, he heard "the harp at the same time. Who shall say that the primitive forces are not still at work?" The sand foliage now reminded him of the "laciniated, lobed, and imbricated thalluses of some lichens,—somewhat linear-laciniate," a closely detailed description that would appear almost without change in "Spring." "They come out from the interior of the earth like bowels," he elaborated, "a rupture in the spring—and bury the snow. The crust of the snow is completely concealed with the sand for an eighth of a mile" (J, III, 348-49).

Having passed from a state of indifference to one of rapture over the sand and clay in the Deep Cut, Thoreau now describes the burgeoning "lobe" in details relating both to the natural shaping of the bankside by Thaw and to the artful shaping of a stream of air by the vocal apparatus in human speech as it articulates the word "lobe" [my comments are in brackets]:

> At any moment the creative stream [of air?] will be seen flowing in a restricted channel or artery [as it is compressed to form the liquid *l* of "lobe"?], but it is forming new lobes [the letters *b* and *B*, lobe-shaped?], and at last, in the ditch [between the teeth and the lips, where the explosive *b* is temporarily withheld in its formulation?], it forms sands [words?], as at the mouths of rivers [of human speakers?], in which the outlines of the different lobes are almost lost, are dissi-

pated [as when the plosive *b* of "lobe" is dispatched or expressed?] into mere shaded outlines on the flat floor. (J, III, 349)

The passage exemplifies Thoreau's instinct for tracing the "double parentage" of a word—to its natural, no less than its linguistic, origins; for Thoreau had what F. O. Matthiessen judged as "a more dogged respect for the thing than any of his companions, and limitless tenacity in waiting to find the word." In "What Music Shall We Have?" Matthiessen remarked the uniqueness, among the Transcendentalists, of Thoreau's grasp of "the organic harmony between body and spirit." In part, this was a function of an acute sense of hearing: he wrote of the aeolian (telegraph harp) "at length no less than thirty times."[4] Bending an ear to its resounding harmonies, with side-of-the-eye vision he caught sight of the word being shaped in the book of Nature laid open at the Deep Cut, a word enabling him to bring the crop of his Walden experience to a harvest in "some upland pasture—where the John's / wort grew" (PJ, I, 352; J, I, 304).

*

By the time the telegraph line was laid in 1851, Thoreau had already established a solid lowland basis for gardening and harvesting in the high pastures of imagination. In 1853 he wrote to H. G. O. Blake, in what was not so much sound advice as it was a report of his own condition, that he should "put on the pack of an Upland Farmer in good earnest the coming spring, the lowland farm being cared for," select his seeds, and do his winter work. "No man," Thoreau proclaimed, "can suspect that he is the proprietor of an Upland farm, upland in the sense that it will produce nobler crops and better repay cultivation in the long run, but he will be perfectly sure that he ought to cultivate it" (C, 298). By this time Thoreau had twice served as gardener and handyman for Emerson, who was absent for prolonged periods traveling and lecturing, had tended his crops through two seasonal harvests on Emerson's land at Walden Pond, and was bringing his journal "gleanings" of that experience to a literary harvest.

Emerson, in the meantime, had eased himself into the pack of an Upland farmer only, which he shouldered with self-reliance in lecturing; but perhaps his similitude was Bronson Alcott, who went a-lecturing at the time of the harvest at Fruitlands, at considerable cost to the "lowland farm" underfoot. Increasingly, Emerson had become a mere proprietor who depended on other gardeners; Thoreau, however, was harvesting not only literal crops from his squatter's rights on Emerson's property, but the cream of the crop—its poetry—as well. Emerson had early suggested the natural origin of abstract words in the "Language" chapter of *Nature* by citing illuminating instances such as "right," "spirit," and "supercilious";

but these were largely gleanings from a growing tradition of etymological musings that might be found in such works as Horne Tooke's *The Diversions of Purley.* Emerson did take delight in the jawing of sailors at Long Wharf, but he was not the coiner of words that Thoreau was. Moreover, as early as 1837 Emerson showed a predilection to avert his eye from the Apocalypse of Nature in order to read books *about* Nature, and found a harbor for both his eye and his ear in one book he repeatedly borrowed. Ironically, the book was by another "gardener"—William Gardiner by name—and its title, *The Music of Nature,* suggests that to seek an answer to the question "What Music Shall We Have?" Emerson characteristically resorted to books. Having a tin ear, as Emerson readily admitted, would not dispose him to such ecstasy as Thoreau felt in hearing the notes of a telegraph harp. (One wonders, on this basis, why Emerson so delighted in owning an aeolian harp—was it only through literary associations, and not for its *natural* music?) At any rate, Emerson quotes a lengthy passage from Gardiner in which the sense of sight governs a search for correspondence between the sounds of the language of man and those of Nature. By relentlessly tracing Nature's shaping of the sand foliage, Thoreau suggests, perhaps unconsciously, a parallel shaping of "lobe" by human speech. In contrast, neither term in the comparison Emerson quotes is unmediated Nature:

> *A* probably represented the figure of the mouth when open and the bar across it the line which the teeth would form while uttering this sound.
>
> The upper part of the small letter *e* would represent the figure of the mouth as but just opened & which would give the true sound of this vowel. The vowel *O* accurately represents the circular form of the mouth for that sound. The letter *U* probably in its original form was an exact representation of the scooped figure of the tongue in uttering that sound.
>
> The two semicircles in *B* represent the lips as closely pressed together in the act of forcing that explosive sound & the consonant *P* having but one curve would intimate a slighter effect of the same kind. (JMN, V, 432-33)

In the passage Emerson here quotes at length, he takes no notice of nature in the process of articulation, and thus deals only with the linguistic parentage of words. Even in *Nature,* he was rather citing words that revealed a double parentage, and not, as Thoreau, persistently attending to the process by which nature seemed to unfold to language.

In the same journal entry where Emerson quotes Gardiner on language, he also quotes him, under the heading "Tone":

> When Barthelemon led, the opera connoisseurs would go into the gallery to hear the effect of his Cremona violin which at this distance predominated greatly above all the other instruments. Though in the orchestra it was not perceptibly louder than any of the rest. (JMN, V, 432)

In this case, too, the ear of Emerson is content to register the note of a violin as expressed in a literary medium, in *The Music of Nature.*[5] In the first weeks after the telegraph line was laid beside Walden Pond, Thoreau, on the other hand, perhaps triggered by some remark of Emerson about the violin, wrote:

> As the wood of an old Cremona, its very fibre, perchance, harmoniously transposed and educated to resound melody, has brought a great price, so methinks these telegraph-posts should bear a great price with musical instrument makers. It is prepared to be the material of harps for ages to come, as it were put asoak in and seasoning in music. (J, III, 37)

Whatever momentary use Thoreau might have made of such verbal mediums as Gardiner (through Emerson—there is no evidence that Thoreau read the book), or perhaps Coleridge ("The Aeolian Harp"), Thoreau's attention focuses on the note in nature as yet unmediated by language, and at a place of sounding where spirit and human art (the wind and the wire) capture the ear and the eye by resounding articulations that inform his Walden experience, giving it a "seasoning in music." In the passage Thoreau devotes to the emergence of "lobe," he concludes with the assertion that "the telegraph harp has *spoken* to me more distinctly and effectually than any man ever did" (J, III, 349; emphasis added).[6]

*

Remarkably, the formulations of nature in the Deep Cut had come to the notice of Emerson at least two years before the laying of the telegraph wire. On August 18, 1849, following a day in which he had walked with Thoreau to Acton, Emerson used as one example of how the Concord Society should report its business, that "Mr C read a paper on the foliaceous & sponge-like formations by spring-thaw in the argillite of the Deep Cut in the Rail Road—and so forth" (JMN, XI, 146). That he did not exploit the symbolic significance of "argillite," a metamorphic rock, underscores the difference between his imagination and Thoreau's, for whom the natural phenomenon of "argillite" would later translate to "sand foliage." No doubt the comparison is unfair to Emerson—each author should be judged by his accomplishments, not his presumed omissions. Nonetheless, the difference it suggests squares with Moncure Conway's judgment that Thoreau "had as a touchstone for authors their degree of ability to deal with supersensual facts and feelings with scientific precision," a quality Emerson seems to have lacked.[7] As an interesting corollary, Charles Darwin, as Stanley Edgar Hyman points out in *The Tangled Bank,* constantly used language as a metaphor for nature, as in writing that "rudimentary organs may be compared with the letters in a word."[8]

But even though Thoreau was able to detect a latent harmony between the burgeoning articulations of the voices of earth and of man, he did not yet have a firm grasp of the word uttered, or had not yet formed a nexus between the act of the articulating globe and the lobe emerging through the workings of a boreal spirit. Two weeks later he again deferred to the classical tongues in writing that the "Greek word ἔαρ [spring]" was running through his head (J, III, 363). Yet he caught a sense of the word he was straining to hear, and wrote, with the same ambiguity he had expressed about the tree of life, that "as long as vibrating wires make music of harps, we do not want [desire? need? lack?] redeemers" (J, III, 418; my comment in brackets).

In his next encounter with the "undecayed oracle" in the Deep Cut, seven months later, the note Thoreau heard was flattened. It was a particularly hot day, and while he was going through the Cut, it occurred to him that he had

> scarcely heard one strain from the telegraph harp this season. Its string is rusted and slackened, relaxed, and now no more it encourages the walker. I miss it much. So it is with all sublunary things. Every poet's lyre loses its tension. (J, IV, 206)

But when he crossed the railroad in the waning moon of a moist warm night in late October, the harp seemed newly tuned, for he felt the vibrations of the telegraph pole communicating its message "to the surrounding earth for a considerable distance" (J, IV, 402). Still later he again fell back on the classics to interpret, punning heavily that he never heard the telegraph harp "without thinking of Greece. How the Greeks *harped* upon the words immortal, ambrosial! they are what it says" (J, IV, 458). In a calmer moment, a few days after hearing the harp for the first time, he had confided to his journal: "Shall I not have words as fresh as my thoughts? Shall I use any other man's word? A genuine thought or feeling can find expression for itself, if it have to invent hieroglyphics" (J, II, 480). Two months later he had retained that faith in writing, "as you *see,* so at length will you *say*" (J, III, 85).

But though his aeolian harp seemed to sting his ears, to ally "Concord to Athens, and both to Elysium" (J, IV, 458-59), the Greek translation failed to satisfy, even as his native tongue failed him as well. Two weeks later he felt the strain of melody might "at last ripen to something glorious. The wire will perhaps labor long . . . before it attains to melody" (J, IV, 473). Listening with delight to his "aeolian harp" again in December, 1853, Thoreau found it among the "truest and loftiest preachers that I know now left on this earth. . . . He that hath ears, let him hear" (J, VI, 39). Two months later the luxuriant sand foliage persuaded Thoreau that

> Nature is still in her youth,—that florid fact about which mythology merely mutters,—that the very soil can fabulate as well as you or I. It stretches forth its baby fingers on every side. . . . This earth is not . . . like the leaves of a book, an object for a museum and an antiquarian, but living poetry, like the leaves of a tree,—not a fossil earth, but a living specimen.

In the face of Nature's extravagant fabulation in the bankside, Thoreau feared only that his expression "may not be extravagant enough,—may not wander far enough . . . to be adequate to the truth of which I have been convinced" (J, VI, 99-100).

Three days later the sand foliage seemed to trace in the Deep Cut, as if with baby fingers, not only a fabulation of the season, but of "spring" as a preverbal, dreamlike expression of nature that "precedes the green and flowery spring, as mythology does ordinary literature and poetry" (J, VI, 109). The next day Thoreau was entranced by "a peculiar softness and luminousness in the air." The morning itself seemed illuminated "tenfold by the sun reflected from broad sheets of rain and melted snow-water, and also, in a peculiar manner, from the snow on the sides of the Deep Cut." In this luminous, dawning season, as the sand foliage burgeoned toward expression, Thoreau on Valentine's Day heard the herald of spring in a "distant crowing of cocks and the divine harmony of the telegraph,—all spring-promising sounds" (J, VI, 122-23) that conjoined as if to announce the word made light.

On March 1, while correcting his *Walden* manuscripts and very possibly inserting the sand foliage material into "Spring," he found the foliage "in its prime" (J, VI, 147), doubtless punning on "prime" to suggest both dawn and spring, as well as a consciousness of what he had referred to in *A Week* as the matutine intellect. The next day, in the soil in which the telegraph harp was rooted as a resonating tree of life and from which nature articulated its primal "lobe" so extravagantly and yet with such reserve, Thoreau stumbled upon his word, *lobe*:

> The sand foliage is vital in its form, reminding me [of] what are called the vitals of the animal body. I am not sure that its arteries are ever hollow. They are rather meandering channels with remarkably distinct sharp edges, formed instantaneously as by magic. How rapidly and perfectly it organizes itself! The material must be sufficiently cohesive. I suspect that a certain portion of clay is necessary. Mixed sand and clay being saturated with melted ice and snow, the most liquid portion flows downward through the mass, forming for itself instantly a perfect canal, using the best materials the mass affords for its banks. It digs and builds it in a

twinkling. The less fluid portions clog the artery, change its course, and form thick stems and leaves. The lobe principle,—lobe of the ear (*labor, lapsus*?).

On the outside all the life of the earth is expressed in the animal or vegetable, but make a deep cut in it and you find it vital; you find in the very sands an anticipation of the vegetable leaf. No wonder, then, that plants grow and spring in it. The atoms have already learned the law. (J, VI, 148)

And Thoreau, too. For if a nick in his brother's finger had drawn him to express in his first book a myth of the Fall, a Deep Cut near Walden Pond drew him to express in his second a myth of Resurrection. With his masterpiece just published, Thoreau wondered, upon seeing some "Castile-soap galls": "Is not Art itself a gall? Nature is stung by God and the seed of man planted in her. The artist changes the direction of Nature and makes her grow according to his idea. . . . Genius stings Nature, and she grows according to its idea" (J, VII, 10). By attention most deliberate, Thoreau had delved in imagination beneath a lapsing phenomenon whose first formulation was an ode to dejection, beneath a layer of silence upon which he had settled at the end of *A Week,* to discover at hard bottom and rocks in place a Reality upon which to posit his Chanticleerian brag:

God himself culminates in the present moment, and will never be more divine in the lapse of all the ages. And we are enabled to apprehend at all what is sublime and noble only by the perpetual instilling and drenching of the reality which surrounds us . . .; whether we travel fast or slow, the track is laid for us. (Wa, 97)

And the telegraph wire as well!

Almost at once after the publication of *Walden,* the sound of the telegraph harp and the sight of the sand foliage in the Deep Cut became matters of indifference to Thoreau, and not simply because his observation of the manufacture of telegraph wire at Quinsigamond Village on January 5, 1855, extracted some of the poetry from his aeolian harp, his "wire redeemer" (J, VII, 101-2). Having caught an expression of eternity in the lapse of the Deep Cut and notched it upon his stick, he seemed thereafter to read the zephyral and boreal spirits with an eye and ear to memory. Perhaps he had more lives to live. Still, a single post-*Walden* journal entry recalls his passionate attention to nature's articulations in the Deep Cut, and serves as their coda. On February 18, 1857, Thoreau wrote of the very note of a bluebird's song as an anticipation of spring, the sound of its lobelike warble:

The very grain of the air seems to have undergone a change and is ready to split into the form of the bluebird's warble. Methinks if it were visible, or I could cast up some fine dust which would betray it, it would take a corresponding shape. . . . The air over these fields is a foundry full of moulds for casting bluebird's warbles.

Any sound uttered now would take that form . . . [of] a softer, flowing, curling warble, like a purling stream or the lobes of flowing sand and clay. . . .

What a poem is this of spring, so often repeated! I am thrilled when I hear it spoken of,—as the *spring* of such a year, that fytte of the glorious epic. (J, IX, 270)

As he lay dying in the spring of 1862, Thoreau told of a dream he had "of being a railroad cut, where they were digging through and laying down the rails," Ellery Channing taking the place to be in his lungs—and, indeed, he did have "rales" in his chest, a punning prospect not likely to be overlooked by Thoreau's walking companion.[9] But was it simply a thrill of pain? Was there, perhaps, a thrill of ecstasy as well at the point of death in his sensing that a deep cut in Nature had a corresponding deep cut in his own lungs? With Nature, he too had been "stung by God," whereby, perhaps, the "seeds of Genius" had been planted in him. Were those seeds, now that he was at the point of death, about to spring in some upland pasture, where the johnswort grew? Achieving, thereby, a "spring of springs"?

*

The tree of life was not only the informing medium of *Walden*; it was the message as well. At the end of "Economy," Thoreau drew upon *The Gulistan* of Sadi to specify the fruit of his tree of life. The quotation from *The Gulistan* poses a riddle: why do some trees, like the date tree, bear fruit in such abundance, while it is only the cypress tree, which bears no fruit, that is termed "azad" or free? Characteristically, Thoreau unriddles in punning language: while the fruit of the date tree is "liberal," it is likewise diurnal, for its crop is "dates." The crop of the cypress tree, on the other hand, is "liberal" in that it is "always flourishing," and thus its fruit is eternal life, without "dates." "Fix not thy heart on that which is transitory," Thoreau urges, "but if it affords nothing to give away, be an azad, or free man, like the cypress" (Wa, 79). In *A Week* he anticipated this passage in remarking "not the *annals* of the country, but the natural facts, or *perennials,* which are ever without date. When out of history the truth shall be extracted, it will have shed its dates like withered leaves" (Wk, 219). And it may be that at some level his stay at Walden Pond extended to two years so as to test his perennial resources, enabling him to convert his experience, by sound seasoning, into a work of art that had shed all dates.

In the penultimate paragraph of *Walden,* Thoreau rehearses the story of the "strong and beautiful bug" that emerged from the "dry leaf of an old table of apple-tree wood" that had stood in a farmer's kitchen in Connecticut, and later in Massachusetts. The egg from which the bug hatched had been deposited in the "living tree many years earlier still, as appeared by counting the annual layers beyond it. . . . Who does not feel his faith in a resurrection and immortality strengthened by hearing of this?" Thoreau analogizes that man himself, "buried for ages under many concentric layers of woodenness in the dead dry life of society," may likewise expand to a "beautiful and winged life" in a way to astonish the family of man "as they sat round the festive board" (Wa, 333). The emergence of the beautiful bug from the "dry leaf of an old table of apple-tree wood" suggests its having been part of the leavings from the tree of knowledge hewn by Thoreau in *A Week.* William J. Wolf conjectures that since "the first edition of *Walden* had the subtitle *Life in the Woods*," Thoreau must have delighted in this final parable because "it dramatized the theme of life-in-the-wood."[10] And on this same point, Martha Banta comments that the apple tree at the end of *Walden* is "Eden's tree of knowledge metamorphosed into the tree of life."[11] Is it not also an illustration of the principle of the work within the wood, but not altogether "*Walled*-in" (Wa, 183)?

In his journal entry for August 30, 1851, on the eve of his first notice of the resonating tree of life in the Deep Cut, Thoreau provided a floral prophecy of his artistic masterpiece. Looking at the Norway cinquefoil's manner of protecting its seeds by the enfolding five leaves of its calyx, he saw there

> evidence of forethought, this simple *reflection* in a double sense of the term, in this flower, [which] is affecting to me, as if it said to me: "Even I am doing my appointed work in this world faithfully. Not even do I, however obscurely I may grow among the other loftier and more famous plants, shirk my work, humble weed as I am. Not even when I have blossomed, and have lost my painted petals and am preparing to die down to my root, do I forget to fall with my arms around my babe, faithful to the last, that the infant may be found preserved in the arms of the frozen mother." (J, II, 430)

The flower of the tree of life, by reflection coming to fruit as his appointed work, *Walden* is Thoreau's perennial child, the infant preserved in the arms of its frozen mother who, faithful to the last, was true to the dreams of his youth and sang them in new song.

11

Instrumental Dreams: The Plectrum and the Harp

. . . At the bottom of my dream
PJ, II, 5; J, I, 438

I look under the lids of Time.
PJ, I, 242; J, I, 188

TWO DAYS before Christmas 1851, Thoreau mused that our dreams come upon us out of "our waking *moods* and *humors*" and might be the result of something "eaten or done," but that our deeper dreams come, paradoxically, from a state when we are "truly awake and serene, and healthy in all our senses, [and] we have memorable visions." When he added "Who that takes up a book wishes for the report of the clogged bowels or the impure blood?" (J, III, 150-51), he could not have foreseen his Freudian and Eriksonian critics who have fastened onto the oral and anal imagery in his dreams and books, especially in the sand foliage section of "Spring," and speculated with such absorption about his digestion and toilet training.[1] Early that November, as a matter of fact, he had suggested—with Wordsworthian allusiveness and some ambiguity—that he was intent upon the dream as a passage to memorable visions, and not as a consequence of clogged bowels:

> Our life is not altogether a forgetting, but also, alas, to a great extent a remembering, of that which perchance we should never have been conscious of,—the consciousness of what should not be permitted to disturb a man's waking hours. As for society, why should we not meet, not always as dyspeptics, but sometimes as eupeptics? (J, III, 103)

This is a judgment he used as the conclusion of "Life Without Principle," first given as a lecture in 1854.[2] A few short weeks before these observations about dreams and their probable causes, Thoreau recorded in his journal, on October 26, the longest description of his dreams he was ever to write. Though critical comment has concentrated on the dreams reported here as testimony of clogged bowels, I here deal with it as testimony of memorable visions. In the period from May 1851 to January 1852, moreover, these visions attend, if they do not cause, the conversion of *Walden* from mechanic to organic form. To get at such matters may appear to be "One Step Backward Taken," as the title of a Robert Frost poem has it. But I pursue Thoreau's dreams only to get at "a little lower layer," as Captain Ahab put it to his crew, as a means for looking "under the lids of Time" (PJ, I, 242; J, I, 188).

In *A Week* Thoreau had written that true friends are "kind to each other's dreams" (Wk, 270), and apparently he tried to procure those of his Worcester disciple, H. G. O. Blake, whom he chided in 1850: "You tell me that you dream, but not what you dream. . . . So do the frogs dream. Would that I knew what" (C, 260). Three years later he urged Blake:

> Hold fast to your most indefinite waking dream. The very green dust on the walls is an organized vegetable; the atmosphere has its fauna & flora in it; & shall we think that dreams are but dust & ashes, are always disintegrated & crumbling thoughts and not dust like thoughts trooping to its standard with music systems beginning to be organized[?][3] (C, 300)

Such remarks indicate that for Thoreau dreams, as well as the works of nature, were not only worthy of inquiry, but were imbued with a dynamic, ordering principle that might inform man's art. Thus considered, dreams are not simply illusions, but allusions to another, inherently transcendental, order of reality, and ought to be prized as a "forgotten language" that Thoreau tried to decipher, translate, and articulate in a way to remember the dreams of his youth and convey his memorable visions.[4] In collective as well as individual dream experience, Thoreau found significance, and in *A Week* brilliantly foreshadowed Carl Jung's "collective unconscious" in writing:

> In the mythus a superhuman intelligence uses the unconscious thoughts and dreams of men as its hieroglyphics to address men unborn. In the history of the human mind, these glowing and ruddy fables precede the noon-day thoughts of men, as Aurora the sun's rays. The matutine intellect of the poet, keeping in advance of the glare of philosophy, always dwells in this auroral atmosphere. (Wk, 61)

For one who made a career out of anticipating the sunrise, it is not surprising that Thoreau was so concerned with the dream, and with the shaping of dreams toward meaning: it might not be too much to say that of his two books published in his lifetime, the first is about a dream and the nature of dreaming, the second is a dream, and one that many of his countrymen, both here and abroad, have dreamed anew and made their own. More precisely, *A Week* is an attempt to recover the dream of an ideal lost youth (Thoreau's own as well as his dead brother's), only to find, foreshadowing Thomas Wolfe, that you can't go home again; and *Walden,* pruned of such nostalgia, is an attempt to realize the dream of perpetual youth—timelessness—that man has only when most fully awake. As *Walden* nears its paradoxical conclusion, it offers as one result of the two-year experiment in awakening that

> if one advances confidently in the direction of his dreams . . . he will put some things behind, will pass an invisible boundary; [and] new, universal, and more liberal laws will begin to establish themselves around and within him. . . . (Wa, 323)

Thoreau's dream of October 26 occurs at a point roughly midway between the publication of his two books—*A Week* (May 30, 1849) and *Walden* (August 9, 1854). When he took leave of *A Week,* Thoreau did so as an aspiring poet who, his lofty aims notwithstanding, dealt with the problem of form by mechanically pouring his book into the mold of a single week; when he takes his leave of *Walden,* he does so as an accomplished poet-priest who expresses in organic form the liberal laws he has unconsciously absorbed from the cycles of nature—those of the day no less than of the season.[5] Thoreau's letter to Blake, in which he writes of dreams as thoughts in the process of organization, prefigures a nine month gestation period when, out of his matutine unconsciousness, Thoreau found that his own "dust like thoughts [were] trooping to its standard with music systems beginning to be organized." As demonstrated, one of these "music systems," the vibrating wires of the telegraph harp, translated a spirit that crossed Thoreau's oneiric threshold, and articulated the seminal organization of *Walden* in a word. But *A Week* served as "the plectrum with which our else silent lyres are struck" (Wk, 392); indeed, were it not for *A Week, Walden,* the "harp articulate" (J, VI, 294), might never have sounded.

When he moved to the shores of Walden Pond on July 4, 1845, Thoreau would not only write *A Week*; he would begin to articulate his dream of natal communion with the Concord upon whose banks he was born, mingling the flow of his life stream with the flow of a river that "meanderest forever / At the bottom of my dream" (J, I, 438).[6] Few works of literature are so persistently concerned with dreams and dreaming. There are sixty-four instances of "dream" (or its variants) in *A Week,* more than three times the number in *Walden* (twenty). According to Jonathan Bishop, "dreaming and waking experience" provides one of the numerous polarities that give the book its loose structure: "Thoreau *sees* what in ordinary life one 'dreams' of."[7] In the "Saturday" chapter, when Thoreau and his traveling companion, outward bound, approach the bend in the river at Ball's Point that will take them out of sight of their native town, their departure is likened to an entry into a lengthening dream: "Gradually the village murmur subsided, and we seemed to be embarked on the placid current of our dreams . . ." (Wk, 19-20). "Current events" and meditations then alternate, and chapter divisions repeatedly draw attention to oneiric thresholds, times of "fresh morning or evening thoughts" (Wk, 20). Two key chapters, "Sunday" and "Wednesday," conclude by reporting in considerable detail the recollected dreams of one or both of the travelers, and the final chapter, "Friday," considers dreams generically in a way to convey Thoreau's thematic purpose in the book: "We linger in manhood to tell the dreams of our childhood, and they are half forgotten ere we have learned the language" (Wk, 380). Not always able to express the impressions of his matutine intellect, Thoreau, perhaps under the influence of Emerson's "The Poet," wrote in "Friday" of "an important difference between men of genius or poets, and men not of genius," the latter

> unable to grasp and confront the thought which visits them . . . because it is too faint for expression, or even conscious impression. What merely quickens or retards the blood in their veins and fills their afternoons with pleasure they know not whence, conveys a distinct assurance to the finer organization of the poet. (Wk, 341)

In part, Thoreau had moved to Walden Pond to give expression to his youthful, dreamlike voyage and to "see, smell, taste, hear, feel, that everlasting Something to which we are allied, at once our maker, our abode, our destiny, our very Selves" (Wk, "Monday," 173). Once near the pure Walden waters with an aspiration to live a "*purely* sensuous life" (Wk, 382), he uncovered the deeper memory of Walden Pond itself. In August of his first summer there, he recalled that when five years old he had been brought to the pond, which then became "one of the most ancient scenes stamped on the tablets of my memory," an "oriental Asiatic valley of my world." He went on to write that thereafter the "woodland vision . . . made the drapery of my dreams." His "spirit" seemed nourished by "that sweet solitude" that seemed to provide both "room to entertain my thronging guests, and that speaking silence that my ears might distinguish the significant sounds" (J, I, 380-81). Then, as if to pinch himself, he detailed some of his daily activities that "at length helped to clothe that fabulous landscape of my imagination." In his first summer at the pond he set aside a broad margin of life in order to entertain his thoughts and dreams, and by listening with the side of the ear began to discern the "significant sounds" from "that speaking silence" that unfolded at his feet, beneath the sod. He would voice his dream in "The Ponds," rejecting notions that his was a fabricated, or merely literary, experience:

> It is no dream of mine,
> To ornament a line;
> I cannot come nearer to God and Heaven
> Than I live to Walden even. (Wa, 193)

But four years after his sojourn at the pond had ended, Thoreau's dream was unrealized in expression, his *Walden* manuscript put aside.

As he began his thirty-fifth year Thoreau, sensing that his youth had slipped through his fingers, wrote of his past experiences having been "all in all" (J, II, 306), echoing a line (75) from Wordsworth's "Lines Composed a Few Miles above Tintern Abbey." Rereading the English laureate the year after his death may have been one means of redirection for Thoreau in his watershed year of 1851, when the Thoreau family settled into their home on Main Street after moving from the outlying "Texas" house.[8] Thoreau's regrets at the time were not only for the experiences of his boyhood, but for those of a "previous state of existence. 'For life is a forgetting,' etc." (J, II, 306), as he warped a line from Wordsworth's Intimations Ode, a poem that gnawed at the psychic vitals of virtually every New England Transcendentalist. In late July Thoreau traveled alone to Hull and Plymouth where he explored a literal shoreline (L. *literalis*) that offered a New World perspective on Wordsworth's figurative "immortal sea / Which brought us hither." It was his only trip of the year.[9]

But life was a forgetting of a friend as well. By 1851 the rift with Emerson had widened, paradoxically because of a growing self-reliance on the part of Thoreau. His intellect having once been made fruitful by reading Emerson's *Nature,* that fact of the imagination had gradually subsided to a fact of the understanding. By July Thoreau was smitten by the genius in the original book of nature, a genius that made "distinctions which my understanding cannot, and which my senses do not report" (J, II, 337). His evolving affair with this genius was not so much an invigoration as a impregnation: "some grains of fertilizing pollen . . . fall on us, . . . and suddenly the sky is all one rainbow, is full of music and fragrance and flavor." It was "the marriage of the soul with Nature," he summarized, that "makes the intellect fruitful, . . . gives birth to imagination" (J, II, 413). In December Thoreau wrote of a desire to "ally myself to the powers that rule the universe" (J, III, 133), but almost immediately thoughts of Emerson intruded. He wrote of picking up one of Emerson's books in which a thought was expressed, good in itself, but so obvious in its moral that he had himself "*thought* the same thing . . . twenty times during the day" (J, III, 135). As he renewed his labors over the *Walden* manuscript in late January, Thoreau quite literally underscored the decline of Emerson's influence from a fact in the imagination: "I never realized so distinctly as this moment that I am peacefully parting company with the best friend I ever had, by each pursuing his proper path. I perceive that it is possible we may have a better *understanding* [the emphasis is Thoreau's] now than when we were more at one" (J, III, 214).

Two differences with Emerson at the turn of the year seem to have been pivotal. Reading a chance sentence in one of Emerson's books, one "that I rarely look at," triggered Thoreau's memory of a conversation in which Emerson had been the critic, Thoreau the apparent defender, of Margaret Fuller, her "whims and superstitions" (J, III, 134). A decade earlier, it had been Emerson who both shielded and promoted Thoreau in the face of Miss Fuller, editor of *The Dial.* The second difference came about when Emerson showed Thoreau a letter from Horatio Greenough that Emerson "liked very much" (J, III, 181). According to Thoreau, Emerson was taken by Greenough's idea of making "architectural ornaments have a core of truth. . . ." But Thoreau regarded this as no more than "common dilettantism," and was afraid of saying "hard things" to Emerson if he should go on. Thoreau's own view was organic, that architectural beauty grew "from within outward . . . without even a thought for mere ornament, but an unconscious nobleness and truthfulness of character and life . . ." (J, III, 182). In this flareup, F. O. Matthiessen sees a "prickly" Thoreau misrepresenting Greenough[10]—could it be to draw to himself the fire of Emerson, and by that means locate himself on the side of the imagination, away from both "pretenders"? Ten days later, when Thoreau attended a lecture by Thomas Wentworth Higginson that stirred his understanding but failed to touch his imagination, he complained that Higginson reminded him of Emerson (J, III, 213). When the moment of creative renewal in his composition of *Walden* was at hand, on January 26, 1852, Thoreau wrote of a growing responsiveness to his own genius, in a metaphor that mixes details of vegetation and horsemanship to roughly suggest that the roots of Thoreau's peculiar genius were burgeoning, while the directive influence of Emerson was being thrown from the saddle:

> Obey the spur of the moment. These accumulated it is that make the impulse and the impetus of the life of genius. These are the spongioles or rootlets by which its trunk is fed. If you neglect the moments, if you cut off your fibrous roots, what but a languishing life is to be expected? Let the spurs of countless moments goad us incessantly into life. I feel the spur of the moment thrust deep into my side. The present is an inexorable rider. The moment always spurs either with a sharp or a blunt spur. Are my sides calloused? Let us trust the rider, that he knows the way,

that he knows when speed and effort are required. What other impulse do we wait for? (J, III, 231)

And later in the same journal entry he harks back to one such impulse of genius, the sound of the harp overhead, "a new Orpheus" (J, III, 235).

The next day—the very day fixed by critics for his tapping into the deep source of inspiration that wells up into *Walden*[11]—Thoreau indirectly evaluates what has been happening to him in the previous nine months by considering the role of the "unconsciousness" in Shakespeare:

Jan. 27. The peculiarity of a work of genius is the absence of the speaker from his speech. He is but the medium. You behold a perfect work, but you do not behold the worker. I read its page, but it is as free from any man that can be remembered as an impassable desert.

I think that the one word which will explain the Shakespeare miracle is "unconsciousness." If he had known his own comparative eminence, he would not have failed to publish it incessantly. . . . (J, III, 236)

Mention of Shakespeare supplies a hint that Thoreau may have been thinking of Coleridge's *Shakespearean Criticism,* specifically the passage delineating the organic from the mechanic form:

The form is mechanic when on any given material we impress a predetermined form . . . as when to a mass of wet clay we give whatever shape we wish it to retain when hardened. The organic form, on the other hand, is innate; it shapes as it develops itself from within, and the fullness of its development is one and the same with the perfection of its outward form.[12]

Notwithstanding his apparent early dismissal of Coleridge, Thoreau, as Alexander Kern has recently affirmed, "was profoundly influenced" by that English Romantic, and it may be that in 1851 he was absorbing what he had earlier been exposed to only. Laraine Fergenson has suggested an affirmative answer to the question "Was Thoreau Rereading Wordsworth in 1851?"; it may be that at the same time, Thoreau was rereading Wordsworth's collaborator. The evidence, no more than circumstantial, is nonetheless suggestively telling—as when Thoreau writes during the period when his own genius is supplanting Emerson's: "Flights of imagination, Coleridgean thoughts" (J, III, 144). In *Biographia Literaria,* Coleridge drew on the language of philosophy and theology to delineate the imaginative powers:

The imagination then I consider either as primary, or secondary. The primary imagination I hold to be the living power and prime agent of all perception, and as a repetition in the finite mind of the eternal act of creation in the infinite I AM.[13]

As early as 1841, Thoreau speculated, in the language of poetry and psychology, that "the unconsciousness of man is the consciousness of God, the end of the world" (J, I, 119).[14]

Perhaps the first, uncertain steps Thoreau took to achieve such "unconsciousness" came in May 1851, when he took ether to have all his teeth removed. On May 12 he offered some observations on this experience of what Emerson in "The Poet" had called a "quasi-mechanical" means of exhilaration: "You are told that it [ether] will make you unconscious, but no one can imagine what it is to be unconscious—how far removed from the state of consciousness and all that we call 'this world'—until he has experienced it" (J, II, 194). A month later, however, he was writing of how "we are clarified and calmed healthily . . . not by an opiate, but by some unconscious obedience to the all-just laws, so that we become like a still lake of purest crystal . . ." (J, II, 268). Thoreau may already have been eyeing Coleridge, whose addiction to opium had compromised his poetic imagination, as the Transcendentalists generally assumed. In September Thoreau wrote of his belief that each moment of inspiration leaves an indelible impression, "like a pot of pure ether" (J, II, 469), even though no poem results. In some such mood he had appraised *A Week* for its "*hypaethral* character . . . open to the heavens above, *under the ether*" (J, II, 274).

To the cerebral thought he had captured in 1840 in writing that "the moon is on the path of her unconscious duty, when the sun lets the light of his genius fall on her" (LJ, 167), he now gave loose rein, dutifully wooing an unconscious genius by tripping out many a night from June until October as the moon neared its full stage. On June 13, 1851, after visiting Walden Pond by moonlight, he wrote at length in a way to echo Wordsworth's Intimations Ode: "There is a certain glory attends on water by night. By it the heavens are related to the earth, undistinguishable from a sky beneath you" (J, II, 249). For what may have been the first time, he noted a halo about his shadow in the moonlight; and three weeks later, he recalled this dreamlike visitation in a lengthy reflection by remarking that

> moonlight, like daylight, is more valuable for what it suggests than for what it actually is. It is a long past season of which I dream. And the reason is perchance because it is a more sacred and glorious season, to which I instantly refer all glorious actions in past time. (J, II, 284)

That he was attempting to recapture a Wordsworthian "glory from the earth" is further borne out by his journal entry the next day: "The intimations of the night are divine, methinks" (J, II, 286).[15]

But while his thoughts dwelt much on the "long past season of which I dream," with regrets for a past youth, and on attempts to consort with the unconscious side of Nature, to "look under the lids of Time" (PJ, I, 242; J, I, 188) as a means of recapturing the glory from the earth, they also dwelt on personal purification and integration as well: in this new phase he wished to make his life a "sacrament" (J, II, 314) and drew from Ecclesiastes in writing "Remember thy Creator in the days of thy youth, i.e., lay up a store of natural influences. Sing while you may, before the evil days come. He that hath ears, let him hear. See, hear, smell, taste, etc., while these senses are fresh and pure" (J, II, 330). Feeling clarified by "unconscious obedience to the all-just laws," on June 22 he "awoke into a music which no one about me heard. . . . To the sane man the world is a musical instrument" (J, II, 268-69). A month later, his attentiveness to a divine harmony even sharper, he was aware of "a kind of fine aeolian harp music" always in the air, "the mellow sound of distant horns . . ., a sound to make all men divinely insane that hear it." He then avowed, "To ears that are expanded what a harp this world is!" (J, II, 330). Of course no harps were to be heard about Concord; but a fortnight later Thoreau *did* hear "the sound of a flute, or a horn, or a human voice" from Bear Garden Hill, and then noted: "I rarely walk by moonlight without hearing . . . a performer I never see by day. . . . He plays but one strain and goes to bed early, but I know by the character of that single strain that he is deeply dissatisfied with the manner in which he spends his day." But the single strain was enough to "remind him of his heavenly descent. It is all that saves him,—his one redeeming trait. It is a reminiscence; he loves to remember his youth . . . is highly related. . . . I never see the man by day who plays that clarionet" (J, II, 373-74). Several days later Thoreau wrote, "No heavenly strain is lost to the ear that is fitted to hear it, for want of money or opportunity" (J, II, 379-80).

Curiously, Thoreau's fit ear soon found opportunity to hear a heavenly strain, for it came upon the heels of "three or four ordinary laborers" (J, II, 428) who appeared along the railroad right-of-way on August 28 to begin putting up the poles and fixtures for a telegraph line to extend from Boston to Burlington. Within a week Thoreau heard these wires "vibrating like a harp high overhead" (J, II, 450); nine days later, "vibrating like an aeolian harp," they reminded him of "infinitely higher, planes of life which it behooved me never to forget" (J, II, 496-97). Keyed by the disaffected clarionet player, Thoreau's expanded ears were alert for divine and divining harmonies, wherever they might be vented.

During the same period Thoreau had been reading *The Autobiography of Benvenuto Cellini,* and in the same journal entry where he first takes notice of the vibrating wires as an aeolian harp, he mentions Cellini's "terrible dream or vision" (J, II, 494) that had prefigured harrowing events that came to pass in his life. From the time of this dream, Cellini had felt a sense of election because of a halo he had seen about the shadow of his head. Thoreau comments on a halo about his own shadow—he noticed it by moonlight on the railroad causeway—remarking that it might, "in the case of an excitable imagination" like Cellini's, be "basis enough for . . superstition." But Thoreau's own state was calm, that of one who by frequent moonlight walks "has travelled to fairyland in the night." What follows, however, is one of the most convoluted passages in his journal: "That kind of life which, sleeping, we dream that we live awake, in our walks by night, we, waking, live, while our daily life appears as a dream" (J, II, 495-96). One of the meanings this suggests is an inversion of the diurnal and nocturnal, conscious and unconscious, states. In the "Baker Farm" chapter of *Walden,* Thoreau draws on such experiences in fancying himself "one of the elect" because of the halo of light about the shadow of his head, for in the "shadows of some Irishmen," he added with a note of facetiousness, there was no halo evident (Wa, 202). During the late summer of 1851, Thoreau's sense of election was reinforced when he was caught in a shower while the sun was setting, and found himself standing in a rainbow: "It was here its arch rested on the earth" (J, II, 382-83; cf. Wa, 202).

On the day he wrote of Cellini's dream, Thoreau's sense of election attained a particularly fine pitch:

> At the entrance to the Deep Cut, I heard the telegraph-wire vibrating like an aeolian harp. It reminded me suddenly,—reservedly, with a beautiful paucity of communication, even silently, such was its effect on my thoughts,—it reminded me, I say, with a certain pathetic moderation, of what finer and deeper stirrings I was susceptible, which grandly set all argument and dispute aside, a triumphant though transient exhibition of the truth. It told me by the faintest imaginable strain, it told me by the finest strain that a human ear can hear, yet conclusively and past all refutation, that there were higher, infinitely higher, planes of life which it behooved me never to forget. As I was entering the Deep Cut, the wind, which was conveying a message to me from heaven, dropped it on the wire of the telegraph which it vibrated as it passed. I instantly sat down on a stone at the foot of the telegraph-pole, and attended to the communication. It merely said: "Bear in mind, Child, and never for an instant forget, that there are higher planes, infinitely higher planes, of life than this thou art now travelling on. Know that the goal is distant, and is upward, and is worthy all your life's efforts to attain to." And then it ceased, and though I sat some minutes longer I heard nothing more. (J, II, 496-97)

Though Nature's divining inspirations at a Deep Cut threshold seemed to sound a sermon "on the mount" (J, IV, 467), Thoreau was brought to earth on September 15 by the mundane task of perambulating the town boundaries accompanied by the town's "Select" men—a term he relished for its irony, for these men seemed to him utterly "common-place and wordly-minded," and he wrote disdainfully that "the poet must keep himself unstained and aloof. Let him perambulate the bounds of Imagination's provinces, the realms of faery, and not the insignificant boundaries of towns. The excursions of the imagination are so boundless, the limits of towns are so petty" (J, III, 5). The following Sunday, he so conscientiously transcribed into his journal certain qualities of moonlight as recorded in Ree's *Cyclopedia* that it seemed as if he were trying to underscore a night and day distinction between his own sense of election as extravagant poet-priest and that of the "Select" men of the town, charged with solidifying the town boundaries (J, III, 7).

In this period when he was moving from conscious to unconscious perception, so, too, in his art activity was he moving from the fanciful and mechanic toward the imaginative and organic, and thus toward that "Sympathy with Intelligence" (W, V, 240) that he prized above knowledge itself. Only days after experiencing ether, he was reading Asa Gray and remarking on the "perfect analogy between the life of the human being and that of the vegetable, both of the body and the mind" (J, II, 201), filling pages of his journal with the topic, and thereby provoking one critic's charge of tedium.[16] But Thoreau blunts such charges in writing near the end of the summer that one should "improve the opportunity to draw analogies. There are innumerable avenues to a perception of the truth. Improve the suggestion of each object however humble, however slight and transient the provocation. What else is there to be improved?" (J, II, 457). On Christmas Day of 1851 Thoreau was playing the terms "understanding" and "imagination" off each other in chastising science for its inability to account for the "beauty in the form or coloring of the clouds which addresses itself to my imagination"; then, as if newly reminded of Coleridge's distinction, he remarked: "Just as inadequate to a pure mechanic would be a poet's account of a steam-engine." He then returned to defend his position: "If we knew all things thus mechanically merely, should we know anything really?" (J, III, 155-56).[17]

It was on New Year's Day that he took issue with Coleridge's desire to have ideas he "could see all round." Such a man, Thoreau complained, "would never look at the moon," could not see "ideas that soar above the earth." Are such ideas so much "moonshine"? "Very well, then," Thoreau feistily defended, "do your night travelling when there is no moon to light you. . . . I will be thankful that I see so much as one side of a celestial idea, one side of the rainbow and the sunset sky, the *face* of God alone" (J, III, 173-74). By this time he was already at the task of improvement, however humble, for he had stepped over the threshold of the unconscious to peer beneath the frost and under the lids of Time. In his journal entry of October 26, 1851, he reported at length the series of dreams he had had:

> I awoke this morning to infinite regret. In my dream I had been riding, but the horses bit each other and occasioned endless trouble and anxiety, and it was my employment to hold their heads apart. Next I sailed over the sea in a small vessel such as the Northmen used, as it were to the Bay of Fundy, and thence overland I sailed, still over the shallows about the sources of rivers toward the deeper *channel* of a stream which emptied into the Gulf beyond,—the Miramichi, was it? Again I was in my own small pleasure-boat, learning to sail on the sea, and I raised my sail before my anchor, which I dragged far into the sea. I saw the buttons which had come off the coats of drowned men, and suddenly I saw my dog—when I knew not that I had one—standing in the sea up to his chin, to warm his legs, which had been wet, which the cool wind numbed. And then I was walking in a meadow, where the dry season permitted me to walk further than usual, and there I met Mr. Alcott, and we fell to quoting and referring to grand and pleasing couplets and single lines which we had read in times past; and I quoted one which in my waking hours I have no knowledge of, but in my dreams it was familiar enough. I only know that those which I quoted expressed regret, and were like the following, though they were not these, *viz.*:—
>
> "The short parenthesis of life was sweet."
>
> "The remembrance of youth is a sigh," etc.
>
> It had the word "memory" in it!! And then again the instant that I awoke, methought I was a musical instrument from which I heard a strain die out,—a bugle, or a clarionet, or a flute. My body was the organ and channel of melody, as a flute is of the music that is breathed through it. My flesh sounded and vibrated still to the strain, and my nerves were the chords of the lyre. I awoke, therefore, to an infinite regret,—to find myself, not the thoroughfare of glorious and world-stirring inspirations, but a scuttle full of dirt, such a thoroughfare only as the street and kennel, where, perchance, the wind may sometimes draw forth a strain of music from a straw.
>
> I can partly account for this. Last evening I was reading Laing's account of the Northmen, and though I did not write in my Journal, I remember feeling a fertile regret, and deriving even an inexpressible satisfaction, as it were, from my ability to feel regret, which made that evening richer than those which had preceded it. I heard the last strain or flourish, as I woke, played on my body as the instrument. Such I knew I had been and might be again, and my regret arose from the consciousness how little like a musical instrument my body was now. (J, III, 80-82)

In this lengthy entry Thoreau describes not only his successive dreams, but also his waking thoughts and his attempts to account for some details of his dream from his experiences awake. The dreams, it is plain, center on traveling and its difficulties: first on the difficulty of managing horses on land, then of managing travel by water. When the dream reverts to land travel, Thoreau finds himself walking with Alcott, and due to the dryness of the season, able to penetrate farther than usual into what is ordinarily a wet meadow, and so the usual difficulty of such travel has evaporated. Next, and in contrast, comes his sight of the buttons from the coats of drowned men, travelers who have succumbed to the difficulties of voyaging by water, and then the sight of a dog up to its chin in the sea. Once Thoreau conjectures a specific stream—"the Miramichi, was it?"—as a deeper channel beyond the sources of the streams he journeys on.[18]

The details of sea travel may have come from reading Laing, though in each of the two preceding years Thoreau had taken a trip to Cape Cod, and during the period 1850-51 had lectured three times on the subject of his first, perhaps also his second, excursion there. In *Cape Cod,* the book that stems from these lectures, his thoughts were much on the sea, and on those Norsemen who had early visited the Cape—Thor, Thorfinn, Thornhall—in whose names Thoreau found an appealing personal lure to his seafaring imagination. The details about exploring a river to its source and to its "deeper *channel*" beyond may be a hint that the trip he and his brother John took to the source of the Merrimack River had not reached its literary destination in *A Week*—he had not there traced the stream of inspiration to its articulating source, but concluded in silence. He may have recalled this dream by means of his third excursion to the Maine woods, in the summer of 1857, for in "The Allegash and East Branch," published posthumously, he writes,

> I remember once dreaming of pushing a canoe up the rivers of Maine, and that, when I had got so high that the channels were dry, I kept on through the ravines and gorges, nearly as well as before, by pushing a little harder, and now it seemed to me that my dream was partially realized. (MW, 246)

As to the details about the buttons from the coats of drowned men, Thoreau on his first trip to the Cape in 1849 had been an eyewitness to the recovery of corpses from the wreck of the Irish brig *St. John.* But the specific details almost surely derive from his trip to Fire Island in 1850 to search for the remains of Margaret Fuller, her husband the Marquis of Ossoli, and their infant, all drowned at sea in July. On that mission Thoreau did find the jacket of the Marquis and ripped a button from it, which then became the focus of a lengthy meditation on the dreamlike nature of the physical:

> I find the actual to be far less real to me than the imagined. Why this singular prominence and importance is given to the former, I do not know. In proportion as that which possesses my thoughts is removed from the actual, it impresses me. . . . I have in my pocket a button which I ripped off the coat of the Marquis of Ossoli on the seashore the other day. Held up, it intercepts the light and casts a shadow,—an *actual* button so called,—and yet all the life it is connected with is less

substantial to me than my faintest dreams. This stream of events which we consent to call actual, and that other mightier stream which alone carries us with it,—what makes the difference? On the one our bodies float, and we have sympathy with it through them; on the other, our spirits. (J, II, 43)

And as if to reinforce the notion of travel as an attempt to discover a source of inspiration, Thoreau queries in the same passage, "Does not the stream still rise to its fountain-head in you?" (J, II, 44).

The dream of attempting to hold apart the heads of horses intent on biting each other might well be related to Thoreau's dreaming of travel by water. In his journal account of traveling the Concord and Merrimack rivers, Thoreau had compared the wind blowing the sail of his boat to "a winged horse, pulling with a strong and steady impulse" (J, I, 155). But he had much difficulty in managing the two currents of *A Week*—he could not make the stream of time, current events, run consistently with the stream of eternity, dreams. And while he may have "mounted" a docile "Saddleback" (curiously, he did not refer to it as "Mt. Greylock"), he seems to have shied away from the more threatening mount, Agiocochook, to which he gave but a few sentences. At the time of his estrangement from Emerson, he had drawn on the equestrian metaphor to write, "We check and repress the divinity that stirs within us, to fall down and worship the divinity that is dead without us" (J, III, 119), and later rejected the Emersonian bridle to respond, instead, to "the spur of the moment" (J, III, 231).[19]

At the next stage of his dream, Thoreau finds himself walking on land with Alcott, and the dream content here turns from physical to mental travel—in this case Thoreau's attempt to grasp a fleeting thought that, apparently familiar in the dream, was not so in his waking hour. What impressed Thoreau in his attempt to recollect were some lines of poetry dealing with the "remembrance of youth," and his exultation at the significance of the single word "memory," which does not itself occur in the lines Thoreau offers as his admittedly imprecise reconstruction of the verse. In "Friday" of *A Week*, Thoreau had written: " 'The remembrance of youth is a sigh.' We linger in manhood to tell the dreams of our childhood, and they are half forgotten ere we have learned the language" (Wk, 380). In fact, this was the period when Thoreau was re-membering, and when the passage from Ecclesiastes, 12:1, came often to mind.[20]

Upon awakening, however, Thoreau has a fleeting perception of his having been used as a musical instrument—the examples he cites are wind instruments—bugle, clarionet, flute. Such examples may be related to his having recently learned how to manage the motive power of other wind "instruments"—sailing vessels. At least a rudimentary knowledge of managing sails had been required for his voyage on the Concord and Merrimack rivers in 1839; on his trip to Hull in 1851, after some attempt at salt water sailing, he wrote that a sailboat "is an admirable invention, by which you compel the wind to transport you even against itself. It is easier to guide than a horse . . ." (J, II, 359). Less than a fortnight before his series of dreams, he described the difficulties of managing an ill-fashioned row-boat that in capricious breezes would "take the bits in its mouth and go round in spite of us" (J, III, 77). Waking from the dream, Thoreau metaphorically compares himself to a lyre, an instrument plucked with the hands, usually, or in the case of an aeolian harp, agitated by the wind and thus become a wind instrument more delicately tuned to the aspirations of Nature than of man. What controls the tone of Thoreau's recollection at the moment of awakening is regret—"infinite regret." The quoted lines of the dimly recalled poem "expressed regret" as well, and Thoreau recalls feeling a "fertile regret" in reading Laing the previous evening, while at the same time deriving an "inexpressible satisfaction" from his "ability to feel regret," which "made that evening richer than those which had preceded it."

In his final two sentences Thoreau emphasizes the musical character of his feeling of regret, and especially because of his "consciousness how little like a musical instrument my body was now." In early May, Thoreau had written of the resemblance between horses, steers, and men and of the relative indifference of one man or another for serving a low use, for "any man can stop a hole to keep the wind away" (J, II, 192), as he writes in an allusion to *Hamlet.* In supplying an interpretation of his dream he suggests a similar low use of himself as "not the thoroughfare of glorious and world-stirring inspirations, but a scuttle full of dirt, such a thoroughfare only as the street and kennel, where, perchance, the wind may sometimes draw forth a strain of music from a straw." Those Thoreauvians who have imbibed deeply in the journals doubtless catch at once the pun on his own name. Delivered with his off-hand, Thoreau glosses his dream in perceiving himself as "a scuttle full of dirt," a "thoroughfare only as the street and kennel"—an open drain or sewer into which, particularly in 19th-century America, horse dung was dropped or scraped. ("Kennel" might have some tenuous relationship to the dream dog that Thoreau did not know he had.) As a "thoroughfare," the street and kennel must await the rain or water-cart to be cleansed, a detail perhaps relating to travel by water in the dream. But in his suggestion that within the kennel the winds—those "glorious and world-stirring inspirations"—"may sometimes draw forth a strain of music from a straw," he pictures himself as the homely and fragile musical instrument.

At one level, Thoreau may have been honest in his regret that "arose from the consciousness how little like a musical instrument my body was now," but in a deeper recess he felt his body a not quite conscious organ of inspiration, a wind instrument whose stops he did not entirely govern (cf. *Hamlet,* 3, 2, 378-89), but which were governed by nature's "world-stirring inspirations." By inspiration, the finer organization of a poet, moved toward unconsciousness, might be converted from a mere straw in the wind to a harp articulate. Thoreau's infinite regret is thus, at the same time, a celebration of his subconscious perception of himself as a musical instrument. In his intimations of the articulating aeolian harp in the Deep Cut, he had not repressed but given vent to "the divinity that stirs within us" to become himself a harp articulate.

*

Early in this chapter—as in chapter 1—I alluded to Freudian critics as our chief expositors of Thoreau's unconsciousness, and not surprisingly, they seem to have fastened upon the dream of October 26, 1851, as an important document in their analyses. In *Dark Thoreau,* Richard Bridgman deals with "the troubled dark year of 1851-1852"—a period Lewis Leary, in an article noted earlier, convincingly discusses as Thoreau's watershed year—and the dream of October 26 as a focal point of his perception of being a "scuttle full of dirt." Bridgman then proposes that "one must approach spring's regeneration, and specifically the thawing sand bank of *Walden,* with the memory of Thoreau's feeling of having been that scuttle full of dirt" in mind. For ten pages Bridgman worries the sand foliage paragraphs, sensing that Thoreau, "genuinely affected by the sand bank," tried to transform the images of blood and excrement he there perceived into "a sacrament of the earth; but in vain, for as both titles of his published books attest, he was a man of water and of air."[21]

It is plain enough that *A Week on the Concord and Merrimack Rivers* shows Thoreau to be a man of water, but how *Walden* reveals him to be a man of air puzzles me. Is it because Professor Bridgman sees in the soaring hawk in "Spring" an expression—ungrounded in his estimation—of Thoreau's hopes? so much spiritual winging it? Bridgman seems unable or—given the restrictions of his thesis—unwilling to follow the articulated progress of the bud to the leaf and to the feathers of the bird as a more finely expressed leaf, and persists in staring blankly at the exuviae, seeing there only a mixture of blood and excrement, as Thoreau clearly did not. To be sure there is evidence, as Thoreau entered the period of gestation I have been discussing, that he anticipated the element of air as a preferred medium of communication with the gods. In July he inverted his schedule of writing in the morning and walking in the afternoon because he sought influences that were "more ethereal than terrestrial. It is the quality of the air much more than the quality of the ground that concerns the walker,—cheers or depresses him. What he may find in the air, not what he may find on the ground" (J, II, 339). But he did not insist on this fleeting preference, for he wrote on December 20, "Be faithful to your genius" (J, III, 144), and on Christmas Day, "Let me not be in haste to detect the *universal law*; let me see more clearly a particular instance of it!" (J, III, 157). Five days later he directed himself to "go to the Deep Cut" (J, III, 161), but the next day seemed to have been too late to see the thawing bank. Nonetheless, he felt he had there tread on a ground that was replete with life; "in the spring bud and blossom" he felt near the "fountainhead."

> The earth I tread on is not a dead, inert mass. It is a body, has a spirit, is organic, and fluid to the influence of its spirit, and to whatever particle of that spirit is in me. She is not dead, but sleepeth . . . this fundamental fertility near to the principle of growth. (J, III, 165)

To be sure Thoreau was directed by the zephyral spirit moving through the wires of the telegraph harp, was then obsessed by the signs of a boreal spirit working out of the earth near the base of this harp, a veritable fountainhead of language. From this hitherto walled-in bankside, he finally managed to draw out—to read and express—an articulation of the language of nature, its earth-voice.

A somewhat reluctant Freudian interpreter of Thoreau's dream of October 26 is Mary Elkins Moller, who in *Thoreau and the Human Community* finds it an expression of Thoreau's revulsion from his own body during a time of sexual fantasy and accompanying guilt feelings over Lidian Emerson. As the title of her book fairly suggests, she finds no occasion to discuss the sand foliage in connection with the dream, or in any other connection. But elsewhere she discusses at length the consequences of a violent explosion of a munitions factory that Thoreau described in horrifying detail—blood, decapitated bodies, limbs, bowels—a "manifestation of brutish force in nature." And she discusses with astute perception how, two days later, Thoreau was entranced by the telegraph harp in the Deep Cut as a sign of the existence of a healing and invigorating power in nature, as well as an avenging power. "How it was," she wonders, "that the humming of the telegraph wire could dissipate the horror of the scene, 'make all the world a lie,' and restore Thoreau's sanity—this question is probably beyond scholarly elucidation, though it may not be wholly beyond our intuitive grasp."[22] In the case of Bridgman, a reading of the October 26 dream is related, in an insistently unsympathetic way, to the exuviae of nature; in the case of Moller, a somewhat obligatory Freudian analysis is undercut elsewhere by an instinctively well-tuned perception of what else was at work in the Deep Cut, and how it affected Thoreau.

Without denying the existence of dark forces operating upon Thoreau's unconsciousness and manifesting themselves in frequent images of revulsion that penetrated into the world of his dreams, I propose as both a fresher and more illuminating gloss of Thoreau's dream a passage from Jacques Maritain's *Creative Intuition in Art and Poetry*:

Everything depends . . . on the recognition of the existence of a spiritual unconscious, or rather, preconscious, of which Plato and the ancient wise men were well aware, and the disregard of which in favor of the Freudian unconscious alone is a sign of the dullness of our times.

Maritain goes on to designate the

first kind of unconscious by the name of *spiritual,* or, for the sake of Plato, *musical* unconscious or preconscious; and the second by the name of *automatic* unconscious or *deaf* unconscious—deaf to the intellect, and structured into a world of its own apart from the intellect; we might also say, in quite a general sense, leaving aside any particular theory, *Freudian unconscious*.[23]

Perhaps the most deliberate—in many ways the most fair and cautious—Freudian critic of Thoreau is Raymond Gozzi, whose unpublished dissertation—"Tropes and Figures: A Psychological Study of David Henry Thoreau" (New York Univ., 1957)—is something of a minor classic amongst Thoreau scholars. At one point, however, Gozzi conjectures, and then makes almost a cornerstone of his edifice, that Thoreau's ear was attuned to sound as acutely as it was because he had been an auditory witness of the "primal scene" of his parents when he occupied a trundle bed in their room; and it was this infantile experience, Gozzi argues, that enlarged and "libidinized" Thoreau's ears to the sounds of nature.[24] Perhaps. But it seems to me there is more evidence in the journal passages adjacent to the lengthy account of Thoreau's dream, and more consistency in such evidence, for reading the musical sounds therein as sounds of the telegraph harp in the Deep Cut—which in turn bore witness to orphic, rather than dionysian, performances. As his work on the final manuscript version of *Walden* drew to a close, Thoreau in April 1854 was waiting at the Lincoln depot where he heard "the telegraph harp," whereupon any memory of a frost would have melted away:

I perceived distinctly that man melts at the sound of music, just like a rock exposed to a furnace heat. They need not have fabled that Orpheus moved the rocks and trees, for there is nothing more insensible than man; he sets the fashion to the rocks, and it is as surprising to see him melted, as when children see the lead begin to flow in a crucible. I observe that it is when I have been intently, and it may be laboriously, at work, and am somewhat listless or abandoned after it, reposing, that the muse visits me, and I see or hear beauty. It is from out the shadow of my toil that I look into the light. The music of the spheres is but another name for the Vulcanic force. May not such a record as this be kept on one page of the Book of Life: "A man was melted to-day." (J, VI, 193-94)

And finally, on May 23, 1854, Thoreau seemed to memorialize the oneness of his poetic genesis with that of *Walden*:

There was a time when the beauty and the music were all within, and I sat and listened to my thoughts, and there was a song in them. I sat for hours on rocks and wrestled with the melody which possessed me. I sat and listened by the hour to a positive though faint and distant music, not sung by any bird, nor vibrating any earthly harp. When you walked with a joy which knew not its own origin. When you were an organ of which the world was but one poor broken pipe. I lay long on the rocks, foundered like a harp on the seashore, that knows not how it is dealt with. You sat on the earth as on a raft, listening to music that was not of the earth, but which ruled and arranged it. Man *should be* the harp articulate. . . . Think of going abroad out of one's self to hear music,—to Europe or Africa! Instead of so living as to be the lyre which the breath of the morning causes to vibrate with that melody which creates worlds. . . . (J, VI, 294-95)

More than five years later, Thoreau may be summarizing the meaning he discovered in this period of his own translation from the conscious and mechanical to the unconscious and organic:

It is foolish for a man to accumulate material wealth chiefly, houses and land. Our stock in life, our real estate, is that amount of thought which we have had, which we have thought out. The ground we have thus created is forever pasturage for our thoughts. I fall back onto visions which I have had. What else adds to my possessions and makes me rich in all lands? If you have ever done any work with these finest tools, the imagination and fancy and reason, it is a new creation, independent on the world, and a possession forever. (J, IX, 350)

V

Epilogue: After *Walden*

12

Rubrics—A Brown Study—Gleanings

Grow green with spring, yellow and ripe with autumn.
J, V, 394

IF THE PERIOD between *Walden* and his late nature essays was one of decay for Thoreau, as Sherman Paul contends,[1] it was nonetheless one of absorption, concentration, reflection, and communion that pointed toward a time of final harvest. It was a period of chromatic transition from green to red and brown as well. The "grass flames" (Wa, 310) that burst from the earth in *Walden*'s "Spring" were, paradoxically, an expression of moisture, and through that, life. In the spring after *Walden* was published, Thoreau pondered the color of vegetation with etymological penetration, noting that it was "more vivid when wet. . . . Green is essentially *vivid,* or the color of life, and is therefore most brilliant when a plant is moist or most alive." And one here senses his compression of "most alive" to "moist," the "i" running like a vivifying rivulet through the middle of the word. "A plant is said to be green in opposition to being withered and dead. The word, according to Webster, is from the Saxon *grene,* to grow, and hence is the color of herbage when growing" (J, VII, 280-81).

*

At the time *Walden* was published, Thoreau's attention was turning with the season to the yellowing, and then to the reddening, year; and for a week in late September 1854, his journal is richly tinctured by the color of nature's flowering. Having once noted that red was "the richest color" (J, II, 489), and that the rose, "from the Celtic *rhos,* red" (J, IV, 218), was preeminent due to its color, he now pursued red intently for more than a year—in cranberry cheeks and hazelnut husks (J, VI, 432-33), in the leaves of the small andromeda (J, VII, 358), in flesh-colored red lichen (J, VII, 105), in some "rose-colored ice" (J, VII, 139, 142) in Walden Pond, and in a flock of lesser redpolls that appeared in early December, 1855 (J, VIII, 42-44).

In the fall of 1858, he reflected that there seemed to be no record of the "autumnal change of our woods" in English poetry, when the trees acquired their bright hues. "October has not *colored* our poetry yet" (J, XI, 254-55). So to remedy this deficiency, he gleaned his journals for materials that would form his lecture "Autumnal Tints," first given in Worcester in 1859. For Thoreau, "autumnal" was a prophecy of the fall, not the fall itself, for it stood as a bright anticipation of the fruitful brown season to follow. "By fall I mean literally the falling of the leaves, though some mean by it the changing or the acquisition of a brighter color. This I call the autumnal tint, the ripening to the fall" (J, XI, 280). Sherman Paul argues that Thoreau planned to write an almanac or "Kalendar," whose contents would not be "hard to imagine, for 'Autumnal Tints' was planned for it, and his résumés, as well as proposed chapters, like 'November Lights,' suggest its scope. . . ."[2] Both "Autumnal Tints" and "Wild Apples" have to do with the end of the season: the former an early fall piece—"October, or Autumnal Tints" (W, V, 251) as Thoreau toyed with a title for a book-length treatment; "November Lights" might then be his mid-fall piece, and "Wild Apples" his late fall piece, with "Walking" as its companion.

In his journal Thoreau pondered this ripening season etymologically, noting that "the word 'ripe' is thought by some to be derived from the verb 'to reap,' according to which that is ripe which is ready to be reaped" (J, XI, 317). Thus the red coloration was a ripening to the fall of a moist, vivid, hopeful green, a conversion of nature's flowing into her flowering and harvest. One of the most remarkable of the autumnal tints was that of the red maple leaf (in his lecture Thoreau held up specimen leaves for his audience to see), which "flashes out conspicuous with all the virtue and beauty of a maple—*Acer rubrum.* We may now read its title, or *rubric* clear. Its *virtues,* not its sins, are as scarlet" (W, V, 261). Thoreau here implies that the Latin name for red maple has religious significance: *Acer* means either sharp in outline or prominent, conspicuous, in color; and he notes that the red maple is the "most intense scarlet of any of our trees." *Rubrum* sets up holy meanings antithetical to "scarlet sins," for *rubric* refers to the directives in holy books of liturgical worship, printed in red, that serve as guides to meaning. Thoreau later offers the scarlet oak leaf as a directive to holy meanings in the book of Nature by the "lightness" of its leaf as much as by its color—a lightness in weight and illumination. Such leaves are most "ethereal," have "so little leafy *terra firma* that they appear melting away in the light . . . lifted higher and higher, and sublimated more and more, putting off some earthiness, and cultivating more intimacy with the light each year." Aloft these leaves would dance "arm in arm with the light. . . . So intimately mingled are they with it, that . . . you can hardly tell at last what in the dance is leaf and what is light." And even when these ethereal leaves fall, the deep scallops in their design as they lie on the ground "suggest that the material must be cheap, or else there has been a lavish expense in their creation, as if so much had been cut out. Or else they seem to us the remnants of the stuff out of which leaves have been cut"—and Thoreau could not resist a quizzical pun—"with a die?" (W, V, 278-79).

To further illustrate, Thoreau furnished the *Atlantic Monthly* with his own approximation of Nature's rubric, a line drawing of a scarlet oak leaf that, by its deeply scalloped lobes, illustrated its lightness. Thoreau's leafy "rubric," literally colorless, was nonetheless the very antithesis of the colorless "rubric" with which the *New England Primer* began, its *A* an illustration of heaviness, the tree of the Fall. Thoreau's natural rubric posed the question: "What meant the fathers by establishing this *perfectly living* institution before the church—this institution which needs no repairing nor repainting, which is continually enlarged and repaired by its growth?" (W, V, 277). Even the fall of leaves, what might seem Nature's waste—a lavish expenditure of leaves ripening only to fall, and therefore not brought to market—is not a failure in Nature's economy, but an expression of it. For in their fall the trees "are only repaying the earth with interest what they have taken from it. They are discounting" (W, V, 268-69). By such means Thoreau might have been summarizing his own life, for, as Robert Sattelmeyer notes, Thoreau was preparing "Autumnal Tints" for publication as his own life was ripening to the fall.[3] But the trees' "discounting" illustrates the literary results of his assiduous economy as well, a means by which he turned an experiment in living into expression in the bright "leaves" of a literary harvest. In "the falling leaves, all over the forest," Thoreau saw an illustration of Nature's redeeming economy, a means of "protecting the roots of my plants" (W, V, 284). And "Autumnal Tints" concludes with a prospect of the whole world as garden of paradise—or, it may be, of a natural order in the process of celebrating its Fortunate Fall, a season when "all leaves, even grasses and mosses, acquire brighter colors just before their fall. When you come to observe faithfully the changes of each humblest plant, you find that each has, sooner or later, its peculiar autumnal tint" (W, V, 288-89).

But like the sparrows in *A Week,* the leaves *do* fall. In November 1853, Thoreau had detected in the wings of sparrows an illustration of the falling leaves: "They have their fall no less than the plants; the bright tints depart from their foliage or feathers, and they flit past like withered leaves in rustling flocks. The sparrow is a withered leaf" (J, V, 489). And what followed was a decaying leaf. As red leaf declined to brown in autumn's discounting season, Thoreau traced the process of vegetal decay philologically. On October 27, 1858, he wrestled with the problem of describing the coloration of leaves in their deciduous dissolution:

> In describing the richly spotted leaves, for instance, how often we find ourselves using ineffectually words which merely indicate faintly our good intentions, giving them in our despair a terminal twist toward our mark,—such as redd*ish,* yellow*ish,* purpl*ish,* etc. (J, XI, 255-56)

And to his suggestion in his terminal "-ish" of the process of decay, Thoreau elaborated, "We cannot make a hue of words, for they are not to be compounded like colors, and hence we are obliged to use such ineffectual expressions as reddish brown, etc." Nor could he resist punning, "They need to be ground together" (J, XI, 255-56). And so they were. For when the reddish leaves did fall to the ground, without hue or cry, they were caught up in the natural process of decay, fulfilling their destiny "to be ground together."

As autumn subsided to fall in 1856, Thoreau studied the once green leaves, now "quite dry and sapless. . . . Who observed when they passed from green to brown? I do not remember the transition. . . . When was it ordained that this leaf should turn brown in the fall?" (J, IX, 185-86). Two days later, pondering the brown leaf as he had the spring leaf in *Walden,* Thoreau wrote:

> Withered leaves! this is our frugal winter diet, instead of the juicy salads of spring and summer. I think I could write a lecture on 'Dry Leaves,' carrying a specimen of each kind that hangs on in the winter into the lecture-room as the heads of my discourse. They have long hung to some extent in vain, and have not found their poet yet. (J, IX, 191)

Over such dry leaves Thoreau seems to have kept vigil, writing on January 24, 1855, that "not a leaf flutters, summer or winter, but its variation and dip and intensity are registered in THE BOOK" (J, VII, 141). Was he suggesting that the fall of the leaf, like the fall of the sparrow, was, in fact, divined and inscribed in the book of life? For when such "leaves" fell to the earth, to be ground, it was as if the "lively decay of autumn promises as infinite duration and freshness as the green leaves of spring" (J, I, 109). If so, to fall was not an entombment in a house of scurvy death, but a preserve in a house (eco-) of life, in a good earth because eternally vital.

But fall was not only the season of decay; it was also the season of the hardening of the husk, the maturation of the seed, when a tight organization made for a hard, protective outer shell that would make the germ impervious to the dry or damp rot of the earth, rendering it perennial. It was a time for seeds, for nuts, for "perfect works, of hard, tough, ripe twigs, not of tender buds and leaves" (J, II, 111), the bare tree being, for Thoreau, a similitude of the nut, with its "myriad new withes stand[ing] up all around pointing to the sky, able to survive the cold." But this hardening of the seed, how could it occur except for the annual's loss of life? Sympathizing with the season, Thoreau wrote of a winter in man "made to concentrate and harden and mature the kernel of his brain, to give tone and firmness and consistency to his thought. . . . All previous harvests are stubble to this, mere fodder and green crop" (J, VI, 85).

As he drew toward that season in his life when, as he put it, "I shall walk the sky" (J, XIII, 141-42), Thoreau seems to have been intent on fall not so much as a time "to be ground," but—never content with the passive voice—as a time for grinding. Shortly after *Walden* was published, Thoreau was haunted by the sound of a flail in the granary, "separating the kernel from the chaff" (J, VI, 486), and surmised that in order to make flour for his winter customers—he was referring to getting winter lectures together from gleaning through his journals—he "must commence his threshing as early as August," and then grind his "fine flour." Thus the leaves were to be ground, not merely reduced to a layer of seeming decay, but converted into a substance from which Nature, together with her consummate artist, was kneading into a bread of life. "You must love the crust of the earth on which you dwell," Thoreau wrote of such communion in the winter of 1858, "more than the sweet crust of any bread or cake" (J, X, 258); and the next winter he gave way to the impulse to devour his crust by studying lichens again: "The lichenist extracts nutriment from the very crust of the earth. . . . The lichenist loves the tripe of the rock,—that which eats and digests the rocks. He eats the eater. 'Eat-all' may be his name" (J, XI, 440). Late that winter he realized that for some weeks he had been "insisting on the beauty and richness of the moist and saturated crust of the earth. It has seemed to me more attractive and living than ever,—a very sensitive cuticle, teeming with life. . . . This brown earth-crust is not dead" (J, XII, 109-10). As he had anticipated in *A Week,* Thoreau found this earth-crust a "bread of life to such as dwell by the seashore" (Wk, 393), a holy communion to nourish a devoted son of Antaeus.

*

Over his own and nature's fall, the rubrics of Thoreau's liturgy pointed to a communion, to a bread of life, a "brown earth-crust . . not dead." Indeed, this was a "peculiar and interesting *Brown Season*" (J, XII, 113) of his life that involved not only trees anchored firmly in the crust of the earth, but walking trees as well, "men as trees walking" (J, I, 204), as he had remarked in 1841. After *Walden,* literal and symbolic trees figure often in his fallings-out with male authority figures. When the maple sap began to flow in 1856, Thoreau's father objected to the "*use* of my making this sugar when I knew it could be done and might have bought sugar cheaper at Holden's. He said it took me from my studies. I said I made it my study; I felt as if I had been to a university" (J, VIII, 217). What impressed Thoreau was the sap dripping from the tube in the maple "about as fast as my pulse beat." His noted dispute with James Russell Lowell stemmed not only from the *Atlantic Monthly* editor's having excised two sentences from "Chesuncook," but more particularly from what those sentences contained: "It is the living spirit of the tree, not its spirit of turpentine, with which I sympathize, and which heals my cuts. It is as immortal as I am, and perchance will go to as high a heaven, there to tower above me still."[4] And when the old Davis Elm was felled in Concord during late January 1856, Thoreau—who was known to balk at entering graveyards and "commonly [did] not attend funerals"—laid this "old citizen" to rest "as it became me to do" (J, VIII, 130), then read the "inscription" on its marker, the one hundred twenty-seven annular rings of its stump (J, VIII, 142-44). He contested the opinion of the men from the village post office who steadfastly maintained the tree was two hundred years old, deciding that they dwelt "within an integument of prejudice thicker than the bark of the cork-tree" (J, VIII, 146).

In each of these instances, Thoreau is suggesting that man's life is analogous to the life of a tree, whose vitality is expressed in its *liber* or cambium layer, and this layer is in turn analogous to the "very sensitive cuticle, teeming with life," that is the earth's crust. In his discussion of clothing in "Economy," Thoreau had recommended that man give up a good bit of his bark—his epidermis or false skin, his thin and fanciful clothes, even his cellular integument or cortex, "thicker garments, constantly worn" (Wa, 24); but he insisted that man should not lose his shirt, his "liber or true bark," for this "cannot be removed without girdling and so destroying the man." Generally, however, man was "cooked" in his cortex, rather than stripped of his liber or true bark, and so ran the risk of turning into dead wood by falling asleep at the post, turning, even, into a post. In the same year in which he held wake over the Davis Elm, Thoreau wrote to H. G. O. Blake of persistently trying to arouse himself from the somnolent, wooden state of a cedar (arbor-vitae) post:

> Blake! Blake! Are you awake? . . .
>
> For my part I am trying to wake up,—to wring slumber out of my pores; For, generally, I take events as unconcernedly as a fence post,—absorb wet & cold like it, and am pleasantly tickled with lichens slowly spreading over me. Could I not be content then to be a cedar post, which lasts 25 years? Would I not rather be that than the farmer that set it? or he that preaches to that farmer?—& go to the

heaven of posts at last? I think I should like that as well as any would like it. But I should not care if I sprouted into a living tree, put forth leaves & flowers, & have fruit. (C, 443)[5]

One such expression of the living tree was political. Often, it seemed, politics seemed to cut a swath across Thoreau's private, liberal pursuits in a way to threaten his freedom. The summer after declaring his personal Independence Day on July 4 by moving to Walden Pond, he was on his way to the village to retrieve a pair of shoes from the cobbler when he was jailed for not paying his taxes. To have done so, as he later argued, would be to support a state that in his estimation had "run 'amok' against society" by fostering a slavery system within its own boundaries, and by making war against Mexico as a means of extending the territory of that system. He touched on the incident briefly in "The Village" (Wa, 171-72), and at length in "Resistance to Civil Government" (1849), complaining in the latter of merely "wooden men" marching at once in uncritical support of the "wooden gun" of its government. In such early works as "The Service" (an 1840 essay rejected by Margaret Fuller when she edited *The Dial*) and "Reform and the Reformers" (a pre-1845 working essay), he had resorted to arboreal terms to describe man. In the former he described the brave man's life standing like "some fair sunlit tree against the western horizon, and by sunrise . . . planted on some eastern hill, to glisten in the first rays of the dawn" (RP, 3); in the latter he advised that whoever would be a genuine reformer must "encourage the flow of sap in your veins, find your soil, strike root and grow." And further, he advised becoming "green and flourishing plants in God's nursery, and not such complaining bleeding trees as Dante saw in the Infernal Regions" (RP, 191).[6]

In the midst of his pondering Asa Gray's *Manual of Botany* five years earlier, Thoreau had mused that "the thought that comes to light . . . is wombed and rooted in darkness, a moist and fertile darkness . . . like the tree of life" (J, II, 204). During the period of his wake over the Davis Elm, at the very threshold of his deepest involvement in public issues, he attenuated in his journals an analogy between arboreal and human communities in a way to underscore his political radicalism. The passage—which must be quoted entire—is richly suggestive of Thoreau's radical politics.

I have seen many a collection of stately elms which better deserved to be represented at the General Court than the manikins beneath—than the barroom and victualling cellar and groceries they overshadowed. When I see their magnificent domes, miles away in the horizon, over intervening valleys and forests, they suggest a village, a community, there. But, after all, it is a secondary consideration whether there are human dwellings beneath them; these may have long since passed away. I find that into my idea of the village has entered more of the elm than of the human being. They are worth many a political borough. They constitute a borough. The poor human representatives of his party sent out from beneath their shade will not suggest a tithe of the dignity, the true nobleness and comprehensiveness of view, the sturdiness and independence, and the serene beneficence that they do. They look from township to township. A fragment of their bark is worth the backs of all the politicians in the union. They are free-soilers in their own broad sense. They send their roots north and south and east and west into many a conservative's Kansas and Carolina, who does not suspect such underground railroads—they improve the subsoil he has never disturbed—and many times their length, if the support of their principles require it. They battle with the tempests of a century. See what scars they bear, what limbs they lost before we were born! Yet they never adjourn; they steadily vote for their principles, and send their roots farther and wider from the *same centre*. They die at their posts, and they leave a tough butt for the choppers to exercise themselves about, and a stump which serves for their monument. They attend no caucus, they make no compromise, they use no policy. Their one principle is growth. They combine a true radicalism with a true conservatism. Their radicalism is not cutting away of roots, but an infinite multiplication and extension of them under all surrounding institutions. They take a firmer hold on the earth that they may rise higher into the heavens. Their conservative heart-wood, in which no sap longer flows, does not impoverish their growth, but is a firm column to support it; and when their expanding trunks no longer require it, it utterly decays. Their conservatism is a dead but solid heartwood, which is the pivot and firm column of support to all this growth, appropriating nothing to itself, but forever by its support assisting to extend the area of their radicalism. Half a century after they are dead at the core, they are preserved by radical reforms. They do not, like men from radicals turn conservative. Their conservative part dies out first; their radical and growing part survives. They acquire new States and Territories, while the old dominions decay and become the habitation of bears and owls and coons. (J, VIII, 139-41)

Not only does the passage recapitulate some of the key principles in the "Economy" chapter of *Walden,* with distinct verbal echoes; it serves as a touchstone of Thoreau's politics as well. "Free-soilers" and "a conservative's Kansas" anticipate his response to John Brown, a "free-soiler" whom he would not meet for another year. The passage is almost a prophecy of the impact of Thoreau upon American social and cultural experience, for he has indeed been a "tough butt for the choppers [critics] to exercise themselves about." Viewed symbolically, the passage also casts doubt upon the conclusion of Leo Stoller that Thoreau's "economic botany . . . attains success because it goes beyond individual plants to deal with the biological community, but he does not apply this ability to think in terms of social organism to the human community."[7] Indeed he does! But the vehicle of his thinking is analogical, his thought decidedly radical.

In "Life Without Principle," published posthumously but first given as a lecture the day after Christmas 1854, Thoreau drew on the arboreal image and its fruit in wondering whether our pursuit of worldly wealth, or fame, or the show of liberty makes us "all husk and shell, with no tender and living kernel to us," and if our institutions are fruitless, "like those chestnut-burs which contain abortive nuts, perfect only to prick the fingers?" (RP, 174). But he concludes more hopefully that the "staple production" of a world, "taxed and drawn out," is "not slaves, nor operatives, but men,—those rare fruits called heroes, saints, poets, philosophers, and redeemers" (RP, 177).

For Thoreau, John Brown was such a rare fruit, a hero who had been party to no Missouri Compromise. Both Thoreau and Brown were native New Englanders: Thoreau had been formally educated at Harvard where, as he once quipped, they taught "all of the branches but none of the roots";[8] Brown was educated in the "great university of the West, where he sedulously pursued the study of Liberty" (RP, 113). Both were "surveyors" in more than the usual sense, Brown sometimes running an imaginary line through a conclave of border ruffians in order to learn their plans against the free-soilers, then resuming his "survey" till he was out of sight (RP, 116); Thoreau using that means of gainful employment to become one with nature, and serve as its "reporter to a journal of no very wide circulation" (Wa, 18).

At once a father figure and an incarnation of the divinely appointed Word of God in his time, John Brown was, for Thoreau, a fruit of the tree of life as well. As extravagant as always, Thoreau found in a name partial confirmation of his expectations of the harvest from this mythic tree; for as Virginia Woolf has sensed, Thoreau seems to have been attached not to John Brown, but to John Brownness.[9] Six months before Brown's raid on Harpers Ferry, Thoreau surmised that "Brown is the color for me, the color of our coats and our daily lives, the color of the poor man's loaf" (J, XII, 97). A week later he reflected that "the peculiar and interesting *Brown Season* of the spring lasts from the time the snow generally begins to go off . . ." (J, XII, 113). His own "Brown Season" would carry through till the end of the year when his journal entries show an obsession with thoughts about John Brown, imprisoned in October. In a season when John Brown was much on his mind, Thoreau ostensibly diverts attention from such matters of politics to note that "the very surface of the earth itself has been rapidly *imbrowned* of late, like the acorns in their cups, in consequence of cold and frost. . . ." (J, XII, 418; emphasis added). In the same entry, significantly, Thoreau disagrees with the general appraisal that the Harper's Ferry raid was a "wild and desperate and insane attempt," calling it, rather, "a well-matured plan" (J, XII, 419). Each one of Brown's party "who there laid down his life for the poor" was thus a "picked man, culled out of many thousands," and he completes the metaphor of arboreal harvest with a ghastly figure, calling these heroes "ripe for the gallows" (J, XII, 420). On December 2, 1859, in seasonal harmony with Thoreau's mythic conception of a hero, John Brown, hanged from the gallows tree, became, for Thoreau, fruit of the tree of life.

Curiously, two days before Brown was captured, Thoreau had been puzzling over the inner sense of humane "letters," an activity that, as we have seen, was a continual source of revelation for him:

> Talk about learning our *letters* and being *literate*! Why the roots of *letters* are *things*. Natural objects and phenomena are the original symbols or types which express our thoughts and feelings, and yet American scholars, having little or no root in the soil, commonly strive with all their might to confine themselves to the imported symbols alone. All the true growth and experience, the living speech, they would fain reject as "Americanisms." It is the old error, which the church, the state, the school ever commit, choosing darkness rather than light, holding fast to the old and to tradition. (J, XII, 389-90)

Certainly by this time—October 16, 1859—John Brown had supplanted Ralph Waldo Emerson in Thoreau's mind as the American Scholar to emulate. Six days after Brown's execution, Thoreau wrote:

> The expression "a *liberal* education" originally meant one worthy of freemen. Such is education simply in a true and broad sense. But education ordinarily so called—the learning of trades and professions which is designed to enable men to earn their living, or to fit them for a particular station in life—is *servile*. (J, XIII, 15)

When Thoreau gleaned this passage for inclusion in "The Last Days of John Brown," he emphasized the philological dimensions of "liberal" that he had found expressed in his ripe hero:

> But taking a hint from the word, I would go a step further and say, that it is not the man of wealth and leisure simply, though devoted to art, or science, or literature, who, in a true sense, is *liberally* educated, but only the earnest and *free* man. In a slaveholding country like this, there can be no such thing as a *liberal* education tolerated by the State; and those scholars of Austria and France who, however learned they may be, are contented under their tyrannies, have received only a *servile* education. (RP, 151)

An influx of long-standing "fossil history" in the terms "frank" and "slave" runs between the journal passage and its essay version. These are terms discussed by Richard Chenevix Trench, whose *On the Study of Words* furnished Thoreau with a hint for his famous "pickerel passage" in "The

Pond in Winter." The "Franks," Trench writes, took to themselves "this proud name of the 'franks' or the free" when they broke up the Roman Empire; and such terms as "frank," "franchise," "enfranchisement," and the like "to express civil liberties and immunities" are outgrowths of this word. He went on to write:

> The word "slave" has undergone a process entirely analogous, although in an opposite direction. The martial superiority of the Teutonic races enabled them to keep their slave markets supplied with captives taken from the Slavonic tribes. Hence, in all the languages of Western Europe, the once glorious name of Slave has come to express the most degraded condition of men. What centuries of violence and warfare does the history of this word disclose.[10]

In Brown's career, Thoreau found the expression of a master of humane letters, letters with Brown being the equivalent of human beings. With a directness of speech that fired his words like a "Sharps' rifle" as straight as a bullet (RP, 127), this free-soiler "would have left a Greek accent slanting the wrong way, and righted up a falling man" (RP, 113). In Thoreau's view, the "Western Humanities" of Brown translated servile, slavish man to an upright condition, a process analogous to Thoreau's translation of the earth's (and man's) servile, lapsarian expression in the Deep Cut (there conveyed by such terms as "lava" and "lapse") to a frank and liberal expression, upright and aspiring.

In his conception of John Brown, the inextricability of Thoreau's language with his vision of the tree of life is clear. It is also discoverable in the sentence that begins what is perhaps the most frequently quoted passage of *Walden*: "I went to the woods because I wished to live deliberately . . ." (Wa, 90-91). In *The Magic Circle of* Walden, Charles Anderson touches on this passage: "Deliberately," he observes, is the "first polysyllable, followed by a marked pause." In Anderson's judgment,

> This is skillful rhetoric, compelling the reader to speak the word slowly in order to take in its full weight (*delibrare*-to weigh). As one critic [F. O. Matthiessen] has summed up the sound effects of this passage: "The measured pace seems in exact correspondence with his carefully measured thoughts, and serves, as effective rhythm always does, to direct the fullest attention to the most important word." The only way to experience life to the full is by meditating on its true values.[11]

Certainly this analysis directs attention to the most significant word in Thoreau's sentence. But for Thoreau, and in part at least subconsciously for the reader with a deep feel for his style, the force of "deliberately" also derives from the "liber" within "deliberately," a product of Thoreau's extended deliberation that opens itself to a flow of life in channels contiguous to those in the "true bark" (Wa, 24) of an archetypal tree of life, and in the moist vital cuticle of the crust of the earth. In such *liber*—as in the volatile truth of a word—life flows, and man experiences this flow of spirits by a fluvial alignment of his own *liber* with that in the tree of life. Flowing through and in such nourishing umbilical cords that link him with divinity (Wk, 78), he frees himself; through a vascular correspondence his expression is liberated. And this is not just by accidental or passive sympathy, but, as the sentence being analyzed suggests, an intentional one that springs from the relation of the speaker to the end perceived, however uncertainly, though clearly with faith: "I *wished* to live *deliberately*. . . ." The co-natural relationship of man and archetypal tree is a flowering of *virtu*, of immortal truth, of the "Chastity" Thoreau wrote of in *Walden* that was "the flower and fruit of a man" (Wa, 77), the highest use to which a thing may be put.

For Thoreau, the flower and fruit of a life of deliberation appeared in the humanities of John Brown, who, when called "to be ground," provided a rich, post-humous soil for the interior life of a people, as Thoreau suggested in his journal entry for March 26, 1856:

> I am sometimes affected by the consideration that a man may spend the whole of his life after boyhood in accomplishing a particular design; as if he were put to a special and petty use, without taking time to look around him and appreciate the phenomenon of his existence. If so many purposes are thus necessarily left unaccomplished, perhaps unthought of, we are reminded of the transient interest we have in *this life*. Our interest in our country, in the spread of liberty, etc., strong and, as it were, innate as it is, cannot be as transient as our present existence here. It cannot be that all those patriots who die in the midst of their career have no further connection with the career of their country. (J, VIII, 229)

Surely this last sentence has a bearing on Thoreau as well, whose incorporated body was laid to rest at age forty-four, but whose in-spirited word, a "tough butt for the choppers" (J, VIII, 140), has tripped up many an incorporated body. When in the 1970s the antiwar movement joined with the civil rights movement against the ecological movement, the former two accused the latter of being a deliberate, politically inspired diversion from their goals: Thoreau's words supplied campaign literature for all three groups. One of our most truly seminal authors, he has supplied words that have been "translated" by Leo Tolstoy and Bertrand Russell; by Henry Salt, Mohandas K. Gandhi, and Martin Luther King; and by John Burroughs, Aldo Leopold, and Rachel Carson. And curiously, behind the visions he projected into all three groups was an intensely relevant philology. Thoreau furnishes a telling example of the unanticipated interrelatedness of apparently disparate human concerns, perhaps the best, certainly the most deliberate, spokesman we have ever had for the liberal arts in America.

*

In his waning years on this globe, Thoreau rejected a suggestion to write a biography of John Brown and instead wrote nature essays on the season of harvests and terminations.[12] Pondering the fall of leaves, the collapse of the year, the diurnal decline of the "Great Western Pioneer" (the sun) that moved with man toward a final Stygian stream, the Pacific (a far-western Concord), Thoreau worked his art to translate such lapses into the dawn of a new life, a final harvest from the tree of life. As a metaphor of his own artistic life, in "Wild Apples" Thoreau describes how the wild apple tree, though annually "cut down" by foraging cattle, does not despair, but puts up more twigs for each one that is chewed off, until the spreading low growth prevents the cattle from coming at the new growth, and then, perhaps twenty years later, "some interior shoot, which their foes cannot reach, darts upward with joy: for it has not forgotten its high calling, and bears its own peculiar fruit in triumph." By such a fall growth the tree, whose shape has come to resemble an hourglass, is similarly inverted, and "lives a second life, as it were" (W, V, 303-5).

Thoreau had anticipated such a second life, an Indian summer and fall harvest after *Walden,* "a second flowering to celebrate the maturity of the fruit" (J, IV, 308). In "Wild Apples," concerned about such a harvest, he ponders the history and myth of the apple tree, and lingers over the name, so inextricably woven into the fabric of man's religion, myth, and language. "Apple" (L. *malus*) provides Thoreau with a philological pun for the thorny apple in which "there is no malice, only some malic acid" (W, V, 304). Singling out the wild apple tree as a fitting symbol for his own life, both having "strayed into the woods from cultivated stock," he tells of his quest for the wild crab-apple: a "half-fabulous" tree that escaped his eye until May 1861, when on his only trip to the western frontier he caught glimpses of it from a moving train in Michigan, and then, eight miles west of St. Anthony's Falls in Minnesota, "touched it and smelled it, and secured a lingering corymb of flowers" for his herbarium (W, V, 301-2). But from this indigenous crab-apple, Thoreau falls back upon the "backwoodsman" among apple trees, descended, like himself, from cultivated stock, "these are the ones whose story we have to tell" (W, V, 302-3).

Less personal, more universal, is the analogy Thoreau draws between the celestial fruit of this tree—the "golden apples of the Hesperides" (W, V, 307)—and knowledge itself. Such "spirited fruit," too commonly left by an indifferent owner who "has not faith enough to look under [his] boughs" (W, V, 309), is ready to hand for the saunterer, though it is palatable only when a touch of frost has mellowed its acrid "*verjuice*." Even then, the fruit is for walkers only, to be eaten out of doors: "The Saunterer's apple not even the saunterer can eat in the house" (W, V, 311). But when time and place are ripe, the saunterer's craving for such "spirited fruit" incites an appeal: "Bring me an apple from the tree of life" (W, V, 314).

To the true saunterer, even the gnarliest apple will "show some redeeming traits" in a Hesperidean redness dashed or sprinkled on its skin, an apple neither like that "which beshrewed the name of wife [Eve], / Nor that whom beauty caused the gold strife [Helen]," an apple "not of Discord, but of Concord . . . apple of the Hesperides, apple of the evening sky" (W, V, 314-15). This is ample harvest from the tree of life whose living waters run their course not in current motions on horizontal planes on the face of the earth, superficially, nor on elevated and empyrean planes without ligature to the earth, in rivers of stars, Milky Ways, but in the veins and liber of an upright tree whose puckery "*verjuice*" flows in vertical planes, then swells the fruit of a "spirited" wild apple, to a ripened, transcendent fruit for the true saunterer.

Thoreau's comment on the appropriate names—"Saunterer's Apple" ("you must lose yourself before you can find the way to that") and "Frozen-Thawed Apple," which must be frozen in order to convert an unpalatable "*verjuice*" to a rich, sweet cider (W, V, 316)—effectively sets up his terminal comment on the "crabbed apple." In the lapse of the year, in the midst of winter in a despairing season, a perfect fruit, "never carried to market" (W, V, 320), is brought to perfection as knowledge, beauty, truth. Thoreau's essay on the fruit of his tree of life closes with a reference to "the word of the Lord that came to Joel," a lament that describes a decadent land and orchards, concluding:

> Be ye ashamed, O ye husbandmen; howl, O ye vinedressers. . . . The vine is dried up, and the fig tree languisheth; the pomegranate tree, the palm tree also, and the apple tree, even all the trees of the field, are withered; because joy is withered away from the sons of men. (W, V, 322; cf. Joel, 1)

This is not a lament that the time of fruit has passed, but that the time of fruition is always passing, and is ever at hand—a time for the harvest of beans, seeds of hope that ripen to seeds of faith. For Thoreau, the lament is epitomized in the apples, especially wild apples whose immortal *verjuice* is a product of a liquid *verite* flowing vertically in the liber of the tree of life, gathering to spirited fruit in heavenly groves, there to be savored by saunterers who, like the apples themselves, have survived a winter of discontent and lost themselves, only to find themselves, like the frozen-thawed apples, with a flavor "borrowed . . . from heaven through the medium of the air in which they hang" (W, V, 320).[13]

*

In "Walking," Thoreau deals with a Hesperidean West complementary to his Hesperidean fruit: that "every tree sends its fibres forth in search of the Wild" applies no less to the saunterer than to the Saunterer's Apple. Thoreau defines the exercise of a "Saunterer" as "no more vagrant than the meandering river," for he is a "Holy Lander" whose "every walk is a sort of crusade . . . to go forth and reconquer this Holy Land from the hands of the Infidels" (W, V, 205-6). To sustain the idea that one must undergo a conversion from the civil to the wild in order to become a "part and parcel of Nature," Thoreau twice paraphrases the Bible, in contending that "You must be born into the family of the Walkers," and in remarking that some of his townsmen can remember "walks which they took ten years ago, in which they were so blessed as to lose themselves for half an hour in the woods."[14] "Like a camel, which is said to be the only beast which ruminates when walking," the true saunterer integrates physical and spiritual exercises to go "in search of the springs of life" (W, V, 209-10). Most walkers, however, are content with a superficial journey to the "trivial or quadrivial place," where all roads tend, to the "village," a word with analogies in the "Latin word *vilis* and our vile: also villain," and these walkers ignore the wilder roads that alone "may be trodden with profit," such as the "Old Marlborough Road."[15]

> Nobody repairs it,
> For nobody wears it;
> It is a living way,
> As the Christians say.

Along such a living way, in the wild places, men should saunter, "before the evil days come" (W, V, 213-16).

By a "subtle magnetism in Nature," Thoreau's own sauntering inclines to a path "perfectly symbolical of the path which we love to travel in the interior and ideal world." For mankind generally this inclination is toward a west of myth and fable, rather than an east of history, where he goes "only by force" (W, V, 217). The southeastward migration of mankind from Europe to Australia is the exceptional "retrograde movement" that only proves the general westering tendency of man. But "something akin to the migratory instincts in birds and quadrupeds" diverts Thoreau's own inclination somewhat to the southwest, toward the Indian heaven, holy land, source of the thawing breezes of spring. Modified by such wild deviations, his general inclination is yet with that "Great Western Pioneer," the sun, whose diurnal lapse "inspires me with the desire to go to a West as distant and as fair as that into which the sun goes down. He appears to migrate westward daily, and tempt us to follow him" to a West perceptible only in dreams and moments of a sudden influx of transcendent light:

> We dream all night of those mountains—ridges in the horizon, though they may be of vapor only, which were last gilded by his [the sun's] rays. The island of Atlantis, and the islands and gardens of the Hesperides, a sort of terrestrial paradise, appear to have been the Great West of the ancients, enveloped in mystery and poetry. Who has not seen in imagination, when looking into the sunset sky, the gardens of the Hesperides, and the foundations of all those fables?" (W, V, 219)

Locally, the saunterer finds a preserving "wildness" in those "impervious and quaking swamps" that to civilization signify the loss of hope—John Bunyan's or any man's "Dismal Swamp" or "Slough of Despond." But deep in the quaking swamps, the Concord saunterer finds himself in a region most provocative of hope. "My spirits infallibly rise in proportion to the outward dreariness. . . . When I would recreate myself, I seek the darkest wood, the thickest and most interminable and, to the citizens, most dismal swamp. I enter a swamp as a sacred place,—a *sanctum sanctorum*." Thoreau later elaborates his veiled allusion to Dante in the "darkest wood" by an account of how he once surveyed a farmer's swamp "at whose entrance might have been written the words which Dante read over the entrance to the infernal regions,—'Leave all hope, ye that enter.' " And yet the farmer "did not despair, but valued his swamps above all the rest of his land" (W, V, 226-30).

An expression of such "Genius," of positive will, is a "light which makes the darkness visible," and whoever would express such light must do so extravagantly:

> Where is the literature which gives expression to Nature? He would be a poet who could impress the winds and streams into his service, to speak for him; who nailed words to their primitive senses; as farmers drive down stakes in the spring, which the frost has heaved; who derived his words as often as he used them,—transplanted them to his page with earth adhering to their roots; whose words were so true and fresh and natural that they would appear to expand like the buds at the approach of spring, though they lay half-smothered between two musty leaves in a library,—ay, to bloom and bear fruit there, after their kind, annually, for the faithful reader, in sympathy with surrounding Nature. (W, V, 231-32)

The extravagant expression of such wild enlightenment is limited by a "Useful Ignorance," for we cannot attain to knowledge, only a "Sympathy with Intelligence," and thus cannot aspire to be a source of illumination, but only to be sun*like,* children of the light, our knowledge being *as*

> the lighting up of the mist by the sun. Man cannot *know* in any higher sense than this, any more than he can look serenely and with impunity in the face of the sun. . . . Live free, child of the mist,—and with respect to knowledge we are all children of the mist. (W, V, 239-40)

Children of the mist, children of the light, are few because man fails to respond to his wild, migratory instinct. "We have to be told that the Greeks called the world κόσμος Beauty, or Order, but we do not see clearly why they did so, and we esteem it at best only a curious philological fact." Thoreau finds his own life in this order, κόσμος, altogether too rare, for he thinks of himself as living only

> a sort of border life, on the confines of a world into which I make occasional and transient forays only, and my patriotism and allegiance to the state into whose territories I seem to retreat are those of a moss-trooper. Unto a life which I call natural I would gladly follow even a will-o'-the-wisp through bogs and sloughs unimaginable, but no moon or firefly has shown me the causeway to it. Nature is a personality so vast and universal that we have never seen one of her features. The walker in the familiar fields which stretch around my native town sometimes finds himself in another land . . . in some faraway field on the confines of the actual Concord, where her jurisdiction ceases, and the idea which the word Concord suggests ceases to be suggested. (W, V, 242)

At this border, Thoreau has sometimes seen farms that "appear dimly still as through a mist," when "the world with which we are commonly acquainted leaves no trace." Some afternoons before at Spaulding Farm he had seen such a farm, inhabited by children of the mist:

> I saw the setting sun lighting up the opposite side of a stately pine wood. Its golden rays straggled into the aisles of the wood as into some noble hall. I was impressed as if some ancient and altogether admirable and shining family had settled there in that part of the land called Concord, unknown to me,—to whom the sun was servant,—who had not gone into society in the village,—who had not been called on. . . . Their house was not obvious to vision; the trees grew through it. I do not know whether I heard the sounds of a suppressed hilarity or not. They seemed to recline on the sunbeams. . . . The farmer's cart-path, which leads directly through their hall, does not in the least put them out, as the muddy bottom of a pool is sometimes seen through the reflected skies. They never heard of Spaulding, and do not know that he is their neighbor. . . . (W, V, 243)

From these children "there was no noise of labor. I did not perceive that they were weaving or spinning." But Thoreau seemed to hear, "when the wind lulled and hearing was done away, the finest imaginable sweet musical hum,—as of a distant hive in May,—which perchance was the sound of their thinking." Yet it was

> difficult to remember them. They fade irrevocably out of my mind even now while I speak, and endeavor to recall them and recollect myself. It is only after a long and serious effort to recollect my best thoughts that I become again aware of their cohabitancy. If it were not for such families as this, I think I should move out of Concord. (W, V, 243-44)

As dawn is the climactic moment in *Walden,* sunset is the climactic moment in "Walking." Amidst the ending of the day, the children of the mist and the light, hope mounts to discovery, matures to faith and possession. If Thoreau sees in the New England scene fewer winged hopes, fewer pigeons returning, "few and fewer thoughts visit[ing] each growing man from year to year," still faith endures. "In some more genial season, perchance, a faint shadow flits across the landscape of the mind, cast by the *wings* of some thought in its vernal or autumnal migration." The shadow cast by such a thought is a corollary to the expression of the hope-filled lobe (*speca*) in *Walden* that rises to a winged faith in the soaring hawk that lives in the light. The shadow of doubt and the wing of faith correlate even if the faithlessness of contemporary society is in winged thoughts that, having been clipped, have "turned to poultry" (paltry?) and "no longer soar" but "attain only to a Shanghai and Cochin-China grandeur" instead of an Oriental wonder. "Those *gra-a-ate* thoughts, those *gra-a-ate* men you hear of!" Thoreau exclaims in exasperation over the persistence of civilization's quiet desperation and avoidance of the light (W, V, 244).

But if civilized man with earthbound thoughts is ever discounting the evidences of faith about him, the uncivil, wild man is "well paid" for entertaining them, as Thoreau indicates in his "account" of climbing a white pine tree. By his climb he discovered "much more of the earth and the heavens" on the ends of the "topmost branches" than he might have by circumambulating the tree for the whole of his "three-score years and ten." For here were some "few minute and delicate red cone-like blossoms, the fertile flower of the white pine looking heavenward." To the village inhabitants, the flower of the white pine was utterly unknown, "not one had ever seen the like before, but they wondered as at a star dropped down. . . . Nature has from the first expanded the minute blossoms of the forest only toward the heavens, above men's heads and unobserved by them." To Thoreau, wild enough to climb this tree of life and discover its fruit, here was "a newer testament,—the gospel according to this moment," a constant "expression of the health and soundness of Nature . . . healthiness as of a spring burst forth . . . to celebrate this last instant of time . . . a pure morning joy" (W, V, 244-46).

While "Walking" concludes with a "remarkable sunset one day last November," the manner of expressing it effectually translates sunset and November, with their terminal implications, to sunrise and spring, with implications of a new life. Walking in a meadow, the source of a small brook, Thoreau notices

when the sun at last, just before setting, after a cold, gray day, reached a clear stratum in the horizon, and the softest, brightest *morning sunlight* fell on the dry grass and on the stems of the trees in the opposite horizon and on the leaves of the shrub oaks on the hillside, while our shadows stretched long over the meadow eastward, as if we were the only motes in its beams. It was such a light as we could not have imagined a moment before, and the air also was so warm and serene that nothing was wanting to make a paradise of that meadow. When we reflected that this was not a solitary phenomenon, never to happen again, but that it would happen forever and ever, an infinite number of evenings, and cheer and reassure the latest child that walked there, it was more glorious still. (W, V, 246-47; emphasis added)

Then, as at the conclusion of "Spring," Thoreau presents a scene bathed in resplendent autumnal twilight:

The sun sets on some retired meadow, where no house is visible, with all the glory and splendor that it lavishes on cities, and perchance as it has never set before,—where there is but a solitary marsh hawk to have his wings gilded by it, or only a musquash looks out from his cabin, and there is some little black-veined brook in the midst of the marsh, just beginning to meander, winding slowly round a decaying stump. We walked in so pure and bright a light, gilding the withered grass and leaves, so softly and serenely bright, I thought I had never bathed in such a golden flood, without a ripple or a murmur to it. The west side of every wood and rising ground gleamed like the boundary of Elysium, and the sun on our backs seemed like a gentle herdsman driving us home at evening. (W, V, 247)

The fall of the sun to the western horizon, and by analogy the Fall of man, is here made tropical, turned, to a spring morning "softly and serenely bright," whose "golden flood" bathes the narrator, sauntering at the boundary of Elysium in close communion with the small, black-veined brook, companion to the frost-sealed brook he had written of in the first months of his journal—meandering through a meadow, just beginning its expression.[16]

The final paragraph of Thoreau's posthumous essay is similarly prospective: "So we saunter toward the Holy Land, till one day the sun shall shine more brightly than ever he has done, shall perchance shine into our minds and hearts, and light up our whole lives with a great awakening light, as warm and serene and golden as on a bankside in autumn" (W, V, 247-48). Wildly, tropically, extravagantly, the passage extends a comment in the "Conclusion" chapter of *Walden* that in view of the future or possible, we should live quite laxly and undefined in front, our outlines dim and misty on that side; as our shadows reveal an insensible perspiration toward the sun. The volatile truth of our words should continually betray the inadequacy of the residual statement. Their truth is instantly *translated*; its literal monument alone remains. The words which express our faith and piety are not definite; yet they are significant and fragrant like frankincense to superior natures. (Wa, 324-25)

In "Wild Apples" and "Walking," the volatile truth is the fruit and flower of the tree of life. The sudden burst of light—"*Ex-Oriente lux*"—in "Walking" overtakes and glorifies man's mythic, westering tendency. From a New World perspective, a Hesperidean sky rays over that broader Concord of the West, the Pacific. A Hesperidean fruit, a Hesperidean light—volatile, fragrant, tantalizing—are all that is permitted to mortal sense of the fruit of the tree of life, and then only to a traveler deep in concord who had stumbled upon "some upland pasture—where the John's / wort grew" (PJ, I, 352; J, I, 304).

*

In a "Summing-Up" of the 1978 conference "Psychology and the Literary Artist: A Case Study of Henry David Thoreau," Norman Holland suggested that for him, at least, any theme-and-variations conception of Thoreau's identity—his "characterology" in the sense of the word borrowed from Lichtenstein—would include the "balancing [of] a movement of loosening and flying out with an opposite movement of tying and binding in."[17] As an illustration of this aspect of Thoreau's characterology, Holland cited the opening four lines of Thoreau's most frequently anthologized poem, "Sic Vita":

I am a parcel of vain strivings tied
By a chance bond together,
Dangling this way and that, their links
Were made so loose and wide,
Methinks,
For milder weather.

The remainder of the poem fittingly projects the radical—should I say "radicle"?—bent of the genius that in Thoreau would unfold to a tree of life:

A bunch of violets without their roots,
And sorrel intermixed,
Encircled by a wisp of straw
Once coiled about their shoots,
The law
By which I'm fixed.

A nosegay which Time clutched from out
Those fair Elysian fields,
With weeds and broken stems, in haste,
Doth make the rabble rout
That waste
The day he yields.

And here I bloom for a short hour unseen,
Drinking my juices up,
With no root in the land
To keep my branches green,
But stand
In a bare cup.

Some tender buds were left upon my stem
In mimicry of life,
But ah! the children will not know,
Till time has withered them,
The woe
With which they're rife.

But now I see I was not plucked for naught,
And after in life's vase
Of glass set while I might survive,
But by a kind hand brought
Alive
To a strange place.

That stock thus thinned will soon redeem its hours,
And by another year,
Such as God knows, with freer air,
More fruits and fairer flowers
Will bear,
While I droop here.

(CP, 81-82)

The story behind the poem has become familiar: to express his adulation of Mrs. Lucy Jackson Brown, Emerson's sister-in-law, Thoreau, while home from college in May 1837, "gathered a bunch of violets and tossed them in through her window" with a copy of his poem, as Walter Harding summarizes.[18] To be sure each stanza of this shaped poem visually resembles Thoreau's casual bouquet and suggests the polarities of the loose and the bound that Holland discerns in the stylistic patterning of Thoreau. But other details of this early poem suggest a precarious moment for Thoreau, about to leave the period of his formal education at

Harvard. Only by putting down roots to grow in a different soil would the growth so far nourished survive to bear fruit.

Fourteen years later, Thoreau would write of being affected by such anomalous workings of Nature "as the various red and yellow excrescences on young oaks. . . . As if a poet were born who had designs in his head" (J, II, 416). In his final saunterings, the workings of Nature clarified the designs in his head in the shape of a tree of life. In life as in art, he had first tracked his peculiar genius as expressed halfway in the law of currents, then, having moved to Walden Pond, halfway in the law of vegetation. If the unfolding design of nature had first been perceived as a gall—a shallow but fatal cut in his brother's finger, a deep cut in a hillside near Walden Pond—it became, through the artistry of Concord's most deliberate saunterer, fit material for translation, fertile ground for a sauntering imagination that in the high pastures of the imagination would discover the tree of life, and eat of its fruit.

*

In the Book of Proverbs are four of the eleven biblical references to the "tree of life":

> She is a tree of life to them that lay hold upon her: and happy is every one that retaineth her. (3:18)
>
> The fruit of the righteous is a tree of life. (11:30)
>
> Hope deferred maketh the heart sick, but when the desire cometh, it is a tree of life. (13:12)
>
> A wholesome tongue is a tree of life. (15:4)

"Backing" Concord in 1850, Thoreau had faced the "oceans and wildernesses far away, the materials out of which a million Concords can be made . . . there too I am at home. Nature is as far from me as God, and sometimes I have thought to go West after her" (J, II, 46-47). In 1861, with hope deferred, Thoreau journeyed to Minnesota in quest of the wild, and of the tree that bore the wildest fruit of all. Though his discovery of an actual wild crab-apple tree in Minnesota was an eleventh-hour boon, what the Concord saunterer sought with side-of-the-eye vision was a mythic *wild* fruit, and a mythic *wild* west. In 1853 he had soberly glossed the meaning of "wild" in the pages of his journal:

> Trench says a wild man is a *willed* man. Well, then, a man of will who does what he wills or wishes, a man of hope and of the future tense, for not only the obstinate is willed, but far more the constant and persevering. The obstinate man, properly

speaking, is one who will not. The perseverance of the saints is positive willedness, not a mere passive willingness. The fates are wild, for they *will*; and the Almighty is wild above all, as fate is. (J, IV, 482)

And so Thoreau, in deliberate sympathy with the divinely wild, stepped west as saunterer in quest of the wild apple of the evening sky and tree of life, the apple not of Discord, but of Concord. To taste its fruit was to taste of an atonement where Nature and the word were one.

Appendix A

The following is Thoreau's commentary on a passage from Asa Gray's Manual of Botany, recorded in Thoreau's journal entry for May 20, 1851. (The whole of the long passage is quoted here, with Gray's words italicized in order to make Thoreau's comments evident. The bracketed portions are Thoreau's.) Thoreau's personal copy was a first edition (Boston & Cambridge: James Munroe and Company, 1848) presently in the Special Collection at Middlebury College, Vermont. I am grateful to Robert Buckeye, Curator, for permission to examine Thoreau's copy.

May 20. Tuesday. There is, no doubt, a perfect analogy between the life of the human being and that of the vegetable, both of the body and the mind. The botanist Gray says:—

> *The organs of plants are of two sorts:— 1. Those of* Vegetation, *which are concerned in growth,—by which the plant takes in the aerial and earthy matters on which it lives, and elaborates them into the materials of its own organized substance; 2. Those of* Fructification *or* Reproduction, *which are concerned with the propagation of the species.*

So is it with the human being. I am concerned first to come to my *Growth,* intellectually and morally (and physically, of course, as a means to this, for the body is the symbol of the soul), and then to bear my *Fruit,* do my *Work, propagate* my kind, not only physically but *morally,* not only in body but in mind.

> *The organs of vegetation are the* Root, Stem, *and* Leaves. *The* Stem *is the axis and original basis of the plant. The first point of the stem preexists in the embryo (i.e. in the rudimentary plantlet contained within the seed): it is here called the radicle.*

Such is the rudiment of mind, already partially developed, more than a bud, but pale, having never been exposed to the light, and slumbering coiled up, packed away in the seed, unfolded [*sic*].

Consider the still pale, rudimentary, infantine, radicle-like thoughts of some students, which who knows what they might expand to, if they should ever come to the light and air, if they do not become rancid and perish in the seed. It is not every seed that will survive a thousand years. Other thoughts further developed, but yet pale and languid, like shoots grown in a cellar.

> *The plant . . . develops from the first in two opposite directions,* viz. *upwards* [to expand in the light and air] *to produce and continue the stem (or ascending*

> *axis), and downwards* [avoiding the light] *to form the root (or* descending *axis). The former is ordinarily or in great part aerial, the latter subterranean.*

So the mind develops from the first in two opposite directions: upwards to expand in the light and air; and downwards avoiding the light to form the root. One half is aerial, the other subterranean. The mind is not well balanced and firmly planted, like the oak, which has not as much root as branch, whose roots like those of the white pine are slight and near the surface. One half of the mind's development must still be root,—in the embryonic state, in the womb of nature, more unborn than at first. For each successive new idea or bud, a new rootlet in the earth. The growing man penetrates yet deeper by his roots into the womb of things. The infant is comparatively near the surface, just covered from the light; but the man sends down a tap-root to the centre of things.

The mere logician, the mere reasoner, who weaves his arguments as a tree its branches in the sky,—nothing equally developed in the roots,—is overthrown by the first wind.

As with the roots of the plant, so with the roots of the mind, the branches and branchlets of the root *"are mere repetitions for the purpose of multiplying the absorbing points, which are chiefly the growing or newly formed extremities, sometimes termed* spongelets. *It bears no other organs."*

So this organ of the mind's development, the *Root,* bears no organs but spongelets or absorbing points.

Annuals, which perish root and all the first season, especially have slender and thread-like fibrous roots. But biennials are particularly characterized by distended, fleshy roots containing starch, a stock for future growth, to be consumed during their second or flowering season,—as carrots, radishes, turnips. Perennials frequently have many thickened roots clustered together, tuberous or palmate roots, fasciculated or clustered as in the dahlia, peony, etc.

Roots may spring from any part of the stem under favorable circumstances; *"that is to say in darkness and moisture, as when covered by the soil or resting on its surface."*

That is, the most clear and ethereal ideas (Antaeus-like) readily ally themselves to the earth, to the primal womb of things. They put forth roots as soon as branches; they are eager to be *soiled.* No thought soars so high that it sunders these apron strings of its mother. The thought that comes to light, that pierces the empyrean on the other side, is wombed and rooted in darkness, a moist and fertile darkness,—its roots in Hades like the tree of life. No idea is so soaring but it will readily put forth roots. Wherever there is an air-and-light-seeking bud about to expand, it may become in the earth a darkness-seeking root. Even swallows and birds-of-paradise *can* walk on the ground. To quote the sentence from Gray entire: *"Roots not only spring from the root-end of the primary stem in germination, but also from any subsequent part of the stem under favorable circumstances, that is to say, in darkness and moisture, as when covered by the soil or resting on its surface."*

No thought but is connected as strictly as a flower, with the earth. The mind flashes not so far on one side but its rootlets, its spongelets, find their way instantly on the other side into a moist darkness, uterine,—a low bottom in the heavens, even miasma-exhaling to such immigrants as are not acclimated. A cloud is uplifted to sustain its roots. Imbosomed in clouds as in a chariot, the mind drives through the boundless fields of space. Even there is the dwelling of Indra.

I might here quote the following, with the last—of roots: "*They may even strike in the open air and light, as is seen in the copious aerial rootlets by which the Ivy, the Poison Ivy, and the Trumpet Creeper climb and adhere to the trunks of trees or other bodies; and also in Epiphytes or Air-plants, of most warm regions, which have no connection whatever with the soil, but germinate and grow high in air on the trunks or branches of trees, etc.; as well as in some terrestrial plants, such as the Banian and Mangrove, that send off aerial roots from their trunks or branches, which finally reach the ground.*"

So, if our light-and-air-seeking tendencies extend too widely for our original root or stem, we must send downward new roots to ally us to the earth.

Also there are parasitic plants which have their roots in the branches or roots of other trees, as the mistletoe, the beech-drops, etc. There are minds which so have their roots in other minds as in the womb of nature,—if, indeed, most are not such?!

(J, II, 201-05)

Appendix B

TABLE I

This is a list of *possible* simple English words of one syllable, constructed on the principles derived from paragraph 7 of "Spring": words constructed with the radical consonants *l* and *b* (or a variation of the latter: *p, f, v*), arranged in that order, with an intervening vowel (*a, e, i, o, u*—digraphs are discounted in this listing). The *e* in parentheses and the terminal *s* suggest variations, chiefly pluralizations, of these possible words, without the addition of a second syllable. The occurrence of an additional initial consonant in a one syllable word is not here given—for instance, *slip*—though numerous possibilities exist and may be entertained by the reader.

lab(e)s	lap(e)s	laf(e)s	lav(e)s
leb(e)s	lep(e)s	lef(e)s	lev(e)s
lib(e)s	lip(e)s	lif(e)s	liv(e)s
lob(e)s	lop(e)s	lof(e)s	lov(e)s
lub(e)s	lup(e)s	luf(e)s	luv(e)s

TABLE II

This is a list of actual words occurring in paragraphs 6 through 9 (the sand foliage paragraphs) of "Spring," that employ the radical letters *l* and *b* (or a variation of the latter: *p, f, v*) arranged in that order, with or without intervening vowels or diagraphy (*pulpy* and *leaves,* for instance, are included here), and comprised of one or more syllables. Foreign words, Greek or Latin, are included in this list—so also such nonwords as *lb* and *glb.* The words are listed in the order in which they occur in each of the four paragraphs.

PARAGRAPH 6
FREQUENCY OF USE

Word	*In this paragraph*	*In paras. 6–9*	*In whole of "Spring"*	*In whole of* Walden*
slopes	1	1	1	1
lava	1	1	1	1
overlap	1	1	1	2
half	2	2	4	63
leaves	2	9	10	49
pulpy	1	2	2	2
lobed	1	1	1	1
leopards'	1	1	1	1
itself	1	6	7	49
Total	11	24	28	169

PARAGRAPH 7
FREQUENCY OF USE

Word	*In this paragraph*	*In paras. 6 8, 8, and 9*	*In whole of "Spring"*	*In whole of* Walden*
laboratory	1	1	1	1
globe	5	6	6	18
leaf	3	8	8	22
itself	3	6	7	49
leaves	4	9	10	49
labors	1	1	1	8
lobe	1	1	1	1
liver	1	2	2	3
leaves	1	1	1	1
λείβω	1	1	1	1
labor	1	2	2	2
lapsus	1	1	1	1
slip	1	1	1	2
lapsing	1	1	1	1
λοβος	1	1	1	1
globus	1	1	1	1
lobe	2	3	3	3
lap	1	1	1	1
flap	1	1	1	1
leaf	1	1	1	1
lb	1	1	1	1
lobed	2	2	2	2
glb	1	1	1	1
pulp	1	1	2	2
Total	37	54	57	173

PARAGRAPH 8
FREQUENCY OF USE

Word	*In this paragraph*	*In paras. 6 8, 8, and 9*	*In whole of "Spring"*	*In whole of* Walden*
itself	2	6	7	49
silvery	1	1	3	6
pulpy	1	2	2	2
leaves	1	9	10	49
leaf	3	8	8	22
lobes	3	3	3	3
lobe	2	3	3	3
lip	1	1	1	1
labium	1	1	1	1
labor	1	2	2	2
laps	1	1	1	1
lapses	1	1	1	1
Total	18	38	42	140

PARAGRAPH 9

leaf	2	8	8	22
hieroglyphic	1	1	1	1
liver	1	2	2	3
globe	1	6	6	18
leaves	2	9	10	49
living	2	2	4	39
life	2	2	10	192
Total	11	30	41	324

*The number in this column, and the means of arriving at the number in the previous column are provided by Stephen Sherwin and Richard Reynolds, *Word Index* to Walden (Charlottesville, Va.: Univ. of Virginia Press, 1960). The *Walden* text I use here is the Princeton edition (1971).

The high incidence of such words in the sand foliage paragraphs is readily apparent and is further emphasized by the fact that in neither of the framing paragraphs—5 or 10 (a combined word count of 143)—is there a single instance of the use of this kind of word. In the whole of "Spring" (26 paragraphs), this word type occurs 138 times, of which 77 (55.8 percent) are in the four sand foliage paragaraphs.

TABLE III

This table attempts to bring together the theoretical and the actual in the sand foliage paragraphs: following each theoretical word of one syllable (in column 1), the actual words occurring in paragraphs 6-9 (sometimes of more than one syllable) that most nearly conform to the type are listed. Words having no vowel intervening between the two radicals are classified by a transposition of the preceding consonant and appear in parentheses, thus: (pulpy).

Theoretical Words	*Actual Words in 6-9*
lab(e)s	laboratory, labors, *labor, lb, glb, labium*
leb(e)s	λείβω
lib(e)s	none
lob(e)s	lobed, globe, *lobe,* λοβος, *globus,* lobe, single lobed, double lobed, lobes
lub(e)s	none
lap(e)s	overlap, *lapsus,* lapsing, lap, flap, laps, lapses
lep(e)s	leopards'
lip(e)s	slip, lip
lop(e)s	slopes
lup(e)s	(pulpy), (pulp)
laf(e)s	(half)
lef(e)s	(itself), leaf, *leaf*
lif(e)s	hieroglyphic, life
lof(e)s	none
luf(e)s	none
lav(e)s	lava
lef(e)s	leaves, *leaves*
lif(e)s	(silvery), liver, living
lov(e)s	none
luv(e)s	none

Of the *theoretical* words listed above, only two of the seven types that Thoreau fails to draw on by actual English words are *real* possibilities. Of the five words beginning with *leb-* that are entered in the *American Heritage Dictionary,* four are proper nouns, the fifth a recently Anglicized Germanic word: *lebensraum. Lub-* presents, to Thoreau, the unreal choices of lube (too modern and mechanically oriented) and *lubber* (too nautical). So too *luf-*: only *luff*—a technical nautical term. *Luv-* presents no possibilities in English; and *lof-* offers only *loft,* though *loaf* and *loaves* are possibilities if a digraph is considered. Only *lib-* and *lov-*, therefore, are solid possibilities not taken advantage of by Thoreau in the sand foliage paragraphs. But *leb-*,[1] *leb-*,[2] *leup-,* and the like, should be consulted in the appendix "Indo-European Roots" of the AHD.

Appendix C

The following four versions of "The first sparrow of spring" passage (paragraph 13 in "Spring"), as printed in parallel columns in J. Lyndon Shanley, *The Making of Walden* (Chicago: Univ. of Chicago Press, 1957), pp. 42-45, furnish evidence of the genetic process whereby Thoreau, over a period of more than ten years, brought into ever sharper focus the "root" myth of *Walden.* The journal source having been dated September 29, 1843, Shanley estimates the composition date of "Version I" as 1846-47 (p. 24), and of "Version V" as 1853 (pp. 31-32). Walden was published on August 9, 1845.

*Journal of September 29, 1843**

HM 13182

The first sparrow of spring. The year beginning with younger hope than ever. The faint [first?] silvery warblings heard over the bare dank fields as if the last flakes of winter tinkled. What then are histories, chronologies—traditions, and written revelations. Flakes of war sunlight fall on the congealed earth—the brooks and rills sing carols and glees for the spring. The marsh hawk already seeks the first slimy life that awakes—The sough of melting snow is heard in the dells of the wood, by the sunny river banks, and the ice dissolves in the seething ponds, evaporating hourly. The earth sends forth as it were an inward green heat and the grass flames up on the warm hill sides like a green spring fire. Methinks the sight

Version I

The first sparrow of spring—the year beginning with younger hope than ever—the faint silvery warblings heard over the bare and moist fields from the song-sparrow—the bluebird—and the red-wing—as if the last flakes of winter tinkled as they fell.—What at such a time are histories—chronologies—traditions, and all written revelations?

The brooks sing carols and glees to the spring—the marsh-hawk—sailing low over the meadow—is already seeking the first slimy life that awakes. The sough of melting snow is heard in all dells and on all hillsides—and by the sunny river banks—and the ice dissolves apace in all ponds. The earth sends forth an inward heat to greet the returning

*For the Princeton edition version of the journal passage, see PJ, I, 469-70.

The Princeton version gives the beginning of the third sentence as "The first silvery . . ." and indicates new paragraphs at "The marsh hawk . . ." and "So the human life. . . ."

Version V

The first sparrow of spring—the year beginning with younger hope than ever—the faint silvery warblings heard over the bare and moist fields from the song-sparrow—the blue-bird & the red-wing, as if the last flakes of winter tinkled as they fell—What at such a time are histories—chronologies—traditions and all written revelations? The brooks sing carols and glees to the spring. The marsh hawk sailing low over the meadow is already seeking the first slimy life that awakes. The sough of melting snow is heard in all dells and on all hillsides, and by the sunny river banks—and the ice dissolves apace in all ponds. As if the earth sent forth an inward heat to greet the returning sun, the grass flames up on all hillsides like a spring fire—not yellow but green is the color of earth's flame; the symbol of perpetual youth, its blade, like a long green ribbon streaming from the sod into the summer, checked indeed by

Published Text

The first sparrow of spring! The year beginning with younger hope than ever! The faint silvery warblings heard over the partially bare and moist fields from the bludebird, the song sparrow, and the red-wing, as if the last flakes of winter tinkled as they fell! What at such a time are histories, chronologies, traditions, and all written revelations? The brooks sing carols and glees to the spring. The marsh hawk, sailing low over the meadow, is already seeking the first slimy life that awakes. The sinking sound of melting snow is heard in all dells, and the ice dissolves apace in the ponds. The grass flames up on the hillsides like a spring fire,—"et primitus oritur herba imbribus primoribus evocata,"—as if the earth sent forth an inward heat to greet the returning sun; not yellow but green is the color of its flame;—the symbol of perpetual youth, the grass-blade, like a long green ribbon, streams from the sod into the summer, of the first sod of fresh grass in the spring would make the reformer reconsider his schemes, the faithless and despairing man revive—The grass blade is a perpetual growth a long green ribbon—streaming from the sod into the summer—checked indeed by the frost—but anon pushing on again lifting its withered hay with fresh life below.—I have seen where early in spring the clumps of grass stood with their three inches of new green upholding their withered spears of the last autumn, and from year to year the herds browse and the mower cuts from this never failing out-welling supply—what their needs require. So the human life but dies down to the surface, but puts forth a green blade to eternity.

The grass blade is as steady a growth as the rill which leaks out of the ground—indeed it is almost identical with that, for in the vigorous fertile days of June when the rills are dry the grass blades are their channel.

sun—not yellow like the sun—but green is the color of its flame.

The grass flames up on all hillsides like a spring fire. Grass is the symbol of perpetual youth its blade like a long green ribbon—longer than was ever woven in the factories of men—streaming from the sod into the summer—checked indeed by the frost, but anon pushing on again—lifting its last year's spear of withered hay with the fresh life below.—It is as steady a growth as the rill which oozes out of the ground, and indeed is almost identical with that—for in the fertile and growing days of June, when the rills are dry—the grass blades are their channels—and from year to year the herds drink at this green stream—and the mower cuts from this out- welling supply—what their several needs require.—So our human life but dies down to the surface of nature—but puts forth its green blade still to eternity.

the frost, but anon pushing on again—lifting its last year's spear of withered hay with the fresh life below. It grows as steadily as the rill which oozes out of the ground, indeed is almost identical with that, for in the growing days of June when the rills are dry, the grass blades are their channels, and from year to year the herds drink at this perennial green stream, and the mower cuts from this out-welling supply what their several needs require. So our human life but dies down to its root, and still puts forth its green blade to eternity.

checked indeed by the frost, but anon pushing on again, lifting its spear of last year's hay with the fresh life below. It grows as steadily as the rill oozes out of the ground. It is almost identical with that, for in the growing days of June, when the rills are dry, the grass-blades are their channels, and from year to year the herds drink at this perennial green stream, and the mower draws from it betimes their winter supply. So our human life but dies down to its root, and still puts forth its green blade to eternity.

Notes

Chapter 1

1. For an account of Emerson's purchase of "The Briars" and Thoreau's residence on that site, see Walter Harding, *The Days of Henry Thoreau* (Princeton: Princeton Univ. Press, 1982), pp. 179- 81; and of the railroad's commerce in the ice of Walden Pond, p. 189. See also Robert D. Richardson, Jr., "The Railroad Comes to Concord," in *Henry Thoreau: A Life of the Mind* (Berkeley: Univ. of California Press, 1986), pp. 137-39.

2. See Leo Marx, *The Machine in the Garden* (New York: Oxford Univ. Press, 1964), pp. 242-65.

3. Gail Sheehy, "The Creative Crisis," in *Passages: Predictable Crises of Adult Life* (New York: E. P. Dutton, 1976), pp. 255-57; Sheehy mentions Thoreau only in passing, p. 237. Richard Lebeaux, *Young Man Thoreau* (Amherst: Univ. of Massachusetts Press, 1977). Lebeaux, *Thoreau's Seasons* (Amherst: Univ. of Massachusetts Press, 1984), discusses the Deep Cut on pp. 149-50, 154, and 191. Daniel J. Levinson, *The Seasons of a Man's Life* (New York: Ballantine, 1978). Lebeaux, in "Thoreau's Lives, Lebeaux's Lives," in *Introspection in Biography,* ed. Samuel H. Baron and Carl Pletsch (Hillsdale, N.J.: Analytic Press, 1985), pp. 225-48, discusses as a psychobiographer his long-term involvement with Thoreau, and the perspectives provided him by Sheehy, Levinson, and others (p. 247).

4. In his third adventure, he was committed—and here the passive voice prevails—to the Concord jail for not paying his taxes, the literary result of which was "Resistance to Civil Government," or, as it is more popularly known, "Civil Disobedience."

5. See LJ, pp. 66-79, 104-27, and passim. See also Richard Bridgman, *Dark Thoreau* (Lincoln: Univ. of Nebraska Press, 1982), p. 146.

6. Richard Chenevix Trench, *On the Lessons in Proverbs: Being the Substance of Lectures Delivered to Young Men's Societies at Portsmouth and Elsewhere* (New York: Redfield, 1853), p. 27. For the use Thoreau made of Trench's *On the Study of Words* (New York: Redfield, 1852), see Gordon V. Boudreau, "Thoreau and Richard C. Trench: Conjectures on the Pickerel Passage of *Walden,*" *ESQ: A Journal of the American Renaissance* 20 (1974): 117-24.

7. For an illuminating discussion of paradox, see Joseph J. Moldenhauer, "Paradox in *Walden,*" in *Twentieth Century Interpretations of Walden,* ed. Richard Ruland (Englewood Cliffs, N. J.: Prentice-Hall, 1968), pp. 73-84.

8. Harding, *Days,* p. 205.

9. Robert D. Richardson, Jr., *Myth and Literature in the American Renaissance* (Bloomington: Indiana Univ. Press, 1978), pp. 105-17. Quotations are from pp. 111, 112, 115, and 116. For the journal account of Thoreau's first trip to the Maine woods, hitherto unpublished, see PJ, II, 270-349 passim.

10. Henry Seidel Canby, *Thoreau* (Boston: Houghton Mifflin, 1939), p. 163, contends that "Thoreau was what the common man would call in love with Emerson's wife"; Harding and Bode, coeditors of Thoreau's *Correspondence,* consider Thoreau's letter of June 20, 1843, to Mrs. Emerson "a love letter" (C, 121).

11. Joel Porte, *Representative Man: Ralph Waldo Emerson in His Time* (New York: Oxford Univ. Press, 1979), p. 302.

12. In a six-page journal entry spanning four days in March 1841, Thoreau attempted a lengthy analysis to unriddle the mystery of Emerson's poem "The Sphinx" (J, I, 229-31).

Chapter 2

1. D. H. Lawrence, *Studies in Classic American Literature* (1923; reprint, New York: Viking Press, 1961), p. 65.

2. Lawrence, p. 6.

3. Joel Porte, "Eastering," in *Representative Man,* pp. 37-54.

4. Oliver Wendell Holmes, *Ralph Waldo Emerson* (Boston: Houghton Mifflin, 1885), p. 103.

5. For an account of the interview, including the whole of William Emerson's journal version, see Stanley M. Vogel, *German Literary Influences on the American Transcendentalists,* Yale Studies in English, vol. 127 (New Haven: Yale Univ. Press, 1955), pp. 45-46; for an extended discussion of the impact of German literature, particularly that of Goethe, on the Concord authors, see pp. 79-108.

6. Johann Wolfgang von Goethe, "The Author relates the History of His Botanical Studies," in *Botanical Writings,* trans. Bertha Mueller (Honolulu: Univ. of Hawaii Press, 1952), pp. 6, 162. Mueller comments (p. 251) that during Goethe's Italian journeys of 1786-88, "The lush vegetation of Italy spurs [Goethe's] interest in botany, and in Naples he is inspired with the idea . . . that all plant organs are but modifications of the embryo leaves, the cotyledons."

7. David Robinson, "Emerson's Natural Theology and the Paris Naturalists," *Journal of the History of Ideas* 41 (1980): 69-88, argues that Emerson's "exposure to science in Paris, which consisted essentially of a face-to-face introduction to the most current system of botanical and zoological classification, was new only in one important respect: it was a first hand exposure to classification rather than an exposure through books" (p. 76). Upon his return from abroad in 1833, Emerson had a yearlong flirtation with being a naturalist and lectured on science four times during the period.

8. *Autobiography of Moncure Daniel Conway* (Boston: Houghton Mifflin, 1905), 1: 137.

9. In "The Lord's Supper," Emerson in 1832 made public his inability to accept the efficacy of the Unitarian communion service, thus signaling his own metamorphosis from minister to lecturer. But the concluding sentence of "The Poet" suggests that for Emerson the metamorphosis retained a sacramental character. In Emerson's "wherever are outlets into celestial space . . . there is Beauty, plenteous as rain, shed for thee" (CW, III, 24), Joseph Slater detects an allusion to "'The Blood of our Lord Jesus Christ, which was shed for thee, preserve thy body and soul unto everlasting life': 'The Order of the Administration of the Lord's Supper, or Holy Communion' in *The Book of Common Prayer.* See also Luke 22:20" (CW, III, 181n).

10. For the impact of Coleridge upon the American Transcendentalists, especially Emerson, see F. O. Matthiessen, *American Renaissance: Art and Expression in the Age of Emerson and Whitman* (New York: Oxford Univ. Press, 1941), pp. 6-9; George Hochfield, Introduction to *Selected Writings of the American Transcendentalists* (New York: New American Library, 1966), pp. xv-xvii; and especially Alexander Kern, "Coleridge and American Romanticism: The Transendentalists and Poe," in *New Approaches to Coleridge: Biographical and Critical Essays,* ed. Donald Sultana (Totowa, N.J.: Barnes and Noble, 1981), pp. 113-36. For a discussion of Emerson's acceptance of Reason as a higher moral faculty, see Robert E. Spiller, "Introduction" (CW, I, xviii-xx). Barry Wood, "The Growth of the Soul: Coleridge's Dialectical Method and the Strategy of Emerson's *Nature," PMLA* 91 (1976): 385-97, contends that the dialectical method of *Nature* was learned from Coleridge, and that "this method . . . carries through Coleridge's important linkage between dialectical logic and

organic growth" (Abstract, p. 357). Joel Porte, "A Living Leaping Logos," in *Representative Man,* pp. 55-63, balances his discussion of Coleridge's impact on Emerson with that of the "financial windfall" (p. 63)—the legacy from his first wife—that came to Emerson at the same time.

11. In 1824, Emerson wrote of his desire to add to the tradition of such wisdom literature as "the Proverbs of Solomon, the Essays of Montaigne, & eminently the Essays of Bacon," though he felt "not so foolhardy as to write Sequel to Bacon on my title-page. . . ." (JMN, II, 265). Ralph C. La Rosa, "Bacon and the 'Organic Method' of Emerson's Early Lectures," *English Language Notes* 8 (1970): 108-09, contends that from 1818 to 1836 Emerson "expressed his enthusiasm for Bacon by referring to and quoting from his works no fewer than two hundred times, in journals, sermons, and lectures," prizing especially the aphoristic sentence; that Emerson owned a set of Bacon's *Works* (London, 1824); but that "after further investigating Bacon's style, Emerson found it based on a method contrary to his own ideal of organic composition." In a review of Emerson's *Nature* that appeared in *The Christian Examiner* 21 (January 1837): 377, Francis Bowen perceived the little book to be "a revival of the Old Platonic school. It rejects the aid of observation, and will not trust to experiment. The Baconian mode of discovery is regarded as obsolete; induction is a slow and tedious process, and the results are uncertain and imperfect" [reprinted in *Emerson's* Nature—*Origin, Growth, Meaning,* ed. Merton M. Sealts, Jr., and Alfred R. Ferguson (New York: Dodd, Mead, 1969), p. 83]. See also Vivian Hopkins, "Emerson and Bacon," *American Literature* 29 (1958): 408-30; Sherman Paul, *Emerson's Angle of Vision* (Cambridge: Harvard Univ. Press, 1952), pp. 48-50; and William M. Wynkoop, "Bacon as the Doer," in *Three Children of the Universe: Emerson's View of Shakespeare, Bacon, and Milton* (The Hague: Mouton, 1966), pp. 116-36.

12. Jonathan Bishop, *Emerson on the Soul* (Cambridge: Harvard Univ. Press, 1964), p. 15. For discussions of the ocular imagery in Emerson, see James M. Cox, "R. W. Emerson: The Circles of the Eye," and Albert Gelpi, "Emerson: The Paradox of Organic Form," in *Emerson: Prophecy, Metamorphosis, and Influence,* ed. David Levin, Selected Papers from the English Institute (New York: Columbia Univ. Press, 1975), pp. 57-81, 149-70; Kenneth Burke, "I, Eye, Ay—Emerson's Early Essay 'Nature': Thoughts on the Machinery of Transcendence," in *Transcendentalism and Its Legacy,* ed. Myron Simon and Thornton H. Parsons (Ann Arbor: Univ. of Michigan Press, 1966), pp. 3-24; and Sherman Paul, *Angle of Vision,* pp. 71-84. Porte, *Representative Man,* p. 334, n. 32, provides a brief bibliography on the subject.

13. See, for example, Stephen E. Whicher, ed., *Selections from Ralph Waldo Emerson* (Boston: Houghton Mifflin, 1957), p. 472n. Burke, pp. 16-21, deals with Emerson's attempt to "pontificate" in this radical sense. Matthiessen, pp. 64-71, discusses Emerson's fluxional tendencies in "The Flowing."

14. Norman Foerster, "Emerson on the Organic Principle of Art," *PMLA* 41 (1926): 195, writes that "like Schlegel and Coleridge, Emerson distinguishes between the organic and mechanic."

15. These lines, spoken by Prospero, are erroneously ascribed to Ariel in the first edition of *Nature* and all editions thereafter (See CW, I, 251-52n). In "Fate," Emerson seems to revert to the ocean imagery of *The Tempest,* but in a way to suggest his sense of confusion: "I seemed in the height of a tempest to see men overboard struggling in the waves, and driven about here and there. They glanced intelligently at each other, but 't was little they could do for one another; 't was much if each could keep afloat alone. Well, they had a right to their eye-beams and all the rest was Fate" (EW, VI, 19). In discussing this passage (without reference to *The Tempest*), Bishop, *Emerson,* p. 210, notes that "the sea was once for Emerson a prime emblem of the resources of the Soul, frequently compared to a nourishing fluid streaming down to feed the receptive sensibility. But here the 'seas of strength,' the 'liquor of my life' that he had more than once complained was measured to

him in too slight quantities, has turned vast and inimical; once it nourished, now it drowns. And here too sight, the sense especially associated with the intellectual freedom of the Soul, has dwindled until it can provide only a bare proof of impotence." Bishop's own language suggests a despondent Emerson who prefigures Eliot's Prufrock, who perceived his life as "measured out in coffee spoons," and felt so completely cut off from the vital fluids that the mermaids calling "each to each" would not call to him, or if they would, their "living voices" would waken, only to drown him. See also Nina Baym, "From Metaphysics to Metaphor: The Image of Water in Emerson and Thoreau," *Studies in Romanticism* 5 (1965-66): 231-41.

16. Porte, *Representative Man,* p. vii.

17. In Perry Miller, *The Transcendentalists: An Anthology* (Cambridge: Harvard Univ. Press, 1950), p. 51.

18. Kenneth W. Cameron, *Emerson the Essayist,* vol. 1 (1945; reprint, Hartford: Transcendental Books, 1972), p.287.

19. Miller, *The Transcendentalists,* p. 54.

20. Richard Adams, "Emerson and the Organic Metaphor," *PMLA* 69 (1954): 121, finds that not only the structure of *Nature,* but its language as well, "fails to assimilate the organic idea which it struggles to express."

21. Daniel Shea, "Emerson and the American Metamorphosis," in Levin, pp. 29-56. William T. Harris, "Emerson's Philosophy of Nature," in *The Genius and Character of Emerson,* ed. Frank B. Sanborn (Boston: Houghton Mifflin, 1898), pp. 339-64, discusses the theory of the "Lapse" that Emerson unfolds in the chapter "Prospects"; reprinted, in part, in Sealts, pp. 124-28. Shea, pp. 44-48, discusses the progressive and regressive metamorphosis, with particular reference to Goethe's influence on Emerson, but with an autobiographical focus. See also B. L. Packer, *Emerson's Fall: A New Interpretation of the Major Essays* (New York: Continuum, 1982).

22. Perry Miller, "Thoreau in the Context of International Romanticism," *New England Quarterly* 34 (1961): 153.

23. Conrad Wright, "Emerson, Barzillai Frost, and the Divinity School Address," in *The Liberal Christians: Essays on American Unitarian History* (Boston: Beacon Press, 1970), p. 51. Other discussions on the use Emerson makes of Frost include Porte, *Representative Man,* pp. 114-33, 336n, 337n, 342n; also Robert E. Spiller, CW, I, 71-72.

24. Porte, *Representative Man,* p. 117.

25. Ltr. March 21, 1838 (L, II, 147).

26. George R. Stewart, *American Given Names: Their Origin and History in the Context of the English Language* (New York: Oxford Univ. Press, 1979), p. 65; Charlotte M. Yonge, *History of Christian Names,* new ed., rev. (London: n.p., 1844), p. xxxii.

27. See Wright, pp. 57 and 130 n. 41 quoting from Nathan Hale, Jr., to Lowell, July 9, 1838, Harvard College Library. For the full text of Lowell's leter to Hale, dated July 23, 1838, see Joel Myerson, "Lowell on Emerson: A New Letter from Concord in 1838," *The New England Quarterly* 44 (1971): 649-52.

28. Published as a pamphlet in Cambridge in 1839, Norton's reply to Emerson's address appears in part in Miller, *The Transcendentalists,* pp. 210-13; the quotation is on p. 210.

29. Randall Stewart, *American Literature and Christian Doctrine* (Baton Rouge: Louisiana State Univ. Press, 1958), pp. 50-53. For texts and commentary on the miracle question in Unitarianism and Transcendentalism, see Miller, *The Transcendentalists,* pp. 157-246. In "The Transcendentalist," Emerson described the Transcendentalist as one who "believes in miracle, in the perpetual openness of the human mind to new influx of light and power; he believes in inspiration and in ecstasy" (CW, I, 204).

30. Samuel T. Coleridge, *Biographia Literaria: or Biographical Sketches of My Literary Life and Opinions,* ed. George Watson (New York: E. P. Dutton, 1965), p. 167.

31. Shea, p. 50.

32. Porte, *Representative Man,* p. 163.

33. In an undated entry in 1842, Emerson complained that Alcott has "no roots, but is an air-plant, which can readily & without any ill consequence be transported to any place" (JMN, VIII, 213). R. W. B. Lewis, "Hold on Hard to the Huckleberry Bushes," *Sewanee Review* 67 (1959); reprinted in *Trials of the Word* (New Haven: Yale Univ. Press, 1965), pp. 97-111. Philip F. Gura, "The Transcendentalists and Language: The Unitarian Exegetical Background," in *Studies in the American Renaissance, 1979,* ed. Joel Myerson (Boston: Twayne, 1979), p. 10, poses as an Emersonian question: "If a realm of intuitive knowledge did exist, could it not be that, just as nature derived its meaning from its relation to the ineffable Oversoul, so too did language have its roots in that universal ether?"

Chapter 3

1. Sherman Paul, *The Shores of America: Thoreau's Inward Exploration* (Urbana: Univ. of Illinois Press, 1958), pp. 3, 16. See also Matthiessen, *American Renaissance,* pp. 5-14. Perry Miller, in "Thoreau in the Context of International Romanticism," contends that "by the time Thoreau graduated from Harvard, this Romantic aesthetic had been widely domesticated in America" (p. 155).

2. Harding, *Days,* pp. 47, 50-51, 59-73.

3. "Everything through which you are bettered is true" (PJ, I, 511n).

4. Cf. Thoreau's letter to Emerson, November 14, 1847: "The world is a cow that is hard to milk,—life does not come so easy,—and oh, how thinly it is watered ere we get it!" (C, 188). Raymond A. Gozzi, "Mother-Nature," in *Henry David Thoreau: A Profile,* ed. Walter Harding (New York: Hill and Wang, 1971), pp. 180-84, discusses Thoreau's "oral satisfaction" with nature. James McIntosh, *Thoreau as Romantic Naturalist: His Shifting Stance Toward Nature* (Ithaca: Cornell Univ. Press, 1974), pp. 69-88, discusses the influence of Goethe on Thoreau. See also Robert D. Richardson, Jr., *Henry Thoreau: A Life of the Mind* (Berkeley: Univ. of California Press, 1986), pp. 28-30, 156-57, with additional passing references; and Robert Sattelmeyer, *Thoreau's Reading: A Study in Intellectual History, With Bibliographical Catalogue* (Princeton: Princeton Univ. Press, 1988), pp. 26-27 and additional passing references.

5. Thoreau elsewhere mentions Goethe in *Literary Notebook, 1840-48, facsimile text,* ed. Kenneth Walter Cameron (Hartford: Transcendental Books, 1964), pp. 26, 357; in "Thomas Carlyle and His Works," published in March 1847 (EEM, pp. 220, 233, 240, 243, 251, 262); and in letters written in 1843 (C, 90), 1848 (C, 222), and 1857 (C, 478). In the latter he advised B. B. Wiley, who desired books "of a half biographical character," to read "Goethe's Autobiography" as well as several other works in that line. See also a journal fragment, dated after December 2, 1846 (PJ, II, 356-57), in which Thoreau quotes from and comments on Goethe, without mention of his name.

6. Kenneth Walter Cameron, *Thoreau Discovers Emerson: A College Reading Record* (New York: New York Public Library, 1953), pp. 12-13.

7. Robert Sattelmeyer and Richard A. Hocks, "Thoreau and Coleridge's *Theory of Life,*" in *Studies in the American Renaissance, 1985,* ed. Joel Myerson (Charlottesville: Univ. Press of Virginia, 1985), pp. 269-84. See Thoreau, *Literary Notebook,* pp. 359-63, for his quotations from Coleridge's *Theory.*

8. I heartily concur with Richardson's view in *HT: Life,* p. 291, that Thoreau "found things in books *after* he had already begun exploring them himself."

9. Chalmer's criticism of Coleridge is repeated in "Night and Moonlight" (W, V, 324).

10. Miller (LJ, 225) reports that among the pages of what he calls the "Ur-journal," Thoreau had copied a passage from Coleridge's "Dejection: An Ode." McIntosh, pp. 150-51, discusses Thoreau's "The Poet's Delay" in the light of the "Ode to Dejection," and alludes to

"Frost at Midnight" (p. 121) in discussing Thoreau's comments on frost and crystallization in "A Natural History of Massachusetts" (W, V, 127). Frederick Garber, *Thoreau's Redemptive Imagination* (New York: New York Univ. Press, 1977), likewise alludes to Coleridge's three poems in discussing Thoreau (pp. 27, 103, 154, 168-69, 208). Sattelmeyer and Hocks, *"Theory,"* see Thoreau's reading of Coleridge's *Theory* in late 1848 as having a "catalytic effect on him" (p. 281) comparable to that of the Jardin des Plantes on Emerson, for it signaled "a subtle but profound shift in Thoreau's stance toward nature, a shift that amounted to adopting the study of natural history, along with writing, as the principal occupation of his life" (p. 279). They argue that Coleridge's *Theory* offered "a philosophical underpinning" for his work that "provided him with a bridge between the transcendental idealism of his youth and the detailed and scientific study of nature that occupied his maturity" (p. 279). While I dispute their contention that Coleridge is *the* catalyst, I agree that for Thoreau, "as for Coleridge, the law would always precede the phenomena that demonstrated it" (p. 282). Quite clearly, however, as I have been arguing, he had already caught glimpses of such law before reading Coleridge's *Theory*. For evidence that Thoreau was familiar with, and quoted from, Coleridge's "Dejection: An Ode," see Linck C. Johnson, *Thoreau's Complex Weave: The Writing of* A Week on the Concord and Merrimack Rivers (Charlottesville: Univ. Press of Virginia, 1986), pp. 72-73.

11. Matthiessen, pp. 68, 69, emphasis added.

12. For different speculations on the punning value of "boyant," see Miller, LJ, 140; and Walter Harding, "Thoreau and Eros," in *Thoreau's Psychology: Eight Essays*, ed. Raymond D. Gozzi (Lanham, Md.: Univ. Press of America, 1983), p. 149.

13. Emerson gave his lecture "Water" on January 17, 1834, and had "long been interested in the symbolic possibilities" of the topic (EL, I, 50). Harding, *Days*, pp. 159-62, and Lebeaux, *Young Man Thoreau*, pp. 209-13, discuss the accidental fire and read through Thoreau's posturing of nonchalance. Lebeaux contends that "on some level of the psyche, Thoreau *wanted* to start a fire which would burn all 'houses that have hearths' in Concord" (p. 212).

14. Randall Stewart, *AL and Christian Doctrine*, p. 55.

15. Perhaps what added to the sting was that Emerson, returning from his trip to the White Mountains on September 2, had there "found few striking experiences" (JMN, VII, 234).

Chapter 4

1. Catherine Albanese, *The Spirituality of the American Transcendentalists: Selected Writings of Ralph Waldo Emerson, Amos Bronson Alcott, Theodore Parker, and Henry David Thoreau* (Macon, Ga.: Mercer Univ. Press, 1988), p. 24ln, suggests that "Thoreau may have absorbed a notion of the cosmic tree from Hindu sources."

2. Harding, *Days*, p. 134.

3. Harding, *Days*, p.136.

4. Jonathan Bishop, *Emerson on the Soul*, p. 188.

5. Joel Porte, *Representative Man*, pp. 179-86.

6. In a letter to Caroline Sturgis, February 4, 1842 (L, III, 9), Emerson wrote of his grief as "a lambent flame that will not burn playing on the surface of my river."

7. Lawrence Buell, *Literary Transcendentalism: Style and Vision in the American Renaissance* (Ithaca: Cornell Univ. Press, 1973), p. 206.

8. D. H. Lawrence, *Classic AL*, p. 2.

9. Stephen L. Tanner, "Current Motions in Thoreau's *A Week*," *Studies in Romanticism* 12 (1973): 763-76.

10. Kevin P. Van Anglen, "A Paradise Regained: Thoreau's *Wild Apples* and the Myth of the American Adam," *ESQ: A Journal of the American Renaissance* 27 (1981): 29.

11. For discussions of this interpolated action, see Sherman Paul, *Shores,* pp. 220-25; Jonathan Bishop, "The Experience of the Sacred in Thoreau's *A Week,*" *ELH* 33 (1966): 73-76; and Robert F. Sayre, *Thoreau and the American Indians* (Princeton: Princeton Univ. Press, 1977), p. 49. Buell, *Literary Transcendentalism,* pp. 220-23, finds the interpolation "like an extra day to the week" one that "serves in some ways as an epitome of the present voyage" (pp. 220-21). Donald Murray, "Symbolic Landscape in the Greylock Episode of Thoreau's *Week,*" *American Transcendental Quarterly* 1 (June 1987): 123-34, offers "a Freudian reading of the Greylock adventure" (p. 130).

12. James Russell Lowell reviewing *A Week* in the *Massachusetts Quarterly Review,* 3 (December 1849): 3.

13. Walter Harding, ed., *A Week on the Concord and Merrimack Rivers* (New York: Holt, Rinehart & Winston, 1963).

14. Paul, *Shores,* p. 231.

15. John Carlos Rowe, "'The Being of Language: The Language of Being' in *A Week on the Concord and Merrimack Rivers,*" *Boundary 2,* 7 (Spring 1979): 99-100, 113 n. 13, calls attention to Thoreau's misquotation of "days" for "day" and the significance thereof.

16. Gordon V. Boudreau, "'Here Lies . . . Rear-Admiral Van': Thoreau's Crowded Grave," *The New England Quarterly* 56 (1983): 523-37.

17. Paul David Johnson, "Thoreau's Redemptive *Week,*" *American Literature* 49 (1977): 29.

18. In a letter to H. G. O. Blake, Sept. 26, 1859 (C, 558), Thoreau wrote, "Men may sit in chambers, seemingly safe and sound, and yet despair, and turn out at last only hollowness and dust within, like a Dead Sea apple." For John Milton's use of the Dead Sea apple, see *Paradise Lost,* X, 504-77.

19. P. 33. Linck C. Johnson, *Complex Weave,* pp. 200-201, points out that "little apple tree" in the first version was changed to "wild apple tree" in the published version. He also finds in this apple tree an "echo" of the meaning of "Elisha's apple tree" in "Friday," an image of renewal and rebirth. As he argues (p. 162), Elisha's apple tree seems to "promise a resurrection" in being linked to "the grave of the prophet Elisha, into which a dead man was cast, 'and when the man was let down, and touched the bones of Elisha, he revived, and stood up' (2 Kings 13:21)."

20. Among critics who, in one way or another, have highlighted "lapse" as an operative word in *A Week* are Walter Hesford, "'Incessant Tragedies': A Reading of *A Week on the Concord and Merrimack Rivers,*" *ELH* 44 (1977): 518; Jamie Hutchinson, "'The Lapse of the Current': Thoreau's Historical Vision in *A Week on the Concord and Merrimack Rivers,*" *ESQ: A Journal of the American Renaissance* 25 (1979): 212 and additional passing references; and Eric J. Sundquist, "'Plowing Homeward': Cultivation and Grafting in Thoreau and the Week," in *Home as Found: Authority and Genealogy in Nineteenth-Century American Literature* (Baltimore: Johns Hopkins Univ. Press, 1979), pp. 82-83. In *A Week* "lapse" appears on pp. 12, 62, 124, 158, 193, 296, 351, 359, and 377.

21. Lawrence Buell, *Literary Transcendentalism,* p. 212.

22. Bibliophile Edition, II, 25.

23. Among the instances where Thoreau confounds "literal" and "littoral," see J, III, 360, 417, and CC, 192.

24. Jonathan Bishop, "Experience of the Sacred," in Thoreau's *A Week, ELH* 33 (1966): 79-80; Bishop discusses the bittern for its sacred meanings, but finds Thoreau's description of the bittern probing the shore a "deliberately banal note which returns us to the profane bittern."

25. See J, III, 54; IV, 334; and XIII, 250.

26. Van Anglen, p. 36 n. 4. On the day Thoreau first heard the telegraph wire vibrating, he wrote as if in anticipation of the fruit of the tree: "The melons and the apples seem at once to feed my brain" (J, II, 450); and four days later, feeling "uncommonly prepared

for some literary work," he wrote, "I feel that the juices of the fruits which I have eaten, the melons and apples, have ascended to my brain and are stimulating it" (J, II, 468).

Chapter 5

1. HM 924 "Folder Before A," 1st line recto: "There lie the sand and clay all winter." This item is reproduced by permission of the Huntington Library, San Marino, California. I am grateful to Thomas Blanding for calling this information to my attention and providing a transcript of this version of the sand foliage passages. The editors of PJ, II, 576-79, provide "Selected Later Revisions" of the heavily revised first extensive draft of the sand foliage passages of "Spring," but these represent the "first level of composition" (p. 501) only, a version that has "inert mass" for "inert bean." Somewhat uncertainly, they assign a date of spring 1848 for the revisions. But in referring to sand "flowing down the sides of *a d*eep *c*ut on the railroad through which I walk" (PJ, II, 382; emphasis added), Thoreau suggests that neither the phenomena nor the place had yet captured his attention forcibly. Two years after the conjectured date, in fact, Thoreau remarks that "the railroad cuts make cliffs for swallows" (J, II, 49) and somewhat later casually versified his indifference to the cut that "sets the sand a-flowing" (J, II, 59). In September 1850, he does note that a seasonal rain will occasionally excite the "Deep Cut" to "productiveness," making it seem "a cave, with all its stalactites turned wrong side outward" (J, II, 70). On the final day of 1850, he is able to delineate the summer stratum of deposit from that of the winter "in the cut by Walden Pond" (J, II, 133). Not till the journal entry for June 13, 1851 (J, II, 249-50), does Thoreau respond obsessively to the phenomena in a way to suggest the beginning of a state of mind commensurate with that which expresses itself in the extensive revisions. (I discuss this period of generativity at length in chapters 10-11.) Curiously, James Russell Lowell in a review of Thoreau's *A Week* remarked that "we trace the lines of successive deposits [in the book] as plainly as on the sides of a deep cut." *Massachusetts Quarterly Review* 3 (December 1849): 40-51, as quoted by Linck C. Johnson, "Contexts of Bravery: Thoreau's Revisions of 'The Service' for *A Week*," in *Studies in the American Renaissance, 1983,* ed. Joel Myerson (Charlottesville: Univ. Press of Virginia, 1983), p. 281.

2. *Coleridge on Imagination* (London, 1934), p. 52, as cited by M. H. Abrams, *The Mirror and the Lamp: Romantic Theory and the Critical Tradition* (New York: Norton, 1953), p. 169.

3. Original name, Carl von Linne (1707-78). Thoreau was pleased to learn that Linnaeus's father appropriated the family name from "a lofty linden tree which stood near his native place" (J, III, 117), and that Linnaeus (Linden-tree-man) took revenge on his enemies by giving their names to "pernicious and unsightly plants" (J, III, 120).

4. John Aldrich Christie, *Thoreau as World Traveller* (New York: Columbia Univ. Press, 1965), p. 116.

5. Joel Porte, *Emerson and Thoreau: Transcendentalists in Conflict* (Middletown, Conn.: Wesleyan Univ. Press, 1965), p. 116.

6. A glance through the index of most critical studies on Thoreau reveals that Asa Gray has been treated slightingly, if at all. A notable exception is Reginald L. Cook, *Passage to Walden,* 2d ed. (New York: Russell & Russell, 1966), p. 204, who mentions Thoreau's use of Gray's *Manual* for directing him to see a correspondence between himself and nature. Unfortunately, Cook gives no details. A recent essay by Ray Angelo, "Thoreau as Botanist," in *Botanical Index to the Journal of Henry David Thoreau* (Salt Lake City: Peregrine Smith, 1984), pp. 15-31, takes into account only the scientific use Thoreau made of Gray.

7. Ethel Seybold, *Thoreau: The Quest and the Classics* (New Haven: Yale Univ. Press, 1951), p. 70; Richardson, *HT: Life,* p. 57.

8. Harold Whitehall, "The English Language," *Webster's New World Dictionary* (Cleveland: World Publishing, 1962), p. xxxiii.

9. F. B. Sanborn, ed. *Thoreau: The Poet-Naturalist,* 2d ed. 1902. Reprint. (Boston: Biblo and Tannen, 1966), p. 77n. See also p. 97n. For his interest in the Indian languages see Sayre, pp. 188-90. As Richardson points out in *HT: Life,* p. 13, Thoreau's course work at Harvard included thirty-one courses of language study, which included Greek, Latin, Italian, French, German, and Spanish.

10. For an appraisal of [John] Horne Tooke, see Hans Aarsleff, *The Study of Language in England, 1780-1860* (Princeton: Princeton Univ. Press, 1967), pp. 44-144.

11. Trench, Archbishop of Dublin, poet, and philologist, was instrumental in articulating a viewpoint that led to the publication of the *New English Dictionary.*

12. One finds a particularly striking illustration in Hamlet's "O, 'tis most sweet, / When in one line two crafts directly meet" (III, iv, 209-10). "Crafts" here extends to two ships at sea that meet without apparent design, to Hamlet's own "craft" in catching the conscience of the king at the very moment that King Claudius and Laertes catch his, the results of which include crafty sword play backed by a crafty plot rendered in a crafty language whose tide ebbs and flows in subtle and reversing interplay throughout the world of Denmark. Thoreau's numerous allusions to *Hamlet* are worthy subject for investigation.

13. Similarly, Thoreau noted that a man with a wagon-load of *Rhododendron maximum* said the name meant "rose of Dendrum" (J, V, 161).

14. David Greene (San Diego: San Diego State College Press, 1966), p. 5.

15. Thoreau worked out this relationship in a journal passage for October 31, 1857, by observing that the "withered leaves" of the skunk-cabbage "fall and are transfixed by a rising bud. Winter and death are ignored; the circle of life is complete. Are these false prophets? Is it a lie or a vain boast underneath the skunk-cabbage bud, pushing it upward and lifting the dead leaves with it? They rest with spears advanced; they rest to shoot!" (J, X, 151).

16. A common weed throughout North America, the St.-John's-wort (*Hypericum Perforatum*) grows up to three feet high. Of the many varieties, most have yellow flowers with five sepals and petals, and paired, undivided, and toothless leaves having translucent spots. Ray Angelo, *Botanical Index,* cites thirty-seven references to "Johnswort" (p. 105) in Thoreau's *Journal,* fifteen to "St.–John's-wort" (p. 166). Interestingly, while Thoreau's preference was for "Johnswort," in the period covered by Vol. II there were but two instances of "Johnswort" and five of "St.–John's-wort."

17. See Milton's Sonnet 18, "On the Late Massacre in Piedmont."

18. The poem "Within the Circuit of this Plodding Life" appeared in 1842 in "Natural History of Massachusetts" (W, V, 103-4). Two paragraphs thereafter, Thoreau wrote that "there is no scent in [society] so wholesome as that of the pines, nor any fragrance so penetrating and restorative as the life-everlasting in high pastures" (W, V, 105).

Chapter 6

1. *American Heritage Dictionary of the English Language* (Boston: Houghton Mifflin, 1969). Frequently cited in text as AHD.

2. Benjamin Franklin, *The Way to Wealth,* in *The Papers of Benjamin Franklin,* ed. Leonard W. Labaree et al. (New Haven: Yale Univ. Press, 1959), 3: 306.

3. Thoreau's posthumously published essay "Life Without Principle" (*Atlantic Monthly,* October 1863), which grew from journal entries for 1851-55, was first delivered as a lecture titled "Getting a Living" (December 6, 1854). Walter Harding gives its title as "What Shall It Profit [a Man If He Gain the Whole World But Lose His Own Soul]?" *A Thoreau Handbook* (New York: New York Univ. Press, 1959), p. 72; and *Days,* p. 342. But no authority is given for the bracketed emendations. Thoreau's difficulty in settling on a title is discussed by Wendell Glick in RP, 369-70. David Gordon Rohman, "An Annotated Edition of Henry David Thoreau's *Walden,*" Ph.D. diss., Syracuse Univ., 1960, Preface, p. vii, contends that

"the whole of *Walden* is a form of the Parable of the Talents, controlled by the morality of the Good Steward, an extended account of the meaning of the Biblical injunction, 'for what is a man profited if he shall gain the whole world, and lose his own soul?'"

4. Undated, but presumed to have been written shortly after August 15, 1844.

5. William Drake, "Walden," in *Thoreau: A Collection of Critical Essays,* ed. Sherman Paul (Englewood Cliffs, N.J.: Prentice-Hall, 1962), p. 71.

6. Thoreau used the phrase "a pilgrimage à la Terre Sainte" (EEM, 43) in a review essay on two biographies of Sir Walter Scott, dated May 3, 1836. In a journal entry for January 10, 1851, Thoreau gives a personal etymology of "saunter": "And this word 'saunter,' by the way, is happily derived 'from idle people who roved about the country [in the Middle Ages] and asked charity under pretence of going *à la Sainte Terre,'* to the Holy Land, till, perchance, the children exclaimed, 'There goes a *Sainte-Terrer'* a Holy-Lander. They who never go to the Holy Land in their walks, as they pretend, are indeed mere idlers and vagabonds" (J, II, 141; the brackets in the passage are Thoreau's).

For Thoreau, the saunterer was directly opposite to the villain, one who lived on the superficial way, so to speak, rather than on the living way. In his journal for January 29, 1854, Thoreau wrote: "The village is the place to which the roads tend, a sort of expansion of the highway, as a lake of a river, the thoroughfare and ordinary of travelers, a trivial or quadrivial place. It is the body of which roads are the arms and legs. It is from the Latin *villa,* which, together with *via* (a way), or more anciently *vea* and *vella,* Varro derives from *veho* (to carry), because the villa is the place to and from which things are carried. The steward or overseer of the villa was a *vilicus,* and those who got their living by teaming (?) (*vexturis*) were said *vellaturam facere.* And whence the Latin *vilis* and our word *villain* (?). The inhabitants are way-worn by the travel that goes by and over them without travelling themselves" (J, VI, 82-83).

7. Harding, "Introduction," *A Week,* p. viii.

8. Edwin Fussell, *Frontier: American Literature and the American West* (Princeton: Princeton Univ. Press, 1965), pp. 15, 197, 199, 175-231 passim.

9. Philip Van Doren Stern, ed., *The Annotated* Walden (New York: Clarkson N. Potter, 1970), p. 156, points out that in the page proofs of *Walden,* "radical" was changed to "radicle," possibly a sign of Thoreau's deliberate ambiguity with the term.

10. Consider Thoreau's extravagance with the verb (tr.) "root" here—"To dig with or as with the snout or nose"; and (intr.) "to give encouragement to a contestant or team; cheer" (AHD), the latter meaning drawn on for the epigraph on the title page of *Walden*: "I do not propose to write an ode to dejection, but to brag as lustily as chanticleer in the morning, standing on his roost, if only to wake my neighbors up" (Wa, facing p. 357).

Chapter 7

1. J. Lyndon Shanley, *The Making of* Walden (Chicago: Univ. of Chicago Press, 1957), p. 31, dates the beginning of the process of the creative reshaping of *Walden* as January 17, 1852; Ronald Clapper, "The Development of *Walden*: A Genetic Text" (Ph.D. diss., Univ. of California at Los Angeles, 1967), p. 22, proposes January 22, 1852. For a broader view of the period, see Lewis Leary, "'Now I Adventured': 1851 as a Watershed Year in Thoreau's Career," *ESQ: A Journal of the American Renaissance* 19 (1973): 141-48.

2. On July 21, 1851, Thoreau had written: "Remember thy Creator in the days of thy youth; *i.e.,* lay up a store of natural influences. Sing while you may, before the evil days come. He that hath ears, let him hear. See, hear, smell, taste, etc., while these senses are fresh and pure" (J, II, 330); and in *Walden,* "Remember thy Creator in the days of thy youth. Rise free

from care before the dawn, and seek adventures" (Wa, 207). The passage paraphrases Ecclesiastes 12:1:

> Remember now thy Creator in the days of thy youth,
> While the evil days come not,
> Nor the years draw nigh, when thou shalt say,
> I have no pleasure in them.

The twelfth verse of this chapter is, "And further, by these, my son, be admonished: of making many books there is no end; and much study is a weariness of the flesh." To this passage Thoreau took exception: "Much study a weariness of the flesh, eh? But did not they intend that we should read and ponder, who covered the whole earth with alphabets—primers or bibles—coarse or fine print?" (J, VI, 132). See Gordon V. Boudreau, "'Remember Thy Creator': Thoreau and St. Augustine," *ESQ: A Journal of the American Renaissance* 19 (1973): 149-60.

3. Paul, *Shores,* p. 335; MA 594, the Pierpont Morgan Library. "Ver" is also the name of the spring goddess.

4. On his Minnesota journey in 1861, Thoreau wrote with obvious pleasure that "all water falls, in the Dakota tongue, are called Ha-ha, never Minnehaha [as Longfellow has it]. The 'h' has a strong gutteral sound. The word is applied because of the curling of the waters. The verb I-ha-ha primarily means to curl; secondarily to laugh because of the curling motion of the mouth in laughter." "Notes on the Journey West," in *Thoreau's Minnesota Journey: Two Documents,* ed. Walter Harding, Thoreau Society Booklet no. 16 (Geneseo, N.Y., 1962), p. 12. The comment in brackets is Thoreau's.

5. In the concluding paragraph of *Cape Cod,* Thoreau wrote: "What are springs and waterfalls? Here is the spring of springs, the waterfall of waterfalls" (CC, 215); and in "Civil Disobedience": "They who know of no purer sources of truth, who have traced up its streams no higher, stand, and wisely stand, by the Bible and the Constitution, and drink at it there with reverence and humility; but they who behold where it comes trickling into this lake or that pool, gird up their loins once more, and continue their pilgrimage toward its fountainhead" (W, IV, 385-86).

6. Harding, *Days,* p. 346, mentions Thoreau's speech "defect," citing William Ellery Channing, *Thoreau, the Poet-Naturalist* (Boston, 1873), p. 2.

7. In 1860 Thoreau wrote that "February may be called *earine* (springlike)" (J, XIII, 129).

8. Thoreau regarded Chaucer as "almost . . . a personification of spring" (Wk, 368), and often quoted or paraphrased Milton's "Lycidas" in his journal, a poem that may have supplied much of the rich suggestiveness in Thoreau's "laves" by the line "With nectar pure his [Lycidas's] oozy locks he [Christ] laves" (l. 175).

9. Harding, *Days,* pp. 357-63, gives an account of Thoreau's being afflicted with weak legs in 1855. Raymond Gozzi, "Tropes and Figures," p. 141, gives a Freudian interpretation that his weak legs were "the response of his unconscious to the success of *Walden.*"

10. "I say that sometimes by their fruits ye shall know them" (J, IV, 306), Thoreau's paraphrase of Matthew 7:16, the parable of the sower.

11. Charles Anderson, *The Magic Circle of* Walden (New York: Holt, Rinehart & Winston, 1968), pp. 136-37, believes that Thoreau did stand in the end of a rainbow: "The incident he reports in *Walden* is not fabulous, though the rainbow itself is central to several fables." Walter Harding, *The Variorum* Walden (New York: Washington Square Press, 1968), p. 279, denies this possibility, advanced earlier by Charles D. Steward, "A Word for Thoreau," *Atlantic Monthly* 116 (1935): 110-16.

12. Cf. John Ruskin, "The Lamp of Memory," in *The Seven Lamps of Architecture* (New York: Longmans, Green, 1909), p. 324: "There are but two strong conquerors of the

forgetfulness of men, Poetry and Architecture; and the latter in some sort includes the former, and is mightier in its reality: it is well to have not only what men have thought and felt, but what their hands have handled, and their strength wrought, and their eyes beheld, all the days of their life." Cf. Thoreau, June 20, 1840: "If we only see clearly enough how mean our lives are, they will be splendid enough. Let us remember not to strive upwards too long, but sometimes drop plumb down the other way, and wallow in meanness. From the deepest pit we may see the stars, if not the sun. Let us have presence of mind enough to sink when we can't swim. At any rate, a carcass had better lie on the bottom than float an offense to all nostrils. It will not be falling, for we shall ride wide of the earth's gravity as a star, and always be drawn upward still,—*semper cadendo nunquam cadit,*—and so, by yielding to universal gravity, at length become fixed stars" (J, I, 146). Thoreau read Ruskin in the fall of 1857; see Richardson, "Autumnal Tints, John Ruskin, and the Innocent Eye," in *HT: Life,* pp. 357-62.

13. Shanley, p. 104. See also Clapper, pp. 837-39.

14. Shanley, p. 207.

15. In "Walking," Thoreau wrote, "When I would recreate myself, I seek the darkest wood . . ."; and in the same essay of how in surveying a line through a swamp that might appear the "entrance to the infernal regions,—'Leave all hope, ye that enter' "—he was cheered as if he were entering "a sacred place,—a *sanctum sanctorum*" (W, V, 228, 230).

Chapter 8

1. Melvin E. Lyon, "Walden Pond as a Symbol," *PMLA* 82 (May 1967): 290.

2. Francis Bacon, *Advancement of Learning, Book I,* in *Essays, Advancement of Learning, New Atlantis, and Other Pieces,* ed. Richard Foster Jones (New York: Odyssey, 1937), p. 220; the quoted passage is italicized in this edition.

3. For a summary of critical discussions on the passages since Miller, see chapter 9, below.

4. Carol F. Yehle, "The Thoreauvian Dialectic: A Study of the Nature Symbolism in *Walden*" (M.A. thesis, Syracuse Univ., 1958), p. 54, remarks that "the term *expresses* may be taken to mean articulates as well as *expresses*: presses out in a physical sense."

5. Saint Augustine, *On Christian Doctrine,* trans. D. W. Robertson, Jr. (Indianapolis: Bobbs-Merrill, 1958), p. 60. (2.24.37).

6. In "Paradise (To Be) Regained," Thoreau wrote of the light of the sun as "but the shadow of love," and quoted Sir Walter Raleigh in support: "The souls of men loving and fearing God . . . receive influence from that divine light itself, whereof the sun's clarity, and that of the stars, is by Plato called but a shadow. *Lumen est umbra Dei, Deus est Lumen Luminis*: Light is the shadow of God's brightness, who is the light of light" (RP, 47).

7. Franklin Benjamin Sanborn, in the Bibliophile Edition of *Walden* (Boston, 1909), 2: 22, comments: "This singular passage is one of those in which, as Ellery Channing somewhere says, Thoreau's 'old trade of schoolmaster stuck to him.' These etymologies and analogies are rather forced, and, introduced here, they interrupt the description and the flow of thought. They were more in fashion when Thoreau was at Harvard College than they have been since, or are likely to be again." Thoreau's struggle to align the seed crop (beans-*speca*-hope) with the germinating "lobe" in the "Spring" passage discussed here is evident in the passage Sanborn prints in the Bibliophile Edition, 2: 225, which attempts to personify the phenomena in the thawing bankside: "The whole face is a continuous broad shore, and narrow below, to which the chin is a Cape of Good Hope. We might say, by the way, that the face itself is a *terra firma* broad above and narrow below, with its bald polar crown, its temperate zone of greatest breadth, and intelligence and inland seas, its equatorial but sensuous mouth, and its Dutch Cape of Good Hope or Shakesperian Patagonia."

8. I am here contesting the opinions of Arthur Christy, *The Orient in American Transcendentalism* (New York: Columbia Univ. Press, 1932), p. 214, that "Thoreau never articulated a complete eschatology," and of Richardson, *HT: Life,* p. 174, that Thoreau "does not use or suggest the language of redemption. The awakening he seeks is Greek, not Christian. . . ." See also pp. 79, 158 in Richardson.

9. On January 2, 1841, Thoreau wrote: "With cheerful heart I could be a sojourner in the wilderness if I were sure to find there the catkins of the alder. . . . They are my little vegetable redeemer. Methinks my virtue will not flag ere they come again" (LJ, 206). Thoreau's journal entry for October 25, 1858—"Even bleak and barren November wears these *gems* [azalea buds] on her breast in sign of the coming year" (J, XI, 246)—was footnoted by Bradford Torrey and Frances H. Allen, editors, in this manner: "Thoreau underscored this word doubtless to emphasize its etymology,—from the Latin *gemma,* a bud."

Chapter 9

1. Perry Miller notes, " 'Filfth' is not a slip of the pen: that is the way Thoreau wrote it and the way he thought of it" (LJ, 186).

2. Philip Wheelwright, *Metaphor and Reality* (Bloomington: Indiana Univ. Press, 1962), p. 143.

3. Philip Wheelwright, "The Semantic Approach to Myth," in *Myth: A Symposium,* ed. Thomas A. Sebeok (Bloomington: Indiana Univ. Press, 1965), p. 156.

4. Pp. 5, 50, 62, 80.

5. Paul, *Shores,* p. 293.

6. Pp. 21-23, 26. For Clapper's dating of the various manuscript versions, see pp. 30-32. Shanley, p. 31, proposes January 17, five days earlier than Clapper's date, for the rebirth of Thoreau's creativity in the shaping of *Walden.*

7. Shanley, p. 112.

8. Shanley, pp. 41, 44-45.

9. Shanley, pp. 99, 104, 204.

10. Clapper, pp. 791-845 passim. Stern, *Annotated* Walden, p. 423, remarks that "MS 906-911 shows that Thoreau had a great deal of trouble with the phrasing [of paragraph 6], for this is one of the most heavily revised sections in the entire manuscript."

11. The conference was sponsored by the Conversations in the Disciplines Program of the State University of New York. Carl Bode, "The Half-Hidden Thoreau," in *Thoreau in Our Season,* ed. John Hicks (Amherst: Univ. of Massachusetts Press, 1962), pp. 104-16; reprinted as "Epilogue by the Editor," in *The Portable Thoreau,* revised edition (New York: Penguin, 1964), pp. 683-96.

12. Lebeaux, "Identity Crisis and Beyond: Eriksonian Perspectives on the Pre-Walden and Post-Walden Thoreau," in *Thoreau's Psychology: Eight Essays,* ed. Raymond D. Gozzi (Lanham, Md.: University Press of America, 1983), pp. 19-66; see also in this collection Raymond D. Gozzi, "Some Comments on an Eriksonian View of Thoreau: Young Man Thoreau and 'Identity Crisis and Beyond,"' pp. 67-78; and Norman N. Holland, "A Summing-Up," pp. 165-87.

13. Holland, pp. 171, 181n, refers to Heinz Lichtenstein's "Identity and Sexuality: A Study of Their Interrelationship in Man," *Journal of the American Psychoanalytic Association* 9 (1961): 179-260; reprinted in Lichtenstein, *The Dilemma of Human Identity* (New York: Jason Aronson, 1977), chap. 2.

14. Extracts of Gozzi's dissertation have been published in *Henry David Thoreau: A Profile,* ed. Walter Harding (New York: Hill and Wang, 1971), pp. 150-87. Gozzi provides a convenient summary of his dissertation in "A Freudian View of Thoreau," in *Thoreau's Psychology:*

Eight Essays, pp. 1-18. To signal his intent to get at the person behind the tropes and figures in Thoreau's writings, Gozzi reversed the familiar order of Thoreau's name to get at the order given at his birth.

15. Lebeaux readily and generously acknowledged his debt to Levinson, especially in his preface, pp. xiv-xv. See also the numerous citations in his index.

16. *Lessons in Proverbs,* p. 27. For the use Thoreau made of *Trench's On the Study of Words* (New York: Redfield, 1852), see Boudreau, "Thoreau and Trench," pp. 117-24.

17. Bridgman, *Dark Thoreau,* p. 146; Miller, LJ, pp. 66-79, 104-27 and other passing references. George Hochfield, "New England Transcendentalism," in *Critical Essays on American Transcendentalism,* ed. Philip F. Gura and Joel Myerson (Boston: G. K. Hall, 1982), pp. 453-82, considers it "patently absurd to speak of Nature publishing its truth (this language comes from Thoreau himself), or of anyone else doing so on Nature's behalf, for that matter. Only writers publish, and whatever truth they manage to convey is their own. The 'truth' that *Walden* conveys is the truth of Thoreau's attempt to create a language which would embody the mystical illumination he found in natural facts." The difference between Hochfield's view and the one I am advancing has to do, of course, with whether one can accept a poet as seer, rather than as maker only. My view is that Thoreau is a poet-seer, which may divide me from the mainstream of literary critics.

18. Shanley, p. 150; the italicized portion represents Thoreau's interlineation, which suggests a reinforcement of meaning. Of course Thoreau's "read" is frustratingly ambiguous here—past or present tense. So while he may not have read Plato while at Walden Pond, he almost certainly had done so earlier. Norman Foerster, "The Intellectual Heritage of Thoreau," *The Texas Review* 2 (1916-17): 192-212, reprinted in *Twentieth Century Interpretations of* Walden, ed. Richard Ruland (Englewood Cliffs, N.J.: Prentice-Hall, 1968), p. 47, discounts Plato as an influence.

19. *Darwin,* ed. Philip Appleman (New York: Norton, 1970), p. 199. For a discussion of Thoreau's reading of Darwin's *Origin,* see Richardson, *HT: Life,* pp. 376-79.

20. Robert Sattelmeyer, *Thoreau's Reading: A Study in Intellectual History, With Bibliographical Catalogue* (Princeton: Princeton Univ. Press, 1988), pp. 76-77, provides a brief summary of criticism that deals with "the linking of language itself to natural phenomena, so evident in the sand foliage passage. . . ."

21. *Richardson, Myth and Literature,* p. 123.

Chapter 10

1. Harding, *Days,* p. 297, remarks that in June 1851 Thoreau "was suddenly struck by the different look of the sandbank in the Deep Cut near Walden Pond at night and decided it was necessary to see his world by moonlight as well as sunlight to get a complete picture of it," and so began to take midnight walks.

2. Willard H. Bonner, "Thoreau's Other Telegraph Figure," *American Notes & Queries* 7 (March 1969): 99-100, calls attention to a "series of twenty-one rhapsodic celebrations of the 'telegraph harp'" in Thoreau's *Journal* between September 3, 1851, and February 14, 1854. But the "two telegraph figures in *Walden* . . . can be read only with the semaphore in mind"; they have nothing to do with the telegraph in the Deep Cut. The earliest instance of Thoreau's noting in any detail the thawing bankside in the Deep Cut may be on p. 112 (verso) of the first version of *Walden* (Huntington MS 924), which appears in Shanley, p. 204, before Thoreau began to capitalize "Deep Cut." Shanley's dating of the early version as 1846-47, if correct, suggests a longer genetic process than I here assume; but I am dubious of this early dating. I am also dubious of assuming that the selected later revisions in PJ, II, 576-79, which Shanley believes "could have been written in early 1847," are even as early as 1848. Thoreau's

"Man should be the harp articulate" (J, VI, 294), on May 23, 1854, may be taken as a coda to the twenty-one journal entries on the telegraph harp, which are conveniently indexed in the *Journal*.

William J. Wolf, *Thoreau: Mystic, Prophet, Ecologist* (Philadelphia: United Church Press, 1974), p. 161, calls attention to the pun in Thoreau's journal entry, "We check and repress the divinity that stirs within us, to fall down and worship the divinity that is dead without us" (J, III, 119).

3. By my count there are twenty-two references to the phenomena of sand foliage in the Deep Cut in Thoreau's *Journal* (though not all of these employ the term "sand foliage"). The *Journal* index lists but four of these. A complete listing, with yearly frequency, is as follows:

1851 one: Dec. 31 (J, III, 164-65).

1852 nine: Jan. 25 (J, III, 226); Jan. 26 (J, III, 235-36); Jan. 29 (J, III, 248); Feb. 14 (J, III, 303); Feb. 24 (J, III, 20); Mar. 9 (J, III, 342-43); Mar. 10 (J, III, 344); Mar. 12 (J, III, 348-49); Apr. 28 (J, III, 478).

1853 none.

1854 four: Feb. 5 (J, VI, 99-100); Feb. 8 (J, VI, 109); Mar. 1 (J, VI, 147); Mar. 2 (J, VI, 148).

1855 two: Feb. 16 (J, VII, 187); Feb. 20 (J, VII, 199).

1856 two: Mar. 23 (J, VIII, 222-23); Mar. 30 (J, VIII, 232).

1857 one: Feb. 24 (J, IX, 280).

1858 none.

1859 two: Mar. 2 (J, XII, 3-5); Mar. 18 (J, XII, 61).

1860 one: Feb. 7 (J, XIII, 128).

Two instances in 1859 actually function as comparisons with the slipping bankside at Clamshell Hill, which has become the center of Thoreau's attention. The last extended lyrical reference to the sand foliage is that for March 23, 1856.

4. Matthiesen, *American Renaissance,* pp. 86, 84, 89.

5. In December 1847, Emerson "just missed seeing Gardiner, author of the Music of Nature," as he wrote to Lidian from England on Christmas Day (L, III, 455).

6. In a portion of an early lecture draft for "Life Without Principle" that may date from the time between the publication of *Walden* (August 9, 1854) and the date the lecture was first given (December 26, 1854), Thoreau alludes to the Cremona violin in a way to suggest a summarizing of the effects of attending to the telegraph harp, and a recalling of the worker in wood in the parable of the Artist of Kouroo. See "C15a," William L. Howarth, *The Literary Manuscripts of Henry David Thoreau* (Columbus: Ohio State Univ. Press, 1974), p. 153, for identification of the MS. I am grateful to the Starr Library of Middlebury College, Vermont, for permission to quote the fragment, which reads:

> of sound timber, & kept tuned always, it was he—so that when the bow of events is drawn across him, he may vibrate & resound in perfect harmony. A sensitive soul will be continually trying its strings to see if they are in tune. A man's body must be rasped down exactly to a shaving. This of far more importance than the wood of a Cremona violin.
>
> There are certain strings which only senses refined and purified may take cognizance of—May such senses be mine! I would that I might truly worship my own body—as the worthiest temple of God—bow down with reverence to his image graven in it—& so love and reverence the very persons of my friends. May I love & serve myself above all the gods that men have ever invented, and never let the vestal fire go out in my recesses!

7. Conway, *Autobiography* 1: 143.

8. Stanley Edgar Hyman, *The Tangled Bank: Marx, Frazer and Freud as Imaginative Writers* (New York: Atheneum, 1962), p. 143.

9. Ellery Channing, *Thoreau: The Poet-Naturalist,* new ed. (New York: Biblo & Tannen, 1902), p. 339.

10. P. 101.

11. Martha Banta, "American Apocalypse: Excrement and Ennui," *Studies in the Literary Imagination* 7 (1974): 20. Similarly, Hyman finds the tree of life a "remarkable extended metaphor" (p. 31) in Darwin's *Origin,* one he first used in a letter to Asa Gray. Hyman sees Darwin's tree of life as a Renaissance figure that mediates between the "ordered, hierarchic, and static, essentially medieval" figure of the "great Chain of Life," and the "disordered, democratic, and subtly interdependent as well as competitive, [and] essentially . . . modern vision" of "the great Tangled Bank" (p. 33).

Chapter 11

1. Carl Bode, in "The Hidden Thoreau," as in the collection of essays in which it appears—*The Half-World of American Culture* (Carbondale: Southern Illinois Univ. Press, 1965)—brings the "insights and valuable hypotheses of Freudian psychology" to bear on the "subconscious side" of Thoreau that had "largely gone unstudied." But he does not explore Thoreau's dreams. Examples of discussions of the oral and anal imagery are Raymond D. Gozzi, "Some Aspects of Thoreau's Personality," in *HDT: A Profile,* pp. 150-71, who takes a Freudian view in discussing the "anal-sadistic" level of Thoreau's "unconscious libidinal regression" (p. 165); and Lebeaux, who in *Young Man Thoreau* takes an Eriksonian approach in speculating on the "toilet-training procedures in the Thoreau household" (p. 51). Walter Harding's call for a paper on Thoreau and the dream (for a conference, "Psychology and the Literary Artist: A Case Study of Henry David Thoreau," April 14-15, 1978, State Univ. of New York, Geneseo) apparently fell on unresponsive ears. See also chapter 1, above.

2. In "Life Without Principle": "Thus our life is not altogether a forgetting, but also, alas! to a great extent, a remembering of that which we should never have been conscious of, certainly not in our waking hours. Why should we not meet, not always as dyspeptics, to tell our bad dreams, but sometimes as eupeptics, to congratulate each other on the ever glorious morning. I do not make an exorbitant demand, surely" (RP, 179).

3. Feb. 27, 1853.

4. See Eric Fromm, *The Forgotten Language: An Introduction to the Understanding of Dreams, Fairy Tales and Myths* (New York: Rinehart, 1951).

5. See A. D. Nostrand's fine chapter "Thoreau Beside Himself," in *Every Man His Own Poet: Romantic Gospels in American Literature* (New York: McGraw-Hill, 1968), pp. 92-112.

6. *The Variorum* Walden, p. 263, n. 53.

7. J. S. Sherwin and R. C. Reynolds, *A Word Index to* Walden*: With Textual Notes* (Charlottesville: Univ. of Virginia Press, 1960); the more recent work by Marlene A. Ogden, Walden: *A Concordance* (New York: Garland, 1985), despite the claim of including "references to *all* the words in the text" (p. x), does not include the Greek words and does not distinguish between capitalized and lowercase words. James Karabatsos, *A Word-Index to* A Week on the Concord and Merrimack Rivers (Hartford: Transcendental Books, 1971). Bishop, "Sacred in *A Week,*" p. 74.

8. Leary, "Watershed Year," pp. 141-48.

9. In "The Beach Again," *Cape Cod,* he wrote of bass fishermen sitting on the sand: "It was literally (or *littorally*) walking down to the shore, and throwing your line into the Atlantic" (CC, 92).

10. Matthiessen, *American Renaissance,* pp. 153-57. Harding, *Days,* pp. 298-304, gives an account of the cooling of the Emerson-Thoreau friendship during the late 1840s and early 1850s.

11. Jan. 17 or Jan. 22, 1852. Moncure Conway's visit to Concord in 1853 occasioned a conversation in which Thoreau "praised Wordsworth, Coleridge, and, to a less extent, Carlyle and Goethe," among the moderns. See Conway, 1: 142.

12. Samuel T. Coleridge, *Coleridge: Shakespearean Criticism*, ed. T. M. Raysor, 2d ed. (New York: Dutton, 1960), 1: 198.

13. Coleridge, *Biographia Literaria*, p. 167.

14. See Kern, pp. 113-36; Laraine Fergenson, *Thoreau Journal Quarterly* 5, no. 3 (July 1973): 20-23.

15. In his journal for November 18, 1851—after writing about the woodchopper who in doing his work "really forgets himself, forgets to observe, and at night he *dreams* of the swamp, its phenomena and events," but that it is not so of the naturalist—Thoreau generalizes that "the man who is bent upon his work is frequently in the best attitude to observe what is irrelevant to his work"; and then he notes, "(*Mem.* Wordsworth's observation on relaxed attention.)" (J, III, 123).

16. Porte, *Emerson and Thoreau*, p. 116.

17. He made the point at length in "Paradise (To Be) Regained," RP, 19-47.

18. The Miramichi River in New Brunswick springs from the mountains perhaps 125 miles northeast of Ktaadn (as Thoreau spelled it) and flows into the Gulf of St. Lawrence.

19. Bridgman, *Dark Thoreau*, p. 140, interprets the biting horses as a "need to control intractably opposed forces in his life," which "was a persistent strain for Thoreau." Gozzi, "Tropes and Figures," pp. 232-33, in connection with another journal passage (J, VIII, 41-45), notes as pertinent that Freud's Little Hans chose a horse as a symbol for his father in part because his father played "horsie" with him. He cites Sigmund Freud, *The Problem of Anxiety*, p. 42; and "Analysis of a Phobia of a Five-Year Old Boy," Collected Papers, 3: 149-288.

20. See Boudreau, "Remember Thy Creator," pp. 149-60.

21. Pp. 140, 147.

22. Mary Elkins Moller, *Thoreau and the Human Community* (Amherst: Univ. of Massachusetts Press, 1980), pp. 29, 115-16, 172.

23. Jacques Maritain, *Creative Intuition in Art and Poetry* (Cleveland: World Publishing, 1954), p. 67. With Plato, Maritain's use of "music" includes "every artistic genus which depends on the inspiration of the Muse" (p. 65). See also Thoreau's "What Music Shall We Have?" in his essay "The Service," submitted to *The Dial* in 1841 but rejected by Margaret Fuller and only published posthumously (RP, 9-12, 261-64).

24. Gozzi, "Tropes and Figures," pp. 10-14, 176, 218, 226, 390, 440.

Chapter 12

1. *Shores*, p. 256.

2. *Shores*, p. 399. See also Robert Sattelmeyer, ed., Introduction to *Henry David Thoreau: The Natural History Essays* (Salt Lake City: Peregrine Smith, 1980), pp. vii-xxxiv, who comments (p. xxvi) that Thoreau in his final years was at work on two lengthy manuscripts—one on seeds, one on fruits—which are scheduled for publication in the Princeton edition.

3. Introduction to *Natural History Essays*, p. xxviii.

4. Joseph J. Moldenhauer discusses the incident in MW, 435.

5. Dec. 6, 1856. In May 1851, Thoreau noted that the posts of the arbor-vitae "last thirty-five or forty years, and the rails sixty, or three or four times as long as those of any other species" (J, II, 200).

6. For historical information on the essays in Thoreau's *Reform Papers*, I am indebted to Wendell Glick's "General Introduction" and "Textual Introduction," RP, 219-388. At the

end of "Slavery in Massachusetts," Thoreau makes a distinction, by way of vegetal analogy, between the white Concord water lily, a "*Nymphoea odorata*" as he identifies it in his journal (J, VI, 352), and the "*Nymphoea douglassii*" (RP, 108). The former, though rooted in "the slime and muck of earth," gives forth the most fragrant aroma, "a confirmation of our hopes. . . . I shall not so soon despair of the world for it, notwithstanding slavery, and the cowardice and want of principle in Northern men." The latter passage seems to be a reference to Stephen Douglas, the Great Compromiser, particularly since Thoreau finds in the water lily that at least "Nature has been partner to no Missouri Compromise." But Glick rightly suggests (RP, 337) the allusion may also be to Frederick Douglass, the Black Abolitionist orator for whom Thoreau was a substitute at the Tremont Temple in Boston on November 1, 1859, delivering "A Plea for Captain John Brown." Cf. PJ, II, 122-23, where Thoreau mentions a man, "[we] dare not tell his name . . . Frederick ," but at once alludes to the "Douglasses out of history or fiction." See Stephen Railton, "Thoreau's 'Resurrection of Virtue!'" *American Quarterly* 24 (1972): 224-27, and Robert C. Albrecht, "Conflict and Resolution: 'Slavery in Massachusetts,'" *ESQ: A Journal of the American Renaissance* 19 (1973): 184. On the odor of the lily, cf. Shakespeare's Sonnet 94: "Lilies that fester smell far worse than weeds."

7. Leo Stoller, *After* Walden*: Thoreau's Changing Views on Economic Man* (Stanford: Stanford Univ. Press, 1957), p. 71. Stoller discusses trees in general, and the Davis Elm in particular, on pp. 72-89. Richard Lebeaux, who in *Young Man Thoreau* offers an Eriksonian interpretation of Thoreau's life to the time he moved to Walden Pond, is particularly neo-Freudian in there discussing Thoreau's dreams (pp. 54, 102, 104, 118, 135, 145-46, 148, 187, 198, 207), though the dream of October 26, 1851, lies outside the scope of his study. Subsequently, however, in "'Sugar Maple Man': Middle-aged Thoreau's Generativity Crisis," in *Studies in the American Renaissance, 1981,* ed. Joel Myerson (Boston: Twayne, 1981), pp. 359-77, Lebeaux sensitively probes "how the unconscious interacts with the conscious" (p. 361), and finds evidence of a generativity principle in Thoreau's unconscious in later years, especially in relationship to trees—Lebeaux refers to Thoreau as a "conscious tree" (p. 365).

8. Harding, Days, p. 51, quoting John Albee, *Remembrances of Emerson* (New York, 1903), p. 33.

9. Edward Wagenknecht, *Henry David Thoreau: What Manner of Man?* (Amherst: Univ. of Massachusetts Press, 1981), p. 121. Ellery Channing, *Poet-Naturalist,* p. 261, wrote that "John Brown 'expected to endure hardness'; and this was the expectation and fruition of Thoreau, naturally and by his culture." Sanborn (*Thoreau: The Poet-Naturalist*) also remarked that Thoreau's "pulses thrilled and his hands involuntarily clenched together at the mention of Captain Brown. . . ." (p. 262).

10. See Boudreau, "Thoreau and Trench," pp. 117-24. The quoted passage from Trench's popular work is from the 29th ed. (New York, 1914), pp. 10-11.

11. P. 35; Anderson cites Matthiessen, pp. 95-96. I recognize the sounder *scientific* truth at the basis of Anderson's comment on the etymology of "deliberately"; however, Thoreau's etymological deliberations are fabulously true. Etymological purists will do well to ponder this, or they will fall into the same trap that the scientific critics of Thoreau have—condemning him for inaccuracies while failing to take note of the imaginative dimensions in Thoreau's observations. On this point Thoreau wrote: "My facts shall be falsehoods to the common sense. I would so state facts that they shall be significant, shall be myths or mythologic" (J, III, 99).

12. Stoller, p. 148, mentions the report of F. B. Sanborn, ed., *The First and Last Journeys of Thoreau,* vol. 2 (Boston, 1905), p. xxxvi, that "Mrs. George L. Stearns, wife of one of Brown's important supporters, asked him to write a biography of John Brown, but that Thoreau

refused, 'because he had his own manuscript to edit, and especially those relating to the red man.' "

13. Kevin P. Van Anglen, "A Paradise Regained," pp. 28-37, argues that Thoreau's essay is "a deliberate effort to find in the American landscape the potential for mythology at the deepest level—one which would render the inherited religious symbolism as obsolete as he felt its theology to be" (p. 29), and that Thoreau "distances himself from the mythic apple tree in favor of the real one" (p. 32). My own view is that Thoreau does not demythologize Christian myth; he rejuvenates it. I can agree with Van Anglen's statement that "Thoreau clearly means to approve of 'the pursuit of knowledge,'" (p. 33), but he was interested not so much in knowledge as in a sympathy with intelligence received through his unconsciousness, his dreams, his matutine intellect, his tapping into the mythos.

14. On leaving father and mother, see Ephesians 5:31, Mark 10:7, Matthew 10:37. On rebirth, see John 3:4: "Jesus answered and said unto him, Verily, verily, I say unto thee, except a man be born again, he cannot see the kingdom of God." On losing one's life, see Matthew 10:39: "He that findeth his life shall lose it: and he that loseth his life for my sake shall find it." This is repeated, nearly verbatim, in Matthew 16:25, Mark 8:35, Luke 9:24, and John 12:25. Interestingly, the verse immediately preceding the passage from John reads, "Verily, verily, I say unto you, Except a corn of wheat fall into the ground and die, it abideth alone; but if it die, it bringeth forth much fruit." Was John's "wheat"—a St. John's "wort"—the hint for Thoreau's "*speca*"?

15. Cf. J, VI, 82-83.

16. Sherman Paul, *Shores,* p. 414, remarks that in the last sentence of the manuscript version of "Walking," omitted in the published text, Thoreau wrote that an "adventurous spirit turns the evening into morning," also noting that "in 'Night and Moonlight,' Thoreau turned dark to light." James McIntosh, p. 287, has also commented on this conversion.

17. P. 179.

18. Harding, *Days,* p. 105.

Bibliography

Aarsleff, Hans. *The Study of Language in England, 1780–1860.* Princeton: Princeton Univ. Press, 1967.

Abrams, M. H. *The Mirror and the Lamp: Romantic Theory and the Critical Tradition.* New York: Norton, 1953.

Adams, Richard. "Emerson and the Organic Metaphor." *PMLA* 69 (1954): 117–30.

Albanese, Catherine. *The Spirituality of the American Transcendentalists: Selected Writings of Ralph Waldo Emerson, Amos Bronson Alcott, Theodore Parker, and Henry David Thoreau.* Macon, Ga.: Mercer Univ. Press, 1988.

Albrecht, Robert C. "Conflict and Resolution: 'Slavery in Massachusetts.' " *ESQ: A Journal of the American Renaissance* 19 (1973): 179–88.

American Heritage Dictionary of the English Language. Boston: Houghton Mifflin, 1978.

Anderson, Charles. *The Magic Circle of* Walden. New York: Holt, Rinehart & Winston, 1968.

Angelo, Ray. "Thoreau as Botanist." In *Botanical Index to the Journal of Henry David Thoreau.* Salt Lake City: Peregrine Smith, 1984.

Augustine, Saint. *On Christian Doctrine.* Translated by D. W. Robertson, Jr. Indianapolis: Bobbs-Merrill, 1958.

Bacon, Francis. *Essays, Advancement of Learning, New Atlantis, and Other Pieces.* Edited by Richard Foster Jones. New York: Odyssey, 1937.

Banta, Martha. "American Apocalypse: Excrement and Ennui." *Studies in the Literary Imagination* 7 (1974): 1–30.

Baym, Nina. "From Metaphysics to Metaphor: The Image of Water in Emerson and Thoreau." *Studies in Romanticism* 5 (1965–66): 231–43.

Bigelow, Gordon E. "Thoreau's Melting Sandbank: Birth of a Symbol." *International Journal of Symbology* 2 (1971): 7–13.

Bishop, Jonathan. *Emerson on the Soul.* Cambridge: Harvard Univ. Press, 1964.

———. "The Experience of the Sacred in Thoreau's *A Week.*" *ELH* 33 (1966): 66–91.

Bode, Carl. "The Half-Hidden Thoreau." In *Thoreau in Our Season,* edited by John Hicks. Amherst: Univ. of Massachusetts Press, 1962. Reprinted as "Epilogue by the Editor," in *The Portable Thoreau.* Rev. ed. New York: Penguin, 1964.

Bonner, Willard H. "Thoreau's Other Telegraph Figure." *American Notes & Queries* 7 (March 1969): 99–100.

Boudreau, Gordon V. " 'Here Lies . . . Rear-Admiral Van': Thoreau's Crowded Grave." *The New England Quarterly* 56 (1983): 523–37.

———. "Thoreau and Richard C. Trench: Conjectures on the Pickerel Passage of *Walden.*" *ESQ: A Journal of the American Renaissance* 20 (1974): 117–24.

———. " 'Remember Thy Creator': Thoreau and St. Augustine." *ESQ: A Journal of the American Renaissance* 19 (1973): 149–60.

Bridgman, Richard. *Dark Thoreau.* Lincoln: Univ. of Nebraska Press, 1982.

Buell, Lawrence. *Literary Transcendentalism: Style and Vision in the American Renaissance.* Ithaca: Cornell Univ. Press, 1973.

Burke, Kenneth. "I, Eye, Ay—Emerson's Early Essay 'Nature': Thoughts on the Machinery of Transcendence." In *Transcendentalism and its Legacy,* edited by Myron Simon and Thornton H. Parsons, 3–24. Ann Arbor: Univ. of Michigan Press, 1966.

Cameron, Kenneth W. *Emerson the Essayist.* 2 vols. 1945. Reprint. Hartford: Transcendental Books, 1972.

———. *Thoreau Discovers Emerson: A College Reading Record.* New York: New York Public Library, 1953.

Canby, Henry Seidel. *Thoreau.* Boston: Houghton Mifflin, 1939.

Cassirer, Ernst. *Language and Myth.* Translated by Susanne K. Langer. New York: Dover, 1946.

Cavell, Stanley. *The Senses of* Walden. New York: Viking Press, 1972.

Channing, Ellery. *Thoreau, the Poet-Naturalist.* New ed. New York: Biblo & Tannen, 1902.

Christie, John Aldrich. *Thoreau as World Traveller.* New York: Columbia Univ. Press, 1965.

Christy, Arthur. *The Orient in American Transcendentalism.* New York: Columbia Univ. Press, 1932.

Clapper, Ronald. "The Development of *Walden:* A Genetic Text." Ph.D. diss., Univ. of California at Los Angeles, 1967.

Coleridge, Samuel T. *Biographia Literaria: or Biographical Sketches of My Literary Life and Opinions.* Edited by George Watson. New York: E. P. Dutton, 1965.

———. *Coleridge: Shakespearean Criticism.* Edited by T. M. Raysor. 2 vols. 2d ed. 1930. Reprint. New York: E. P. Dutton, 1960.

Conway, Moncure Daniel. *Autobiography of Moncure Daniel Conway.* 2 vols. Boston: Houghton Mifflin, 1905.

Cook, Reginald. *Passage to* Walden. 2d ed. New York: Russell & Russell, 1966.

Cox, James M. "R. W. Emerson: The Circles of the Eye." In *Emerson: Prophecy, Metamorphosis, and Influence,* edited by David Levin. Selected Papers from the English Institute, 57–81. New York: Columbia Univ. Press, 1975.

Darwin, Charles. *Darwin.* Edited by Philip Appleman. New York: Norton, 1970.

Drake, William. "*Walden.*" In *Thoreau: A Collection of Critical Essays,* edited by Sherman Paul, 71–91. Englewood Cliffs, N. J.: Prentice-Hall, 1962.

Duncan, Jeffrey L. "The Logic of Metamorphosis in Thoreau." *The Missouri Review* 3 (Winter 1980): 90–102.

Eliade, Mircea. *The Sacred and the Profane.* Translated by Willard R. Trask. New York: Harcourt, Brace, 1959.

Emerson, Ralph Waldo. *The Collected Works of Ralph Waldo Emerson.* Edited by Alfred R. Ferguson et al. 4 vols. Cambridge: Harvard Univ. Press, 1971–87.

———. *The Complete Works of Ralph Waldo Emerson.* 12 vols. Centenary Ed. Boston: Houghton Mifflin, 1903.

———. *The Early Lectures of Ralph Waldo Emerson.* Edited by Stephen E. Whicher, Robert E. Spiller, and Wallace E. Williams. 3 vols. Cambridge: Harvard Univ. Press, 1959–72.

———. *The Journals and Miscellaneous Notebooks of Ralph Waldo Emerson.* Edited by William H. Gilman et al. 16 vols. Cambridge: Harvard Univ. Press, 1960–82.

———. *The Letters of Ralph Waldo Emerson.* Edited by Ralph L. Rusk. 6 vols. New York: Columbia Univ. Press, 1939.

———. *Selections from Ralph Waldo Emerson.* Edited by Stephen E. Whicher. Boston: Houghton Mifflin, 1957.

Fergenson, Laraine. "Was Thoreau Rereading Wordsworth in 1851?" *Thoreau Journal Quarterly* 5, no. 3 (July 1973): 20–23.

Foerster, Norman. "Emerson on the Organic Principle of Art." *PMLA* 41 (1926): 193–208.

———. "The Intellectual Heritage of Thoreau." In *Twentieth Century Interpretations of* Walden. Edited by Richard Ruland, 34–49. Englewood Cliffs, N. J.: Prentice-Hall, 1968. Originally published in *The Texas Review* 2 (1916–17): 192–212.

Franklin, Benjamin. *The Way to Wealth.* In *The Papers of Benjamin Franklin,* edited by Leonard W. Labaree et al. New Haven: Yale Univ. Press, 1959.

Fromm, Eric. *The Forgotten Language: An Introduction to the Understanding of Dreams, Fairy Tales and Myths.* New York: Rinehart, 1951.

Fussell, Edwin. *Frontier: American Literature and the American West.* Princeton: Princeton Univ. Press, 1965.

Garber, Frederick. *Thoreau's Redemptive Imagination.* New York: New York Univ. Press, 1977.

Gelpi, Albert. "Emerson: The Paradox of Organic Form." In *Emerson: Prophecy, Metamorphosis and Influence,* edited by David Levin. Selected Papers from the English Institute. New York: Columbia Univ. Press, 1975.

Goethe, Johann Wolfgang von. *Botanical Writings.* Translated by Bertha Mueller. Honolulu: Univ. of Hawaii Press, 1952.

Gozzi, Raymond D. "A Freudian View of Thoreau." In *Thoreau's Psychology: Eight Essays,* edited by Raymond D. Gozzi, 1–18. Lanham, Md.: University Press of America, 1983.

———. "Mother- Nature." In *Henry David Thoreau: A Profile,* edited by Walter Harding, 180–84. New York: Hill and Wang, 1971.

———. "Some Aspects of Thoreau's Personality." In *Henry David Thoreau: A Profile,* edited by Walter Harding, 150–71. New York: Hill and Wang, 1971.

———. "Some Comments on an Eriksonian View of Thoreau: Young Man Thoreau and 'Identity Crisis and Beyond.' " In *Thoreau's Psychology: Eight Essays,* edited by Raymond D. Gozzi, 67–78. Lanham, Md.: University Press of America, 1983.

———. "Tropes and Figures: A Psychological Study of David Henry Thoreau." Ph.D. diss., New York Univ., 1957.

Greene, David. *A Frail Duration.* San Diego: San Diego State College Press, 1966.

Gura, Philip F. "Elizabeth Palmer Peabody and the Philosophy of Language." *ESQ: A Journal of the American Renaissance* 23 (1977): 154–63.

———. "Henry Thoreau and the Wisdom of Words." *New England Quarterly* 52 (1979): 38–54.

———. "The Transcendentalists and Language: The Unitarian Exegetical Background." In *Studies in the American Renaissance, 1979,* edited by Joel Myerson, 1–16. Boston: Twayne, 1979.

———. *The Wisdom of Words: Language, Theology, and Literature in the New England Renaissance.* Middletown, Conn.: Wesleyan Univ. Press, 1981.

Harding, Walter. *The Days of Henry Thoreau.* Princeton: Princeton Univ. Press, 1982.

———. "Thoreau and Eros." In *Thoreau's Psychology: Eight Essays,* edited by Raymond D. Gozzi, 145–64. Lanham, Md.: University Press of America, 1983.

———. *A Thoreau Handbook.* New York: New York Univ. Press, 1959.

———, ed. *Henry David Thoreau: A Profile.* New York: Hill and Wang, 1971.

———, ed. Introduction to *A Week on the Concord and Merrimack Rivers.* New York: Holt, Rinehart & Winston, 1963.

———, ed. "Notes on the Journey West." In *Thoreau's Minnesota Journey: Two Documents.* Thoreau Society Booklet no. 16. Geneseo, N.Y., 1962.

———, ed. *The Variorum* Walden. New York: Washington Square Press, 1968.

Harris, William T. "Emerson's Philosophy of Nature." In *The Genius and Character of Emerson,* edited by Frank B. Sanborn, 339–64. Boston: Houghton Mifflin, 1898.

Harvey, Roderick W. "Thoreau: Psychology." *Canadian Review of American Studies* 17 (1986): 211–17.

Henry David Thoreau: A Profile. Edited by Walter Harding. New York: Hill and Wang, 1971.

Hesford, Walter. " 'Incessant Tragedies': A Reading of *A Week on the Concord and Merrimack Rivers.*" *ELH* 44 (1977): 515–25.

Hochfield, George, ed. Introduction to *Selected Writings of the American Transcendentalists.* New York: New American Library, 1966.

———. "New England Transcendentalism." In *Critical Essays on American Transcendentalism,* edited by Philip F. Gura and Joel Myerson, 453–82. Boston: G. K. Hall, 1982.

Holland, Norman N. "A Summing-Up." In *Thoreau's Psychology: Eight Essays,* edited by Raymond D. Gozzi, 165–87. Lanham, Md.: University Press of America, 1983.

Holmes, Oliver Wendell. *Ralph Waldo Emerson.* Boston: Houghton Mifflin, 1885.

Hopkins, Vivian. "Emerson and Bacon." *American Literature* 29 (1958): 408–30.

Howarth, William L. *The Literary Manuscripts of Henry David Thoreau.* Columbus: Ohio State Univ. Press, 1974.

Hutchinson, Jamie. " 'The Lapse of the Current': Thoreau's Historical Vision in *A Week on the Concord and Merrimack Rivers.*" *ESQ: A Journal of the American Renaissance* 25 (1979): 211–23.

Hyman, Stanley Edgar. *The Tangled Bank: Marx, Frazer and Freud as Imaginative Writers.* New York: Atheneum, 1962.

Irwin, John T. *American Hieroglyphics: The Symbol of the Egyptian Hieroglyphics in the American Renaissance.* New Haven: Yale Univ. Press, 1980.

———. "The Symbol of the Hieroglyphics in the American Renaissance." *American Quarterly* 26 (1974): 103–26.

Johnson, Linck C. "Contexts of Bravery: Thoreau's Revisions of 'The Service' for *A Week*." In *Studies in the American Renaissance, 1983,* edited by Joel Myerson, 281–96. Charlottesville: Univ. Press of Virginia, 1983.

———. *Thoreau's Complex Weave: The Writing of* A Week on the Concord and Merrimack Rivers. Charlottesville: Univ. Press of Virginia Press, 1986.

Johnson, Paul David. "Thoreau's Redemptive *Week*." *American Literature* 49 (1977): 22–33.

Karabatsos, James. *A Word-Index to* A Week on the Concord and Merrimack Rivers. Hartford: Transcendental Books, 1971.

Kern, Alexander. "Coleridge and American Romanticism: The Transcendentalists and Poe." In *New Approaches to Coleridge: Biographical and Critical Essays,* edited by Donald Sultana, 113–36. Totowa, N.J.: Barnes and Noble, 1981.

Kim, Kichung. "Thoreau's Science and Teleology." *ESQ: A Journal of the American Renaissance* 18 (1972): 125–33.

La Rosa, Ralph C. "Bacon and the 'Organic Method' of Emerson's Early Lectures." *English Language Notes* 8 (1970): 107–14.

Lawrence, D. H. *Studies in Classic American Literature.* 1923. Reprint. New York: Viking Press, 1964.

Leary, Lewis. " 'Now I Adventured': 1851 as a Watershed Year in Thoreau's Career." *ESQ: A Journal of the American Renaissance* 19 (1973): 141–48.

Lebeaux, Richard. "Identity Crisis and Beyond: Eriksonian Perspectives on the Pre-Walden and Post-Walden Thoreau." In *Thoreau's Psychology: Eight Essays,* edited by Raymond D. Gozzi, 19–66. Lanham, Md.: University Press of America, 1983.

———. " 'Sugar Maple Man': Middle-aged Thoreau's Generativity Crisis." In *Studies in the American Renaissance, 1981,* edited by Joel Myerson, 359–77. Boston: Twayne, 1981.

———. "Thoreau's Lives, Lebeaux's Lives." In *Introspection in Biography: The Biographer's Quest for Self-Awareness,* edited by Samuel H. Baron and Carl Pletsch, 225–48. Hillsdale, N.J.: The Analytic Press, distributed by Lawrence Erlbaum, 1985.

———. *Thoreau's Seasons.* Amherst: Univ. of Massachusetts Press, 1984.

———. *Young Man Thoreau.* Amherst: Univ. of Massachusetts Press, 1977.

Levinson, Daniel J. *The Seasons of a Man's Life.* New York: Ballantine Books, 1978.

Lewis, R. W. B. *The American Adam: Innocence, Tragedy, and Tradition in the Nineteenth Century.* Chicago: Univ. of Chicago Press, 1955.

———. *Trials of the Word.* New Haven: Yale Univ. Press, 1965.

Lowell, James Russell. Review of *A Week* in *Massachusetts Quarterly Review* 3 (December 1849): 3.

Lyon, Melvin E. "Walden Pond as a Symbol." *PMLA* 82 (1967): 289–300.

McIntosh, James. *Thoreau as Romantic Naturalist: His Shifting Stance Toward Nature.* Ithaca: Cornell Univ. Press, 1974.

McShane, Frank. "Walden and Yoga." *New England Quarterly* 37 (1964): 322–42.

Maritain, Jacques. *Creative Intuition in Art and Poetry*. Cleveland: World Publishing, 1954.

Marx, Leo. *The Machine in the Garden: Technology and the Pastoral Ideal in America*. New York: Oxford Univ. Press, 1964.

Matthiessen, F. O. *American Renaissance: Art and Expression in the Age of Emerson and Whitman*. New York: Oxford Univ. Press, 1941.

Miller, Perry. "Thoreau in the Context of International Romanticism." *New England Quarterly* 34 (1961): 147–59.

———, ed. *The Transcendentalists: An Anthology*. Cambridge: Harvard Univ. Press, 1950.

Moldenhauer, Joseph J. "Paradox in *Walden*." In *Twentieth Century Interpretations of* Walden, edited by Richard Ruland, 73–84. Englewood Cliffs, N.J.: Prentice-Hall, 1968.

Moller, Mary Elkins. *Thoreau and the Human Community*. Amherst: Univ. of Massachusetts Press, 1980.

Murray, Donald. "Symbolic Landscape in the Greylock Episode of Thoreau's *Week*." *American Transcendental Quarterly* 1 (June 1987): 123–34.

Myerson, Joel. "Lowell on Emerson: A New Letter from Concord in 1838." *New England Quarterly* 44 (1971): 649–52.

Ogden, Marlene A. Walden: *A Concordance*. New York: Garland, 1985.

Orth, Michael. "The Prose Style of Henry David Thoreau." *Language and Style: An International Journal* 7 (Winter 1974): 36–52.

Packer, B. L. *Emerson's Fall: A New Interpretation of the Major Essays*. New York: Continuum Pub., 1982.

Paul, Sherman. *Emerson's Angle of Vision*. Cambridge: Harvard Univ. Press, 1952.

———. *The Shores of America: Thoreau's Inward Exploration*. Urbana: Univ. of Illinois Press, 1958.

Poirier, Richard. *A World Elsewhere: The Place of Style in American Literature*. New York: Oxford Univ. Press, 1966.

Porte, Joel. *Emerson and Thoreau: Transcendentalists in Conflict*. Middletown, Conn.: Wesleyan Univ. Press, 1965.

———. *Representative Man: Ralph Waldo Emerson in His Time*. New York: Oxford Univ. Press, 1979.

Railton, Stephen. "Thoreau's 'Resurrection of Virtue!' " *American Quarterly* 24 (1972): 210–27.

Richardson, Robert D., Jr. *Henry Thoreau: A Life of the Mind*. Berkeley: Univ. of California Press, 1986.

———. *Myth and Literature in the American Renaissance*. Bloomington: Indiana Univ. Press, 1978.

Robbins, Deborah. "The Ascetic Winter and Excremental Spring of *Walden*." *ESQ: A Journal of the American Renaissance* 24 (1978): 77–82.

Robinson, David. "Emerson's Natural Theology and the Paris Naturalists." *Journal of the History of Ideas* 41 (1980): 69–88.

Rohman, David Gordon. "An Annotated Edition of Henry David Thoreau's *Walden*." Ph.D. diss. Syracuse Univ., 1960.

Rowe, John Carlos. " 'The Being of Language: The Language of Being' in *A Week on the Concord and Merrimack Rivers.*" *Boundary 2,* 7 (Spring 1979): 91–115.

Ruskin, John. "The Lamp of Memory." In *The Seven Lamps of Architecture.* New York: Longmans, Green, 1909.

Sanborn, F. B., ed. *The Genius and Character of Emerson.* Boston: Houghton Mifflin, 1898.

———, ed. *Thoreau: The Poet-Naturalist.* 2nd ed. 1902. Reprint. Boston: Biblo & Tannen, 1966.

———, ed. *Walden.* 2 vols. Bibliophile Ed. Boston: Bibliophile Society, 1909.

Sattelmeyer, Robert. *Thoreau's Reading: A Study in Intellectual History, With Bibliographical Catalogue.* Princeton: Princeton Univ. Press, 1988.

———, ed. Introduction to *Henry David Thoreau: The Natural History Essays.* Salt Lake City: Peregrine Smith, 1980.

Sattelmeyer, Robert, and Richard A. Hocks. "Thoreau and Coleridge's *Theory of Life.*" In *Studies in the American Renaissance, 1985,* edited by Joel Meyerson, 269–84. Charlotesville: Univ. Press of Virginia, 1985.

Sayre, Robert F. *Thoreau and the American Indians.* Princeton: Princeton Univ. Press, 1977.

Sealts, Merton M., Jr. and Alfred R. Ferguson, eds. *Emerson's* Nature—*Origin, Growth, Meaning.* New York: Dodd, Mead, 1969.

Seybold, Ethel. *Thoreau: The Quest and the Classics.* New Haven: Yale Univ. Press, 1951.

Shanley, J. Lyndon. *The Making of* Walden. Chicago: Univ. of Chicago Press, 1957.

Shea, Daniel. "Emerson and the American Metamorphosis." In *Emerson: Prophecy, Metamorphosis, and Influence,* edited by David Levin. Selected Papers from the English Institute, 29–56. New York: Columbia Univ. Press, 1975.

Sheehy, Gail. *Passages: Predictable Crises of Adult Life.* New York: E. P. Dutton, 1976.

Sherwin, J. S., and R. C. Reynolds. *A Word Index to* Walden: *With Textual Notes.* Charlottesville: Univ. of Virginia Press, 1960.

Stern, Philip Van Doren, ed. *The Annotated* Walden. New York: Clarkson N. Potter, 1970.

Stewart, George R. *American Given Names: Their Origin and History in the Context of the English Language.* New York: Oxford Univ. Press, 1979.

Stewart, Randall. *American Literature and Christian Doctrine.* Baton Rouge: Louisiana State Univ. Press, 1958.

Stoller, Leo. *After* Walden: *Thoreau's Changing Views on Economic Man.* Stanford: Stanford Univ. Press, 1957.

Sundquist, Eric J. *Home as Found: Authority and Genealogy in Nineteenth-Century American Literature.* Baltimore: Johns Hopkins Univ. Press, 1979.

Sweeney, James R. "The Cosmic Drama in Thoreau's 'Spring.' " *ESQ: A Journal of the American Renaissance* 24 (Autumn 1961): 3–6.

Tanner, Stephen L. "Current Motions in Thoreau's *A Week.*" *Studies in Romanticism* 12 (1973): 763–76.

Thoreau, Henry D. *The Annotated* Walden. Edited by Philip Van Doren Stern. New York: Clarkson N. Potter, 1970.

———. *Cape Cod.* Edited by Joseph J. Moldenhauer. Princeton: Princeton Univ. Press, 1988.

———. *Collected Poems of Henry Thoreau.* Enlarged ed. Edited by Carl Bode. Baltimore: Johns Hopkins Univ. Press, 1965.

———. *Consciousness in Concord: The Text of Thoreau's Hitherto "Lost Journal" (1840–1841) Together with Notes and a Commentary.* Edited by Perry Miller. Boston: Houghton Mifflin, 1959.

———. *The Correspondence of Henry David Thoreau.* Edited by Walter Harding and Carl Bode. New York: New York Univ. Press, 1958.

———. *Early Essays and Miscellanies.* Edited by Joseph J. Moldenhauer and Edwin Moser, with Alexander C. Kern. Princeton: Princeton Univ. Press, 1975.

———. *Excursions and Poems.* Vol. 5 of *The Writings of Henry David Thoreau.* Boston: Houghton Mifflin, 1906.

———. "Huckleberries." Edited by Leo Stoller. 1970. Reprinted in *The Natural History Essays,* edited by Robert Sattelmeyer. Salt Lake City: Peregrine Smith, 1980.

———. *The Journal of Henry David Thoreau.* Edited by Bradford Torrey and Francis H. Allen. Vols. 7–14 of *The Writings of Henry David Thoreau.* 20 vols. Walden Edition. Boston: Houghton Mifflin, 1906; herein cited by the alternate numbering, I–XIV.

———. *Journal, Volume 1: 1837–1844.* Edited by Elizabeth Hall Witherell et al. Princeton: Princeton Univ. Press, 1984.

———. *Journal, Volume 2: 1842–1848.* Edited by Robert Sattelmeyer. Princeton: Princeton Univ. Press, 1984.

———. *Literary Notebook, 1840–48, facsimile text.* Edited by Kenneth Walter Cameron. Hartford: Transcendental Books, 1964.

———. *The Maine Woods.* Edited by Joseph J. Moldenhauer. Princeton: Princeton Univ. Press, 1973.

———. *Reform Papers.* Edited by Wendell Glick. Princeton: Princeton Univ. Press, 1973.

———. *The Variorum* Walden. Edited by Walter Harding. New York: Washington Square, 1968.

———. *Walden.* Edited by J. Lyndon Shanley. Princeton: Princeton Univ. Press, 1971.

———. *A Week on the Concord and Merimack Rivers.* Edited by Walter Harding. New York: Holt, Rinehart & Winston, 1963.

———. *A Week on the Concord and Merrimack Rivers.* Edited by Carl Hovde. Princeton: Princeton Univ. Press, 1980.

Thoreau's Psychology: Eight Essays. Edited by Raymond D. Gozzi. Lanham, Md.: Univ. Press of America, 1983.

Trench, Richard Chenevix. *On the Lessons in Proverbs: Being the Substance of Lectures Delivered to Young Men's Societies at Portsmouth and Elsewhere.* New York: Redfield, 1853.

———. *On the Study of Words.* New York: Redfield, 1852.

Van Anglen, Kevin P. "A Paradise Regained: Thoreau's *Wild Apples* and the Myth

of the American Adam." *ESQ: A Journal of the American Renaissance* 27 (1981): 28–37.
Van Nostrand, Albert D. "Thoreau Beside Himself." In *Every Man His Own Poet: Romantic Gospels in American Literature.* New York: McGraw-Hill, 1968.
Vogel, Stanley M. *German Literary Influences on the American Transcendentalists.* Yale Studies in English, vol. 127. New Haven: Yale Univ. Press, 1955.
Wagenknecht, Edward. *Henry David Thoreau: What Manner of Man?* Amherst: Univ. of Massachusetts Press, 1981.
West, Michael. "Charles Kraitsir's Influence on Thoreau's Theory of Language." *ESQ: A Journal of the American Renaissance* 19 (1973): 262–74.
———. "Scatology and Eschatology: The Heroic Dimensions of Thoreau's Wordplay." *PMLA* 89 (1974): 1043–64.
———. "Thoreau and the Language Theories of the French Enlightenment." *ELH* 51 (1984): 747–70.
———. "*Walden*'s Dirty Language: Thoreau and Walter Whiter's Geocentric Etymological Theories." *Harvard Library Bulletin* 22 (1974): 117–28.
Wheelwright, Philip. *Metaphor and Reality.* Bloomington: Indiana Univ. Press, 1962.
———. "The Semantic Approach to Myth." In *Myth: A Symposium,* edited by Thomas A. Sebeok, 154–68. Bloomington: Indiana Univ. Press, 1965.
Whicher, Stephen E., ed. *Selections from Ralph Waldo Emerson.* Boston: Houghton Mifflin, 1957.
Whitehall, Harold. "The English Language." In *Webster's New World Dictionary.* Cleveland: World Publshing, 1962.
Wolf, William J. *Thoreau: Mystic, Prophet, Ecologist.* Philadelphia: United Church Press, 1974.
Wood, Barry. "The Growth of the Soul: Coleridge's Dialectical Method and the Strategy of Emerson's *Nature.*" *PMLA* 91 (1976): 385–97.
Wright, Conrad. "Emerson, Barzillai Frost, and the Divinity School Address." In *The Liberal Christians: Essays on American Unitarian History,* 41–61. Boston: Beacon Press, 1970.
Wynkoop, William M. "Bacon as the Doer." In *Three Children of the Universe: Emerson's View of Shakespeare, Bacon, and Milton,* 116–36. The Hague: Mouton, 1966.
Yehle, Carol F. "The Thoreauvian Dialectic: A Study of the Nature Symbolism in *Walden.*" M.A. thesis, Syracuse Univ., 1958.
Yonge, Charlotte M. *History of Christian Names.* New ed., rev. London: N.p., 1844.

Index